COMMUNITY INVOLVEMENT AND LEISURE

Community involvement and leisure

edited by
JOHN T. HAWORTH
Department of Psychology,
University of Manchester

LEPUS BOOKS • LONDON

© Lepus Books 1979
An associate company of Henry Kimpton Ltd
7 Leighton Place, Leighton Road, London NW5 2QL

ISBN 0 86019 018 8

British Library Cataloguing in Publication Data
Community involvement and leisure.
   1. City planning — Great Britain — Citizen
participation
   2. Regional planning — Great
Britain — Citizen participation
   I. Haworth, John Trevor
   309.2'3'0941   HT169.G7

Typesetting by Malvern Typesetting Services Ltd.
Printed in Great Britain at the
University Press, Cambridge

CONTENTS

RESEARCH

CONTRIBUTORS

John Barrett
  Advisor to Pembrokeshire Countryside Unit, Wales

John Eggleston
  Professor, Department of Education, University of Keele

Rod Hackney
  Architect, Macclesfield

David Harding
  Town Artist, Glenrothes Development Corporation, Fife

John T. Haworth
  Lecturer, Department of Psychology, University of Manchester

Chris Horn
  Institute of Local Government Studies, University of Birmingham

Arfon Jones
  Principal, Sidney Stringer School and Community College, Coventry

Terry J. Marsh
  Assistant Director of Leisure, Wigan Metropolitan Borough Council

Tim Mason
  Youth and Community Worker, Lancashire County Council

George Smith
  Social Evaluation Unit, Department of Social and Administrative Studies, Oxford

Paul Soames
  Playleader, Chelsea Adventure Playground, London

Phil Topping
  Social Evaluation Unit, Department of Social and Administrative Studies, Oxford

Tony S. Travis
  Professor, Director, Centre for Urban and Regional Studies, University of Birmingham

Michael Tempest
  Architect, Nottingham County Council

INTRODUCTION

There is today a considerable interest in the idea of community involvement and the term can mean many things. But to an increasing number of people an essential ingredient is participation in decision making: the opportunity to have some say in and control over events. This participation, which can take various forms, is a prime consideration of this book. It makes the link with leisure, particularly appropriate, with its emphasis on discretionary time and choice. Expectations and aspirations for some control over events may be even greater in leisure than in other areas of life.

The book is concerned with community involvement and leisure in a broad context, and is divided into sections on management, design and research. However, it will readily be seen that many of the projects described cross traditional divisions.

COMMUNITY INVOLVEMENT

Community involvement has been advocated for a number of reasons, not least of which is the better use of resources. Examples of development schemes which have not involved the community in decision making, and which have failed, are numerous. Housing estates have been built without any community and play facilities. Families with children have been allocated accommodation at the top of multi-storey flats. There has been little attempt to find out what tenants want and in some cases flats recently built are becoming unpopular and difficult to let, so much so that some blocks only ten years old are being considered for demolition. In inner cities, resources have often not reached those in greatest need and cities have been planned on the basis of the requirements of commuters at the expense of residents. Motorways have destroyed communities. Whole new towns have been criticised, in some cases for their clinical atmosphere and 'over planning' and giving little scope for individual initiative, and in other cases for creating conditions conducive to isolation and loneliness. Without public participation in decision making the administrators' aim of efficient use of resources may come to mean financial efficiency through large scale organisation and this can produce large scale solutions insensitive to varying individual requirements. The values and priorities of one group of people can come to dominate decision making. [1]

Community involvement has been promoted for another economic reason. In times of financial stringency, the providers are unable to meet demand. Encouraging self-help is viewed as one way of trying to ameliorate the situation. Voluntary work in the social and health services, housing cooperatives, the improvement of residential areas and the management of recreation facilities are just a few of the areas where community involvement has been encouraged. However, the opportunities for involvement have not always been authentic. Often it has been a case of responsibility without decision making power. Volunteers have been used as cheap labour and denied an effective voice in running affairs.

Another reason why community involvement has been advocated is to help improve democracy. There is concern over the growth of direct community action such as protest marches and squatting. Yet, for an increasing number of people, there is the belief that direct community action is simply the best and often the only way by which local issues can be tackled. The main reasons given for direct community action are: 'that proper channels don't work well because most MPs and councillors are too remote from the people they are supposed to represent; officials have too much power; people are dealt with as numbers or 'cases'; burning issues are turned into technical or financial problems; party politics have less and less to do with everyday life; the two main parties being in the pockets of big business and the big trade unions'.[2]

Disenchantment with official channels of democracy, such as local and general elections, has generated some attempts amongst politicians to find ways of involving the public in decision making. Consultation is the *modus operandi* of the moment and of course in structure planning this form of public participation is now mandatory. However, not all moves towards consultation comes from sincere attempts to improve democracy. One danger of public participation is that it is used to legitimise the decisions of those in authority and thereby make it difficult for the public to object at a later date.[3]

Some consultation, however, is genuine. And some participation is accompanied by direct involvement in decision making. In town planning, for example, the difficulty of prediction is now becoming recognised with the realisation that planning cannot prescribe in detail and that it must learn to live with uncertainty.[4] Public participation is becoming seen as necessary if one is to plan for human needs, wants and desires which are influenced by each individual's perception of reality and affected by social change. As outlined later, one particular planning scheme is allocating money to local residents for them to organise the improvement of their area with the back-up of officials and councillors.

Perhaps one of the main reasons for advocating community involvement is the emerging recognition of an active view of man.[5] Man is now being seen not just as a creature of comfort, a consumer, but also as an agent of change; a person who creates his own reality and who has the potential to shape his own future. Creativity, curiosity and exploratory behaviour are the hallmarks of each individual. The psychology of need may not be the psychology of participation, but the dynamic nature of each individual would seem to demand that effective opportunities for involvement are available as of right, even if the individual chooses not to use them.

A final reason to be noted for advocating community involvement is also connected with shaping the future. It is now claimed that there are physical, social and political limits to growth and the present day competitive life style.[6, 7] Changes in life style may not just make community involvement in decision making desirable, they may necessitate it if the imposition of ideas is to be avoided.

Difficulties. Of course there are many difficulties associated with community involvement. Bowden[3] has pointed to the complexity of planning with its many levels of decision making and processes which extend over time. Participants are not always clear where and when involvement would be most productive. Public participation can delay projects for a considerable time. It may make the implementation of large schemes very difficult. Facilities may be curtailed and projects may even have to be abandoned.[8] There is concern in Government that planning must not be made impotent by prolonged delays on the participation and objection stages.[9] In management there is similar concern that considerable staff time and finance can be used in undertaking public participation. However, as already pointed out, provision without participation can be very detrimental.

This question of the time taken by public participation is not only a concern of those in authority. It is also an issue amongst some community groups who consider that public participation can drain energy and cause the group to lose direction. Such groups can also feel that participation is a subtle means of control by the local authority. Perhaps authentic participation would be beneficial for both sides.

Another difficulty is that involvement of the community in official decision making processes may heighten conflict between residents and the local authority, and between different groups in the community. There is also concern by those in authority that those from the community who are participating are not representative. However, conflict may well occur even if there is no participation offered. Direct action by marches, sit-ins, use of the media, etc., are now recognised ways of stimulating those in power to take notice.[10] And representativeness may not be a key issue. The achievements of the group in its work for the community is more important and this may be enhanced by the active participation of those in authority.

Local authorities are often concerned that public participation will mean the abrogation of their responsibilities. The view is that councillors are elected to make the decisions and that community groups are not financially accountable to the public. Councillors and officials may also feel that public participation will mean that their specialist role would be usurped and their technical skills not put to the best use. However this has not prevented some authorities from working successfully with community groups, with councillors taking an active enabling role, and the authority devising new systems of financial accounting where necessary. And, of course, it is not suggested that local authorities should neglect their responsibility to see that all sections of the community are being served.

An underlying worry concerning much public participation is that the public will not make the 'right' decision. There is concern that the public either do not really understand the situation fully or that they do not know what they want, or if they do it will be detrimental to society in the longterm. These worries may be felt by politicians and officials alike. Realising that policymaking is often a complex and tortuous business many people in authority believe in 'guided democracy', maximum participation being reserved for those with appropriate views.

In some cases such worries may be justified. The general public are often in the dark and policymaking can be complex. But, while acknowledging that community involvement is not a panacea, it must be recognised that the public should be given more information and that community involvement can take many forms. Participation in official decision making is only one form. Another important way is for authorities to help community groups and individuals run their own affairs, whether it be housing matters or recreation activities, etc.

Experiments. There have been a number of experiments in recent years which between them cover both these approaches to community involvement. A brief outline of some of the major ones may serve as an indication of the range of activity, as well as acting as a perspective for the topics discussed in this book.

In the broad community sphere, the Educational Priority Area Projects (sponsored by the Government in the late 1960's) were concerned with, amongst other things, trying to help schools in deprived areas.[11] Besides trying to raise the educational performance of children and improve the morale of teachers, the projects were also trying to increase the involvement of parents in the education of their children and increase the sense of responsibility for their communities of the people living in them. Although these projects have been criticised for not producing successful guidelines for national policy, one development, which was partly a result of these projects, was the resurgence of community schools and colleges with their concern for involving pupils and parents in decision making and developing a curriculum and activities relevant to the needs of the local community. Sidney Stringer School and Community College is one such project. The management of this centre is discussed in Chapter 3 by the principal Arfon Jones, who emphasises the crucial role of the professional in relation to participation. Chapter 10 by Michael Tempest, a Nottinghamshire county architect, also stresses the importance of community schools, in this case, in relation to involving the community in the local authority design process. And Chapter 7 by John Eggleston, educationalist, discusses the importance in a changing society of linking education and design with community involvement generally.

The Government-sponsored Community Development Projects, begun in 1970, were also concerned with finding ways of helping people living in areas of multiple deprivation.[12] They consisted of twelve schemes in different urban areas. While there was a range of objectives, all projects included the objectives of citizen involvement and self-help. The projects were concerned with many subjects including housing, social services, welfare matters, planning law and citizen's rights. One of the projects resulted in the Vauxhall Neighbourhood Council being formed in the Scotland Road area of Liverpool. In this scheme, funds from the Government are allocated to local residents for them to employ officers to assist them with their projects. While some difficulties have been experienced, there have been achievements in· a number of areas including housing, civil rights, welfare and recreation.[13]

However, not all Community Development Projects put all their eggs in the community involvement basket. A joint report by five of these teams sees the problem of inner cities not as local difficulties which can be cleared up with government- and self-help, but as the inevitable products of capitalistic society. They believe the answers lie in measures designed to stop capital and industry moving freely about the country and the world with scant regard to the welfare of local communities.[14] Of course while urban problems need to be tackled at many levels, this analysis does not lessen the importance of community involvement in many areas, even if it is only to temper the actions of bureaucracies. The lessons of the Educational Priority

Area and Community Development Projects for research and policy formulation are discussed in Chapter 13 by George Smith and Phil Topping. And the necessity for integrating research, policy formulation and community involvement is outlined in Chapter 11 by the editor.

There have been a number of area management schemes concerned with new approaches to the improvement of the environment. One area-based initiative sponsored by the Government is of note in the context of community involvement. As part of an experiment in a number of urban areas, money was made available in Newcastle upon Tyne to help with positive discrimination in favour of social priority areas. The local authority is saying to the people 'there is the money, you can spend it!' There are ten priority area teams each consisting of ward councillors and officers at field level from different departments of the local authority. Each team is responsible for involving as many people as possible in its area. The general aim is to improve the quality of life of people subjected to urban stress. Although different wards may have different priorities, there is a clear desire to improve community facilities and to bring people together. Each area knows how much is available and it decides its own problems and, to a large extent, its own methods. Project organisers have noted that the devolution of power has brought with it responsibility; local groups have concentrated on organising things for the general good, like recreation and education facilities and measures to help the young and old.[15]

Two chapters in this volume are concerned with community involvement and leisure on the broad scale: Chapter 2, by Terry Marsh, while pointing to some of the difficulties of involving the public in decision making, puts a case for its importance in local authorities; and Chapter 1, by Tony Travis, in discussing the role of the Government and Regional Agencies in leisure provision, points to the opportunities for developing widely based public participatory approaches, particularly at the regional level.

Another National Government experiment indicating that local residents can be successfully involved in decision making in the leisure sphere is the recent Leisure and the Quality of Life Project.[16] In 1973 four Government departments, in association with the Arts Council of Great Britain and the Sports Council, invited four local authorities and local arts and sports groups to participate in a programme of local leisure experiments. The aim of the experiments was to see what could be achieved in different urban areas by locally led campaigns to develop and increase a full range of leisure activities including those of a cultural, recreational and sporting variety, and also to record and learn from the experience.

Although there were dissimilarities between the experiments in the four areas, the groups on the whole focused their action programmes on a relatively similar range of activities; namely, information services, transport, mobile leisure facilities, community theatre, community festivals, equipment pools, projects for young people, and projects for the disadvantaged. All the groups were very successful in developing activities.

One of the main lessons of the experiments is that there is a great potential for self-help within the community and that what is needed to harness it, and make the best use of existing resources, is not just financial support but also sympathetic and flexible relationships between public and voluntary agencies and individuals. The need for better access to information for the public and innovatory financial procedures in local government are also highlighted.

These studies provide a challenge to traditional approaches to provision, management and research in departments of recreation and also in many other departments in the local authority where the need for community involvement is at first sight not so readily apparent as it is in the leisure area with its focus on discretionary time. Chapter 12 by Chris Horn, project evaluator of the Quality of Life Experiments in Sunderland, discusses the Sunderland experience in the context of research and community involvement.

The need for innovatory approaches in local authority to encourage community involvement is also highlighted in a recent Government report entitled 'Recreation and Deprivation in Inner Urban Areas'.[17] The report indicates that the policy of providing sport and recreational facilities for the whole community has not benefited the disadvantaged who make proportionately less use of them. Sports centres, for instance, in inner city areas are mainly catering for the better-off. The report considers that the way local authority facilities are managed, and the detailed control exercised by councillors, make it difficult to vary policies and provisions for different social groups and areas. Teenagers, for instance, the report noted, have little opportunity to do things for themselves in the active and law-abiding recreations. The report indicates that groups need to be consulted in the planning stages and have a say in the management of facilities. It also notes the value of animators or community workers in helping to increase recreational opportunities. In suggesting the exploration of alternative ways of providing and managing local recreational buildings, the report recognises that this would mean a radical change in the attitudes of the local authority. Chapter 4 describes one innovatory attempt at management at a local authority Community Centre and highlights some of the difficulties encountered.

The use of animators, or enablers as they are sometimes called, to increase opportunities by encouraging the community to articulate its requirements, and helping them bring this about, is a developing approach in many countries, including the UK. Community arts affords one important example, as indicated by the reports on the work of the Arts Council in this sphere over a two year period from April 1975. [18, 19] Community art has many aims. While relating art to life more closely and involving the public in the creative process are important aims, another is to stimulate people to an active concern for the needs and aspirations of the community of which they form a part. The aims of 'Sociocultural community development', as expressed in the European Cultural Convention at Oslo in June 1976, are supported. One of these is that cultural policy at the local level should particularly aim at allowing all sections of the population to be involved in the process of change which affects them.

As the 1976 interim report on community arts indicates, the community artist works to achieve objectives such as these by 'working in consultation with the community, meeting its needs, motivating participation, acting as a catalyst to evolve creative ideas and language'. Their work also involves 'stimulating new areas of activity through performance or specific projects, demystifying the media, and passing on skills through workshops on such activities as drama, dance, jazz, clowning, poster printing, wood and metal work, singing, weaving, pottery, printing and video, etc.' For many community artists a fundamental aspect of this is to enable people to gain confidence in their own ability and potential by starting with areas of life which do not overwhelm them before moving on to problems with housing, work, transport and education, etc., where relevant.

As is perhaps apparent, an essential aim of community arts is to breakdown some of the barriers of official classification between the arts, education and social development, etc. [20] Of course community art has not been without its critics. Some fear that community art propagates ultra radical values and political philosophies. While there is no doubt that good animators do foster political awareness, where relevant, this is done from a basis of belief in non-violent action and a desire to get people to analyse situations for themselves. Other critics have viewed much of community art as, at best, mere entertainment. While entertainment is not to be denigrated, it is interesting to note that some local authority councillors and officers have stated that where community arts work has been of a high quality, it is this side of community activity which is doing most to create a continuing and active interest in local community development. Community action groups may form for specific purposes, such as support for a bus stop or pedestrian crossing. But it is considered that community art activities often provide the more general and continuing stimulus. For example, one community and writing project in Birmingham worked with a residents association to successfully encourage the local council to develop a programme for urban renewal for the area rather than demolition or rebuilding. It has also set up a steel band workshop.[19] It would seem that the link between leisure and community development has considerable potential.

In Chapter 8, David Harding illustrates some of the possibilities for activities allied to community arts to include children and other members of the public in the design of the environment. Chapter 6 by Paul Soames, in discussing the importance of play, emphasises the relevance of animation and community involvement. This chapter refers to the work of the National Playing Fields Association who have also done much to further the work of animators. And John Barrett, in Chapter 5, discusses the work of the Pembrokeshire Countryside Unit and illustrates the crucial importance of informal education in creating opportunities for participation.

Animation projects and community involvement have not, of course, been linked solely to official experiments. Many small projects have sprung up, including community law centres, community newspapers, community printers and publishers, and community murals, etc. A whole series of these are reviewed briefly in 'Animation projects in the UK',[21] and the Council of Europe is sponsoring an information service in the UK to collate activities in this sphere.[22] The Directory of Social Change has produced the resource book 'Community', which highlights developments over a wide area,[23] and the Community Foundations Project has produced the series of handbooks on community involvement, referred to earlier. Useful manuals are produced by The Interaction Centre,[24] and the magazine 'Community Action' features current projects and issues.[25] All of this activity demonstrates that community involvement can be linked to a wide range of endeavours with leisure playing a crucial role. As Chapter 9 by the architect Rod Hackney shows, this includes such fundamental necessities as housing.

The chapters in this book, then, have affinities with a range of experiments in community involvement. They highlight the potential and difficulties associated with a number of approaches, including regional councils and pressure groups, area advisory committees, participatory groups, animation and informal education, to name but a few. They are not blue prints for action, but they do offer some very useful insights and raise questions and issues which need to be resolved in the light of particular situations.

While it must be recognised that it is not always possible to involve the public in authentic participation in decision making, it would seem from the experiments cited, and the chapters in this book, that there is much more scope and need than many in authority seem willing to acknowledge. Perhaps this book will play some small part in helping to remedy this.

REFERENCES AND NOTES

1. Gladstone, F. G. (1976) *The Politics of Planning*. Maurice Temple Smith, London
2. Community Projects Foundation (1977) *Community Action and Society*. A Community Groups Handbook, London
3. Bowden, N. (1975) Public participation in planning. In *Work and Leisure* by Haworth, J. T. and Smith, M. A. (eds). Lepus Books, London
4. Metropolitan Development and Change, The West Midlands (1977) *A Policy Review* by F. Joyce (ed). Joint Unit for the Research on the Urban Environment. University of Aston
5. Haworth, J. T. and Smith, M. A. (1975) Introduction. In *Work and Leisure*. Lepus Books, London
6. Hirsch, F. (1977) *The Social Limits to Growth*. Routledge and Kegan Paul, London
7. Miles, R. E. (1977) *Awakening from the American Dream: The Social and Political Limits to Growth*. Boyars/Open Forum, New York
8. Crompton, J. (1975) Problems of provision and planning for leisure. In *Work and Leisure* by Haworth, J. T. and Smith, M. A. (eds). Lepus Books, London
9. Ardel, J. (1974) *The New Citizens Guide to Town and Country Planning*. Charles Knight, London
10. Community Projects Foundation (1977) *Taking Action*. A Community Groups Handbook, London
11. Report of the Research Project (1972–1975) *Educational Priority*. 5 Vols. H.M.S.O., London
12. Community Development Project Reports can be obtained from the CDP library, Mary Ward House, 5 Tavistock Place, London WC1H 9SS
13. Vauxhall Neighbourhood Council (1976) *Annual Report*. Vauxhall Community Services Centre, Liverpool
14. The Cost of Industrial Change. The Home Office, Urban Deprivation Unit. London
15. Public Service Vol. 51 No. 2 p. 8 and 9. February, 1977
16. Department of the Environment (1977) *Leisure and the Quality of Life*. Volumes 1 and 2. H.M.S.O., London. (Volume 1

(Chairman W. N. Fox) discusses and evaluates the experiments; Volume 2 (Chairman R. Shaw) contains the supporting research papers. A Government circular 92/77 (DOE) summarises the main lessons of the experiments and a thirty minute film, showing some of the experiments, can be borrowed from the Central Film Library, Government Buildings, Bromyard, Acton, London W.2.)

17. Department of the Environment (1977) *Recreation and Deprivation in Inner Urban Areas*. H.M.S.O., London
18. The Arts Council of Great Britain (1976) *Community Arts: A Reassessment of the First Year's Work of the Arts Council's Community Arts Committee*. The Arts Council, London
19. The Arts Council of Great Britain (1977) *Community Arts: A Report by the Arts Council's Community Arts Evaluation Working Group*. The Arts Council, London
20. A new project, for which the editor is research director, views the educational content of community activity as fundamental and sees community arts as an important creative arm of community development. Based in the North West Region, the project is attempting to combine these elements in the work of community organisers. For details write to: Chris Elphick, Unit, Co-ordinator, C.E.T.U., 17–21 Mumps, Oldham, Lancs
21. Berrigan, F. (1976) *Animation Projects in the U.K.* National Youth Bureau, Leicester
22. Ann Davis, Animation Service, National Youth Bureau, 17–23 Albion Street, Leicester, LEI 6GD
23. The Directory of Social Change (1977) *Community*. 9 Mansfield Place, London, N.W.3
24. Interaction, 14 Talacre Road, London N.W.5
25. Community Action Magazine, P.O. Box 665, London S.W.1

PLANNING AND
MANAGEMENT

This section deals with involvement of the community in the planning and management of community projects. It begins with a discussion of the role of Central Government and Regional Agencies in planning and management for leisure. The great diversity of those agencies and departments whose work impinges on leisure is shown, as well as their potential for involvement in decision making, particularly at the regional as distinct from the central level.

Chapter 2 discusses the evolving role of local government and examines the opportunities for public involvement in decision making. The author outlines different levels of participation and notes that most is at the consultation level even though statutes permit much more than this. It is suggested that a major factor inhibiting genuine participation is a lack of appreciation of the value of local government involvement.

In Chapter 3 the focus moves to a case study of community involvement in the management of a school and community college. The author makes an important distinction between community participation and democratic control. He believes that the development of the community college he describes, which has proved valuable to the public, would not have been possible if there had been only democratic control without leadership by professionals.

The importance of the contribution by professionals is also recognised in Chapter 4, a case study of a community centre. However, the authors also point to the necessity for individuals and groups to have some genuine control over events if community involvement is to succeed.

The following chapter provides a change in tempo by illustrating a case study of participation relevant to countryside centres and urban country parks. The chapter concerns itself with decision making at the level of individual choices and the author shows the importance of uniformally presented education in extending the range of knowledge, thereby increasing the options for participation.

The last chapter in this section moves to a more general approach and discusses the importance of adventure playgrounds in helping with creative play and community involvement in decision making. The work of the playleader as animator is considered crucial, as is the involvement of members of the community in the planning and management of the playground.

1 LEISURE AND INVOLVEMENT
The role of government and the national and regional agencies

by Tony S. Travis

In reviewing the emergent roles of governmental and regional agencies in Britain in relation to the activities, facilities and use of time we call leisure, it is first necessary to explain both the extraordinary complexity of the existing arrangements and state why they have grown up in so Topsy-like a fashion. By comparison with leisure services, the historical emergence of agencies concerned with public health, housing and education provisions, may be viewed as relatively simple and clear, for they do not straddle nor overlap many facets and sectors of governmental responsibility. In consequence, it is this diffusion of responsibilities and powers, a random scatter of enabling legislation, different agencies and divisions of overviewing responsibilities at the central and regional levels of government, which lie at the heart of many of the problems in making public provisions for leisure. Furthermore, variations in initiative and enterprise, or the ways in which powers are interpreted and used, show that in the system, as it now functions, the questions of 'how' and 'what' is done, 'by whom' and 'for whom', are more important than the simpler question of 'under which powers?'. Paradoxically, the current complexity and confusion of arrangements, with so many organisations involved, may well represent an extraordinary potential for developing widely based public participatory approaches to future policymaking in the realms of the planning and management of leisure and tourism.

HISTORICAL AND LEGISLATIVE FACTORS

Whilst it would be inappropriate, at this point, to go into a lengthy historical explanation of the growth of time available for leisure use, of the financial means and energy available to the population for its recreation, and the provision and use of leisure facilities created by the public and private sectors, it is essential to make some summary comments. However, fuller historical explanations and descriptions of the development of these aspects of leisure are given by Patmore in Land and Leisure;[1] by Burkart and Medlik in Tourism: Past, Present and Future;[2] and in Turner and Ash's more recently published The

Golden Hordes.[3] Mellor's book Leisure and the Changing City 1870–1914[4] is also essential reading in this context.

In the last one hundred years, British society has completed its major phases of industrialisation and urbanisation. The cumulative build up of legislation, under which provision for leisure is made, has grown out of the needs for survival and growth of a market economy. Recent tourism legislation has grown out of recognition of the economic benefits to the nation of a major new industry and the sequence of governmental interventions has been one of marginally adjusting the processes of industrialisation, urbanisation and sub-urbanisation. The actions reflect reluctant responses (under pressure from effective political lobbies, electoral ground-swells, and interest groups) to ameliorate and humanise our urban settlements, urban life and pattern of work to a level which is tolerable; a level at which the processes of production and profit-making could be more satisfactorily conducted. Whether one finds their evidence in the writings of Charles Dickens[5] or of Lord Shaftesbury,[6] this balances up the rather idealised impressions given by reading the key pieces of nineteenth century legislation in the health and environmental fields.

The so-called Sanitary Movement (the evolution of governmental responses to enable the physical survival of an urban society, through defining and meeting basic standards and safeguards for public health) developed through several phases. From an early stage, to enable survival at a minimal level, it developed through to more sophisticated levels of response concerned with the positive nurturing of human wellbeing. In other words, the progress and process was one from minimal remedial interventions, eventually through to preventative actions, and then even as far as some normative actions aimed at creating positively good conditions. Planning for leisure, in specific and explicit terms, was thus an inevitable latecomer in this historical progression. Government action was slow, if not belated, but ultimately benign and paternalistic.

The early urban industrial economy assumed and accepted a human loss, or wastage rate, as a consequence of progress. The slightly more mature industrial economy of the market place, in the late nineteenth century, accepted the notion of the economic advantages which might accrue from having a healthy labour force with higher productivity. Innovators in industry proved, at first in exceptional cases, these principles which could only become norms much later. However, the battles for reducing the numbers of hours of work, for improvements in conditions of work and in the setting aside of non-work time, all inevitably preceded the gradual recognition of the needs for rest as such, the need for adequate holidays and the positive provision of time and means for recreation, for play as opposed to improvement, for sport and leisure in relation to the needs of physical health and mental balance. Such concepts did not fit easily with the permeating Protestant Ethic of Work, which had necessarily and effectively underpinned the industrialisation and urbanisation processes. The implicit hint that to have substantial time for recreation is 'sinful', or to give over maximum time to painful work is 'good', is still to be found in our industrial society.

Legislation for trades and industrial holidays, for libraries, baths and cemeteries, parks and allotments, followed on later, but naturally from the legislative roots to which reference has already been made. Similarly, the emergence of the formal public education system in Britain permitted the economic survival of the society in terms of its changed training needs for a basic spectrum of work tasks in manufacture and commerce. If one says that late nineteenth century public education was designed for society's economic survival, with minor spin-offs or incidental benefits for human development, it may also be said that it took until the second half of the twentieth century to get the basic elements of our public education system geared to selective aspects of preparation for life and not just for work. Developments or innovations in education have come via new orientations, such as learning through play, sport and other aspects of leisure, and broader concepts of human personality development. The evolution of moral conscience and a creative social or welfare response in legislative terms is very much a product of this century. It has indeed been a long path, in terms of time, from the ameliorative phase of industrial and living conditions to the concerns with balanced diet, good health, special social needs and general societal acceptance (via legislation) of planning for sport and recreation,[7, 8] both as positive and important facets of the role of government in Britain.

GOVERNMENTAL RESPONSIBILITY FOR LEISURE

The diffuse nature of public sector responsibilities in relation to leisure was clearly reflected in the wide ranging Second Report of the Cobham Committee of the House of Lords on Sport and Leisure,[7] published in 1973. However, even that important review was limited by its terms of reference: 'to consider the demand for facilities for participation in sport, and in the *enjoyment of leisure out of doors*, and to examine what impediments may exist to the fuller use of existing facilities or the development of new ones, and how they might be removed'.

The analytical sections of that report touched on home-based leisure as well as upon physical recreation. The national agencies to which it referred (in 1973) included the three Sports Councils (England, Wales, Scotland); the two Countryside Commissions (England & Wales; Scotland); the Tourist Boards (1 international, 3 national, 11 regional); the one Forestry Commission; the Nature Conservancy; the Water Space Amenity Commission. Reference is also made in the report to the secondary roles, relating to recreation, of other arms of Central Government. Government Ministries, then defined as Environment, Agriculture, Fisheries and Food, Education and Science, Health and Social Security, Trades and Industry, were shown to have vital interests in or even control of sections of recreation and tourism. Fragmentation of responsibilities within the Super-Ministries, as well as between them, is a subject which also should have merited comment.

In addition, there are the basic roles of the local authorities under the Education Acts, under the Planning Acts and so on, and these were explained and in part evaluated by Cobham. In paragraph 114 of the Report, [7] the attitude is summarised:

> The multiplicity of organisations involved with recreation nationally is reflected in the fragmentary nature of Government responsibility. The organisations report to different Ministers, and nowhere can one say that Governmental interest in recreation is centred. To some extent this is inevitable. Since recreation is often a by-product of some primary function—forestry and education are examples—there can be no hope of collecting into one Department all those bodies whose decisions impinge on recreation. The primary functions of each body will decide where it is located and to which Minister it is responsible.

The Government follow-up to the Cobham Committee's Report, and modification of this stance at least as far as *active recreation* is concerned, came with the publication in August 1975 of the White Paper of the Department of the Environment, on Sport and Recreation, [8] in which, on page 4, it was stated that (para 16):

> The House of Lords Select Committee emphasized the need for the Government to adopt a positive attitude to recreation planning and to promote action within government departments along common and co-ordinated lines. To this end it recommended the appointment of a co-ordinating Minister of Recreation, and in July 1974 the Prime Minister announced the appointment of Mr. Denis Howell as Minister of State for Sport and Recreation, to exercise on behalf of the Secretary of State for the Environment a leading responsibility for co-ordination of policies and promotion of research in the field of active recreation. This arrangement involved *no change* in the functions and departmental responsibilities of other Ministers.

Thus, by 1977, in terms of formal responsibilities in relation to the whole leisure sector, some interests are clustered under key government ministers, whilst others are still scattered. Under the Secretary of State for the Environment, the Minister of State for Sport and Recreation has formal responsibility for the Sports Council, one of the Countryside Commissions, for selected conservation and development functions of Government. Therefore, much of the active recreation sector is grouped together but this excludes the arts, physical education and the media. The Minister has two mechanisms for attempting the wider coordination of Governmental policies on leisure. They are via quarterly meetings of all relevant Government Ministers, and by quarterly meetings of Chairmen and Directors of all key national recreational, tourism and conservation agencies. The question of special coordination at the regional level will be returned to at a later stage.

Within the Department of Education and Science (DES) at Central Government level, all the arts and education responsibilities, plus those for libraries and museums, are clustered. Thus major bodies, such as the Arts Council dating in origin back to 1945, are responsible to a separate Minister of State in the DES. The redefined aims of the Arts Council since 1967 are to: 'improve the knowledge, understanding and practice of the arts; and to increase the accessibility of the arts to the public.'

The Minister of State for Education has responsibilities for many of the specialist forms of education, interpretation and play, recreation, as well as physical education, and regulatory responsibilities for much of the stock of community sports and arts buildings, as well as for the school buildings with multi-use functions. The scale of Mr Howell's challenging tasks in coordination and liaison may be appreciated further when it is noted that tourism development is firmly placed as an economic function under the Secretary of State for Trade; environmental protection and heritage conservation are within the Department of the Environment; forestry and its major recreational uses under the Agriculture, Fisheries, and Food Minister; water planning and land planning under Environment, and so on. The challenge to Central Government to coordinate, and the magnitude of the problem of a non-fit between Central and Local Government structures in these fields, has thus become evident. All recreational sports, tourism and environmental functions of Government affecting Scotland are vested in the Secretary of State for Scotland.

The structural problem for Central and Regional Government may be appreciated when it is noted that at least seven different Secretaries of State have direct major roles and responsibilities affecting leisure, ten Central Government Departments are involved, seventeen Central Government bodies, nine types of Regional Government body, and some five types of Local Government bodies are all involved. These major hazards are there before one can start to examine the viability of arrangements for participation and involvement of interest groups in the leisure realm in the decisions of government which affect them!

Housing and transportation responsibilities — key areas of State intervention and of Central Government responsibility in Britain — give rise to massive public sector budgets. What is done by Government under these headings has a critical effect on the leisure opportunities, choice and access of the whole population. However, it is only recently that the leisure implications of these critical activities have been explicitly recognised by government. Similarly, major new fields of endeavour, such as social tourism which in Britain has been a discretionary facet of the Department of Health and Social Security's realm, is basically a local authority social service activity and has only recently been the subject of a basic review by the Tourist Boards and the Trades Union Congress. Action in such an area now poses a challenge for Local and Central Government, in taking a role in which they have shown scant interest or ability to date.

From these comments it will be seen that not only are responsibilities still diffuse within Central Government, despite recent changes, but also that it is only in the last year or so that the need for coordination in relation to leisure provisions has been given formal recognition within Central Government. The means initiated for attempting such coordination are weak. These highly desirable but extremely difficult intentions to realise *within* government are made all the harder by the vastly variable levels of budget, the power vested in the Ministers mentioned, their ranking and influence, and the great variations in enabling legislation, to mention but a few of the key factors involved. Central Government's encouragements and incentives to Local Government and to Regional bodies to take action in the sphere of leisure are generally weaker in legislative terms than the mandatory or statutory obligations placed upon them to carry out other activities. Strong obligations, such as those in respect of housing, education, planning and transport, vested by National Government in Local Government are repeated in very few of the range of items that come under leisure services; be they related to active or passive recreation, or to outdoor or indoor recreation provisions. Thus, as a majority of activities and expenditures come in the permissive as opposed to the obligatory realm, the levels of innovation, application and pressure by local authorities, and regional and voluntary bodies, are critical variables. Mandatory services in the leisure realm currently include library services, youth service and provision of allotments.

One may well ask, in relation to this extremely complex and confused situation, how far there is clear accountability to the public? How far is the public, or the 'many publics' of a pluralist society, directly or indirectly involved in these critical areas of public policymaking, decision making and decision taking? How far is Government, at the national and regional levels, responsive to public pressures? These are questions which this chapter will attempt to answer.

The history of any of the areas mentioned of Government responsibility differs. The size, effectiveness and length of time that identifiable interests have been involved and politically exerting pressures to certain ends, also differs. The 'provider' side of leisure services included a major commercial component in addition to that part provided by Government. Sampson writing on the New Anatomy of Britain[9] in 1971 has a chapter in relation to 'Arts and Leisure', in which he drew a distinct line between the world of free leisure, and the leisure industries, where profitability has led to a wide range of justified commercial initiatives in terms of returns. Demand satisfaction via supply and justified financial returns can give an adequate explanation in the latter area, but what of involvement in the free leisure area. Television, gardening and the large scale home-based pastimes all relate to the leisure industries. Leisure here has stimulated a commercial response whereby free leisure involves a generated consumption of more and more special consumer products: gardening equipment, track suits, barbecues, deck chairs, etc. Marketing increasingly identifies the images of who should take what, when, where and how, thus affecting involvement.

Sampson's analysis of the Arts and Government gives the impression of the arts being tackled at Government level by a few lay figures as though they are uninfluenced manipulators — albeit benign, in intent and manner, whether referring to the Lords Eccles, Goodman, or Jennie Lee. Sampson's chapter on Leisure and the Workers implies that organised labour in the industrial society is 'other-directed' (to use David Riesman's term in sociology) and work-orientated in the perception of life. Direct and indirect pressures upon Government in the leisure realm are not dealt with in Sampson's work.

If we momentarily consider Central Government artificially as a closed system, then its implicit values and goals in key pieces of leisure legislation need disentangling. Whilst social benefit and wellbeing are made apparent in sports legislation, by contrast tourism legislation is seen largely in terms of economic development and balance of payments. Conservation legislation, like some earlier housing legislation, is viewed in terms of the nation husbanding its physical resources and stock. This sort of preliminary disentanglement of motives is necessary in order to see who participates in such processes and for what reasons.

MULTILOGUE AND CHANGE

It is inadequate to analyse leisure and involvement in terms of two parties, namely the Government, on the one hand, and the public on the other. For it can be easily seen that several political, professional and bureaucratic criteria are being traded-off in the sector we call government, whilst on the side of the public, one may quickly identify several 'publics', i.e. many types of sporting and activity-based groups, professional associations, commercial and industrial lobbies, land interests, and so on. It is hard to suggest a better realm than one such as leisure to reveal the pluralist interests, roles and needs in a complex developed society. The pressure groups and vested interests are not necessarily fundamentally constituted to back leisure interests, but may serve them critically on occasions, i.e. the role of the Automobile Association, conservation groups, hotel groups or brewers versus that of football, racing, or other individual sports interests or associations. If in Schon's[10] terms we see Government as a learning system, then though the many leisure elements of Government may have developed belatedly, they have shown a ready and creative responsiveness to lobbies and pressure and interest groups. The responsiveness of Government to the large voluntary sector (in sport and recreation in Britain) has been ready and significant if one examines the history of the Sports Council and the annual listing in its reports[11] of bodies receiving grant support, or of the Arts Council, and its recent nurturing of the community arts movement, as well as its longer established role in serving 'high culture'. The special relationship of Central to Local Government in Britain, and the slow evolution of the regional level as an intermediate level of Government as an interchange or interface, or diffusion or switching point in devolved Central Government decision making, must be noted. Until literally the late 1970s the Regional Government in England has been assumed to be part of a marginally decentralised national bureaucracy, with selective local political and/or technical representatives joining them. Even now, the idea of regional elected assemblies in England[12] is barely getting a fair hearing, though equivalent or, in fact, very much smaller groups of population in Scotland and Wales are seen to have a right to such involvement in deciding their own affairs, including such issues as leisure, conservation and environment. In the leisure field, the informal idea of the multilogue (a discussion involving many contributors) has been with us for some time — a continuing discussion between parts of government and many interests in the community, but with effective final decision making left, until recently, on a centralised basis. At best, perhaps, the new Regional Councils for Sport and Recreation will function as a representative body for the Local Authorities in the region, but with some advice from Central Government.

GOVERNMENT PRIORITIES FOR LEISURE

Unlike quantitative questions of jobs, prices and houses, the qualitative question of leisure, its provision and access, is still a low priority in terms of direct electoral appeal and the choice of 'planks' which win or lose general elections in this country. A qualitative view of housing is a more recent phenomenon. Indeed, though 'quality of life', environmental and leisure questions have appeared in political manifestos in Britain in the 1960s and 1970s, the percentage of total words devoted to this field in these documents is low, but it is still a higher proportion of the total than is the percentage of government-spending earmarked for this sphere. However, one cannot overemphasise the difficulties in accurately estimating the total public sector expenditure in leisure because of the number of concealed budgetary items and spin-offs to leisure from other named items of expenditure, such as community use of school buildings, recreation on water supplies, and service centres and picnic grounds associated with roads.

If, however, a few items are taken which may be seen as directly and easily identifiable Government expenditures on leisure, some interesting differences of scale and implied priorities come to light. In 1976/77, £38 million was received by the Arts Council from the Government in order to grant aid and promote the arts. This sum was more than four times the size of the operational budget given to the Sports Council in 1976 (some £9 million). Furthermore, payments to bodies such as the Countryside Commissions and to the Statutory Tourist Boards have been at an appreciably lower level than to the Sports Council.

Before one can fully consider the responsiveness of Government to the public in the field of leisure, one needs to get a wider picture of what Government commitment to leisure exists now and this is best formed by examining Government's direct and indirect spending on leisure services. Analysing the returns for National Income and Expenditure[12] from 1964 to 1974, it can be seen that whilst the expenditure of Central and of Local Government has increased about three to four fold in this period, the weights allocated to various budgetary heads has generally been fairly constant, but with a few notable exceptions. The big spenders have remained Defence, Housing, Health, and Education at the Central Government level, but with the lowest proportionate increase on defence and the highest on housing. However, much of the public sector intentions are realised via grants from Central to Local Government, whose policies and expenditure patterns are quite critical for the leisure and recreation fields. In 1964, local authorities received one-third of their income from Central Government. By 1974 nearly half of the local authority budgets were met by income from Central Government. Budgets relating specifically to leisure fared better than average in terms of growth in the 1964–1974 period, but this was a relative 'boom' period in economic terms and a time of growing interest in and concern about recreation opportunities. However, it must be added that leisure started from a low base in expenditure terms and therefore needed proportionately greater boosts to catch up. In the analysis of total public expenditure 1964–1974, annual spending on libraries, museums and the arts increased from £47 million per annum to £222 million per annum and, of this, local authority current account expenditure represented an increase from £31 million per annum up to £128 million per annum. National public expenditure on parks and pleasure grounds increased from £66 million per annum to £265 million per annum. It might be noted, though, that these two distinct leisure categories of public expenditure, combined in 1974, amounted to £487 million per annum compared to a Defence Budget then of £4221 million per annum, but this in no way allows for the proportion of Education, Housing, Health and Transport budgets that contributed towards leisure wellbeing of the community.

The dates of Government initiatives in creating special agencies in relation to the leisure field (Sports Council, Arts Council, etc.), or of converting them from voluntary to statutory bodies, is in itself significant. Whilst the Arts Council dates back to 1945, with its roots in key wartime initiatives, the Statutory Tourist Boards were not created until 1969 and the Statutory and Executive Sports Councils did not come into being until the 1970s as compared to the functioning of statutory Housing and Education Departments in local government dating back to the nineteenth century, and even the Forestry Commission (with a different brief) dating back to the end of the First World War. Though the National Parks Commission was introduced in 1949, the successor Countryside Commissions are of relatively recent origin (the late 1960s) as are the radically-changed water authorities in this country. From the range of agencies and of legislation have emerged an array of permissive powers and sometimes grant support from Central Government to Local Government, with very few obligatory or statutory requirements vested by government in local authorities in respect of leisure functions.

Until recently, only minor coordinative and allocative functions in respect of leisure have been vested at the regional scale of government. The changing roles of Regional Water Authorities, of Regional Tourist Boards, of the important new Regional Councils for Sport and Recreation, of Regional Arts Associations, and of Regional Offices of the Department of the Environment, together provide opportunities for coordinated bureaucratised responses, some regional initiatives and expanded processes of publicity, and consultation in leisure planning and management. Local authority staff are in the main expected to provide the executive in this area. Since August 1975, coordinating meetings of regional arms of government concerned with leisure have been initiated. With little possibility of elected regional assemblies in England, the notion of involvement of a wide public as opposed to representatives of organisations at the regional scale of thought and action is an academic one, unless the functions of the Regional Councils for Sport and Recreation are extended and developed and complemented by twin regional councils of the voluntary bodies to represent all key user interests, as in the equivalent Danish 'Friluftsradet' (discussed later in this chapter).

LIMITS OF PUBLIC INVOLVEMENT

National and regional policies, strategies and priorities cannot be merely an aggregative process, i.e. the simple adding up of local needs. They involve weights, responsiveness to effective needs and to pressure groups and the ranking of significance of certain orders or levels of facility. Just as in town planning, wide participation and involvement is easiest at a very local scale and is selective at the more abstract larger urban and regional scales, so the same general principle applies with leisure planning. However, just as one needs national roads, ports and airport policies with selective public involvement, so with leisure planning. Recent debates on the conflicts between the provision of national and regional major prestigious leisure facilities versus investment in local small and discreet leisure provisions bring out some of the issues involved. The twenty-six year plus terminal history of the ill-fated Opera House to serve the Edinburgh Festival, the contrasting hundred year plus history of the completed National Theatre in London reflect the struggle and often the ineffectiveness of the lobbies supporting the 'few but

Roses' approach to major provisions. The failure to achieve, as opposed to planning, a balanced distribution of regional sports and
leisure centres at the major centres of population, our failure to get
more extended use, as well as multiple-use of facilities such as the
major football grounds in Britain, reflect the sectoral interests and
ineffective political lobbying at definable levels. The Sport for
All campaign and the shift from a focus on 'elites' and 'excellence'
can be seen not only in sports, but in the arts (with the Community
Arts movement) in attitudes to education and in those towards
countryside recreation. The Report of the Sandford Committee on
National Parks[13] reflects the switchover from an earlier lobbying for
minority use and conservation to the current problem of reconciling
mass use for recreation, with what is still seen as the over-riding need
for maintenance of a selective conservation role. The power of
economic arguments and pressure groups associated with mineral
exploitation in modifying the character of national parks in England
and Wales, and potential national parks in Scotland, makes a
strange contrast to the effective containment of market forces in such
places as the national parks in the United States of America.

In respect of leisure planning, accountability to the public is
divided according to a complex range of functions and scales. Whilst
at the local level, local authority leisure service departments are
accountable, via their chief officers, to their Councils and through
them to the public, it is less easy to comprehend when one
examines functions nationally. The public is ill-informed on which
agencies have which responsibilities and to which Government
Ministers they should turn if they want things changed. The lines of
responsibility of agencies and organisations to Parliament is
sometimes difficult to establish. Public needs and dissatisfactions
may be voiced in the House by specific Members of Parliament as a
result of lobbying, petitions and correspondence, but little recourse
to using the Ombudsman in redressing assumed wrongs in this realm
has been had to date. The recent focus on inner city questions by
Government, and potential attention to the leisure and other needs
of disadvantaged populations, has been more an instance of belated
Government initiative than of Government responding to major
pressures placed upon it.

OPPORTUNITIES FOR CHANGE

Is the pluralist nature of leisure and leisure interests such that
the scatter and diversity of user or activity groups will always lose
politically as compared to organised commercial and industrial
lobbies, or, for that matter, public bodies themselves? The answer is
that potentially the broader basis could be a beginning of greater

strength if this is coherently organised. The precedent in Denmark of the 'Friluftsradet', a coordinating national organisation of all the sports and recreational activity interests, enables them to employ their own consultants, become their own strong advocate planners and to talk from strength to the regional and national bodies which are responsible for planning for recreation and conservation. It creates the possibility not simply of negotiation by the public authority staff with a scatter of leisure interests, but also with a strong central representative body acting on behalf of user interests, when talking with and contributing to the ideas of the providers. In Britain, such a development might build upon the more limited approach of bodies like the Central Council for Physical Recreation or the Scottish Countryside Activities Committee, but should be at the regional scale.

In the current political and economic climate in Britain it is unlikely that a single, comprehensive and powerful Ministry of Leisure will be created to match and fit with the two hundred or more comprehensive leisure services departments now found in Local Government. Accountability to the public for decisions about leisure planning remains primarily vested in the elected councils and paid officials in Local Government, as well as the electoral support of Central Government and the large number of private and voluntary sector initiatives in the leisure field. The processes of public participation, which were introduced via town planning activities, have allowed for some direct consultation of recreation and tourism at the local, urban and county or subregional scales. In fact national park planning now has a formalised consultative process associated with it and the preparation of national (if not the regional) tourism strategies is beginning to introduce wider consultations that move towards a more participatory philosophy. However, it is possibly the new Regional Strategies for Sport and Recreation, to be prepared by the new Regional Councils for Sport and Recreation, that represents the biggest opportunity for consciously and directly involving the many recreation-publics in planning for recreation? The regional level is a critical bridge to build in this field. Perhaps, too, at the regional level, the complexity of interests, activities, organisations, responsibilities for leisure provisions by the public, and voluntary and commercial sectors, reflects a richness and mix of participants which has great possibilities for future participation.

The recreation resources *are* more extensive because of the numbers of provider and user organisations involved, and the very large number participating both in activities and management. Club 'umbrellas' at a regional scale effectively act on behalf of vast numbers of recreation activists who are thought of as 'non-clubbable' or non-joiners. For example, one may take the Birmingham Angling Club with its half a million members in an urban region of under three million population which can apparently successfully negotiate access to sufficient water areas to meet the vast scale of implied need. Simplification in the number of provider and user organisations has its risks in the possible loss of this range of vital initiatives.

Adequate budgets, executive staff and formalised processes both of consultation and involvement are needed at the regional level, with improved guidelines from Central Government to both the regional and local levels on how they can plan and manage in this field. Adaptation and use of the 'Examination in Public' type of mechanism for leisure planning at the regional scale warrants investigation. The allocative roles of Central and especially Local Government in leisure makes a coherent regional overview and responsiveness to the initiatives of others essential. The drawing together and recodifying of all the scattered bits of legislation, statutory and permissive that impinge upon leisure services, into a single consolidating Act of Parliament could give the recognition and underpinning to leisure services before 1980, that the 1947 Act gave to the town planning field.

Guidelines, participatory mechanisms, recodified acts, etc., will *not* however change the variable responsiveness, innovativeness and amount of drive found amongst different local authorities and regions. The last fifty years of experience have shown that, almost regardless of the level of legislation, high performing local authorities of the Left have stretched legislation to the limit in providing, directly from public funds, what they saw as key needs; and high performing local authorities of the Right have shown the maximum of responsiveness to private and commercial initiatives in realising leisure provisions in their areas. There is also a danger if legislation is focused in too specific a way, i.e. the provision of country parks has been at the neglect of other countryside recreation provisions; the provision of Sports Centres partly because of fashion and private enthusiasms, for a limited time, was at the expense of the provision of opportunities for indoor passive leisure opportunities, etc. Voluntary and private bodies have often set the pace in specific innovations. The work of the National Trust for Scotland, or of individual entrepreneurs like Michael Sobell, Lord Montagu of Beaulieu, the Duke of Bedford, or the more imaginative Brewers, Hotel Groups, and Theme Park sponsors can be cited.

In a period when constraints upon expenditure have become notable in the public sector, so responsiveness to joint public/private investments, the coming together of different levels of government and various public agencies and voluntary groups now take on a new urgency especially as the activities of many 'charities' have given way to action by local authorities. Leisure is a field of activity that particularly lends itself to guidelines, incentives and participatory planning and management. The low growth or no growth economy could be the unwitting catalyst which enabled Central, Regional and Local Government in Britain to move rapidly forward into such a revised style and character of joint planning and management for leisure.

REFERENCES

 1. Patmore, J. A. (1972) *Land and Leisure*. Penguin, London
 2. Burkart, A. J. and Medlik, S. (1974) *Tourism: Past, Present and Future*. Heinemann, London
 3. Turner, A. and Ash, J. (1975) *The Golden Hordes*. Constable, London
 4. Mellor, H. E. (1976) *Leisure and the Changing City: 1870–1914*. Routledge and Kegan Paul, London
 5. Dickens, C. (undated) Vide Hard Times; Sketches by Boz; Oliver Twist; The Life and Adventures of Nicholas Nickleby. In *Works of Charles Dickens Series*. Cassell & Co., London
 6. Hodder E. (1888) *The Life and Work of the Seventh Earl of Shaftesbury K.G.* Cassell & Co., London
 7. House of Lords Select Committee (1973) *Sport and Recreation*. Second Report (Cobham Report). H.M.S.O., London
 8. Department of the Environment (1975) *Sport and Recreation*. Cmnd 6200. H.M.S.O., London
 9. Sampson, A. (1971) Arts and Leisure. In *The New Anatomy of Britain*. Hodder and Stoughton, London
10. Schon, D. A. (1977) *Beyond the Stable State*. Penguin, London
11. The Sports Council (1977) *Annual Report for 1975/1976*. The Sports Council, London
12. Central Statistical Office (1975) *National Income and Expenditure 1964–1974*. H.M.S.O., London
13. National Park Policies Review (Sandford) Committee (1974) *Report of the National Park Policies Review Committee*. Department of the Environment. H.M.S.O., London

2 THE ROLE OF LOCAL GOVERNMENT

by Terry J. Marsh

That local government should have a role in the developing pattern of community participation is itself a contradiction of the traditional concept of democracy—government of the people, by the people, for the people. The concern of this chapter is to examine that role, its history and development, and perhaps, too, its future.

Local government in this country has recently undergone great change. Why? For two basic reasons:

> One is that scientific discovery and industrial progress are reshaping the life and work of the people of England faster and more fundamentally than in any previous period of our history. The material on which local government has to work, the situations that confront it, the patterns of settlement in town and country, have never stood still; but in recent years and in the years ahead they have altered and will alter in a quite new way. The second reason is of a different kind. In a period of great change, when huge unrepresentative organisations seem to control the lives of individuals and restrict personal freedom, people might be tempted to give up as a bad job the effort to master these impersonal forces. If they yielded, the loss would be irreparable. In this situation, local self-government should be a crucial influence. It should represent the citizen and be the means whereby he brings his views to bear on those public problems that touch most nearly his personal and domestic life. If local self-government withers the roots of democracy grow dry. If it is genuinely alive, it nourishes the reality of democratic freedom. [1]

CONCEPT OF DEMOCRACY

Democratic life depends on a close relationship between the public and the Council members. It is on this base that the system of representative government, democracy, purports to stand; yet it is one of the unfortunate facets of democracy that Council members cannot even hope to truly represent the whole range of views and requirements of their constituents. Instead, because of this impossibility of satisfying all groups of the community, the Councillor comes to represent a set of values. Whether this is a satisfactory arrangement is, of course, a political issue, it does not affect the general acceptance of the democratic system as a starting point for the policymaking process. What it does affect, however, is the tradition which at one time accepted the democratic processes without question. Now there is increasingly more attention being given to the interface between 'them' and 'us': between the public and his councillor, and the public and the officers of local government.

Within the traditional concept of democracy, the true role of the local government officer was never readily apparent. It was the relationship between the elected representative and his constituents which formed the main theme behind the principles of democracy. Records of Council meetings, during the early part of this century, showed that in many authorities even the most insignificant aspect of the authority's work was the subject of a report to Committee. It does not appear to have been until some time during the late 1950s that the day-to-day work of authorities increased to such an extent that Councils found it necessary to delegate aspects of their work to officers. From this time the strength and influence of officers has grown considerably, though not necessarily at the expense of democratic principles. It can clearly be seen, however, that the powers of local Councils have always in some way been fettered by the need to comply with Central Government direction. For example, the appointment of certain officers was not only obligatory, but in some cases subject to the approval of a Central Government Department. This, together with the growing delegation, vested more and more security and, with increasing confidence, power into the hands of officers.

For many years, membership of a Council provided power and prestige, as did service in the employ of the Council. Councillors were figureheads in their local community and their advice and wisdom was greatly respected. They were the representatives of the people, as were their actions. The role of Councillors, however, is not the subject of this discourse and, although it has become far more complicated and calls for a much greater sense of public duty, the principles of that role have changed little over the years. What has changed has been the attitude of the man in the street to the consequences of decisions, particularly where they affect him directly.

ACTIVE MAN

One can trace the influence of local government on people at least 150 years into history, starting in the early nineteenth century in matters of public health and the environment. In the statutes of these days are found the regulations affecting the construction and maintenance of sewers and drains, provisions for the protection of water and for the paving and cleaning of streets, and power even to purchase premises for the improvement of streets. All of these are indicative of the power vested in local authorities to impinge upon the freedom of the individual or groups of individuals. All these powers, however, derive from Parliament and in practice local authorities were seen and used as convenient instruments for implementing the will of national government:

> Local authorities occupy a wide range of subsidiary or dependant positions in relation to Parliament and the central Government. Even where a local authority has legal independence of action, it owes it to statute, and in any case is likely to be dependant on the central Government in finance. It would be wrong to say that local authorities have no life other than that which Parliament breathes into them; but they have no authority other than that which Parliament allows. [2]

These days one can ask why it was that man accepted the role of local government without question. Any answer, however, can at best only be an amalgamation of conjecture and hypothesis. For example, the very fact that the local authority's power derived from Parliament may have influenced many into the belief that the local Councils were inexplicably bound with Parliament and were therefore in some way unapproachable. The author, however, subscribes to the more mundane view that, for the vast proportion of the population, the struggle to keep a house and home together, and to earn enough to live during a period subjected to wars, industrial revolution and acute poverty, totally preoccupied the mind of the individual. There is, too, the further point that even as recent as the early 1960s the Town Hall was seen as a forbidding place from which rate demands and instructions to do or not to do were despatched; a place representing an authority which was seldom challenged or questioned and which created, within the author's experience, a sense of awe sufficient to overpower initiative in many and which exuded the notion that the Town Hall knew best.

Academic research is, however, now revealing a development of profound importance which is occurring and which is already affecting the way local government formulates it plans for recreation and other activities: 'Stated very simply, a more active view of the nature of man is emerging, a view in which consciousness, or brain function as it has been called, is seen to have a greater part in the shaping of beliefs and events than has been granted in the past. Man is seen to act on and influence his position, rather than just reacting passively to events.'[3] Indeed the view is expressed by some psychologists that within each person is the potential to identify and shape his own future, rather than merely reacting to social trends. A view which puts upon each person the responsibility to question his own actions. The validity of this point is substantiated by reference simply to a growing number of complaints received by local authorities, since each of them quite clearly indicates a departure from the hitherto passivity.

Experience in a professional situation demonstrates a growing awareness in the minds of the public to the effects of recreation planning decisions or lack of them. This awareness is heightened when a particular decision has a direct effect, positive or negative, upon an individual, i.e. a decision not to construct a play area within a particular housing community, or one which promotes the construction of a Sports Centre at the rear of the individual's property. Public reaction is, at the present time however, more of a rebellious nature than of constructive criticism: 'I stress at the beginning of this letter that I have never written to a public official before and from that fact you may conclude that I feel strongly . . .', or words to that effect, are so often, these days, met in correspondence. Very often, however, letters of this nature tend largely to express uninformed opinion and are founded on a lack of knowledge of the circumstances within which decisions were made. From this, the public are beginning to recognise that lack of information is instrumental in depriving them of the power to put forward cogent arguments and there is now an element which seeks to clarify before it criticises.

PUBLIC INVOLVEMENT

Reference was made earlier to the increasing attention which is being given to interface areas, the areas where the public and the local authority meet. A fundamental problem, however, has been that these areas have in the past been no-one's responsibility, they were a no man's land and so, even today when procedures were being formulated for the running of the new local authorities, provision for these points of contact were never designed. Indeed, evidence indicates that in many cases their existence was not even suspected. As a result, decisions can often be made without any test against objective reality. There is, however, some realisation that every decision made by local authorities is value laden and that the erstwhile presumption of local sovereignty may now be no longer relevant, or indeed, in the fact of 'active man', appropriate to the majority of local issues:

> Over the last 50 years we have moved away from the situation where individuals in society were relatively unsophisticated, many preoccupied with survival or at least with the struggle for an improved standard of living to a state where, for a powerful number, horizons are infinitely wider. Conflicting interests, opposing values and opinions as to what is and what is not in the 'public interest' have emerged. Very few if any decisions can be regarded as right, as they were 50 years ago. Many of the beliefs and practices taken for granted for many years now can be seen for

PLANNING AND MANAGEMENT33

what they are, merely expressions of certain sets of values, or instruments to protect certain interests—tree preservation, listed buildings, the many prejudices of the experts and so on.[4]

Almost the first essential in any transition towards the development of public involvement in recreation planning is the need for politicians and officers alike to understand the form and true extent of their power. They need to come to appreciate that each decision they make will affect the whole or sections of the population to varying degrees, and to accept that public participation invariably improves the quality of decisions, sometimes avoiding disastrous situations, and gives no small measure of satisfaction to those affected by the decisions. This is equally true of public involvement in any sphere of decision making whether it be recreation provision, town planning, housing schemes, etc., and many are the points of similarity.

Degrees of Involvement. If one examines objectively the levels of opportunity for public involvement, one can assess the extent to which each authority is falling down. It is suggested that a useful guide for this purpose is Sherry Arnstein's[5] interpretation of the participation spectrum, which she claims is a useful framework in which to judge examples from current practice.

The lowest levels of participation are manipulation and therapy. These points describe levels of non-participation with the real objective not of enabling people to participate in planning, but to enable those who hold the reins to educate or cure the participants. The next stage of information and then consultation progress to what Arnstein describes as 'degrees of tokenism', allow the public to hear and to have a voice. At this level, however, the public lack the power to ensure that their views will be heeded and if participation is restricted to these levels there is and can be no assurance that a change in the status quo will emerge. Placation, therefore, is basically a higher degree of tokenism, allowing the public to advise but retaining with the powerholders the continued right to decide. It is the three higher levels of participation that, at the moment, form the most difficult barrier to the development and application of public involvement techniques. These levels, which speak for themselves, are partnership, which would enable the public to negotiate with the local authority, delegated power, and public control.

OVERTURES OF CHANGE

Although discussing the development of the role of local government in providing for public involvement in planning for leisure and recreation, one cannot overlook the suggestion in Skeffington (which was concerned primarily with planning departments per se) that the issue is a much wider one than allows attention on one isolated department. It is a matter for application to the whole authority.

It is felt, however, that local government is not yet, nor may ever be, ready for the higher degrees of Arnstein's ladder. But those with their hands on their hearts in local (and central) government today cannot deny that:

> When governments did little more than wage war with the help of a professional army and keep order with the help of a voluntary magistracy, it did not matter so much that the ordinary citizen had little part to play in public affairs. Now that the Government is omnipotent and ubiquitous; its finger in every pie, a citizen who has no personal contact with the authorities can become utterly bewildered or blissfully irresponsible. [6]

Now the realisation is dawning that public participation is a two-way thing and the local community is seen to be capable of giving as well as receiving. Local government officers are having to recognise that they need (and can save much time and money by utilising) local help and that the forms of participation put forward by Skeffington in People and Planning, viz: the supply of information to the public, the promotion of community forums, opinion surveys, and the appointment of community development officers, whilst increasing to some extent the pressure on members and officers alike, go only part of the way to a realisation of the potential wealth of ideas and constructive observation. Dare I suggest that too few members or officers are prepared to demonstrate their political or professional acumen in the spontaneous atmosphere of public debate?

One of the first contributions to the development of public involvement appeared in 1960 in the form of the Local Government (Admission to Meetings) Act 1960, which compelled local authorities to admit the press and public to all meetings of the Council and its committees. The extension to encompass all committees, irrespective of their constitution, only appeared following much parliamentary and press controversy:

> The object, averred by the champions of this change, was to give the public a greater insight into the detailed workings of the system, in which so much preparatory and executive work has always, hitherto, been done in committees. [7]

Time precludes an extensive investigation into the extent to which this provision, consolidated in the Local Government Act 1972, has been used to advantage, but cursory examination reveals little active desire to tackle opportunities to understand the machinery of local government. Perhaps the time is not yet right? Perhaps awareness of these opportunities is lacking? Perhaps the vast majority of the population are still struggling for survival or self-betterment, and react only when prodded by the local press? Yet, if the Royal Commission's Report[1] is to be believed, the whole concept of reorganisation is in no small way fashioned to permit local self-government to be the means whereby each of us bring our own views to bear on those public problems that affect our personal and domestic life. Perhaps local government does not yet have this necessary cross to bear? Perhaps it should do something about it!

Apathy, however, still abounds. Only when some deficiency is highlighted, by the press media or personal experience, do most individuals seek amends, and when wrong has been put right, or justice seen to be done, peace returns. But present day local authorities were set up to *promote* and *encourage* local self-government and the development of community life; a target at which local authorities are in a unique position to aim. Multi-purpose authorities now abound, possessing the capacity and power to pursue the development of a wide range of services and to realise the full potential of their critical role in the government of local communities. How can this be achieved?

To this end there are two main requirements. Firstly to understand the need to maintain a comprehensive overview of the services provided and, secondly, to accept that the consequences of their decisions often affect the individual (or groups of individuals) in ways that can frequently be enhanced by a process of public involvement. The overview requirement is now widely if not universally accepted and finds its expression through the medium of corporate management. The processes of public involvement, alas, have a long way to go.

The Skeffington Committee advocated participation after the authority had decided which of a number of alternatives it preferred and, in so doing, attracted criticism that it failed to contribute effectively to the encouragement of participation by prohibiting involvement in the choice of properly explained alternatives. To follow this latter course, and to explain what each alternative meant both as a direct consequence and as having an affect on other possibly equally desirable alternatives, would vest with the ordinary citizen any value judgements he has the right to make.[6] Reference, however, to Arnstein's[5] ladder will show that even this level of participation carries no guarantee and that there would be a change in the status quo. The right to decide still rests with the powerholders.

Yet if participation is to be more than a public relations exercise, the people of a locality need to feel that there is a real chance of their case being accepted as well as being heard.[6]

When powerholders restrict the input of citizens' ideas solely to this level, participation remains just a window dressing ritual . . . participation is measured by how many come to meetings . . . or answer a questionnaire. What citizens achieve in all this activity is that they have 'participated in participation'. And what powerholders achieve is the evidence that they have gone through the required motions of involving 'those people'.[5]

Local government, as a general principle, requires no statutory authority to meet the public and discuss proposals with them, or to allow participation in decision making, so what, one might question, is the significance of a change in local government law which creates a situation in which it is possible for non-elected people to actually determine local government policies and practices?[8] Most people in local government are aware of the power to coopt on to committees a limited number of non-elected people, but few, it is suspected, are aware of the change in legislation introduced by Sections 101 and 102 of the Local Government Act 1972. Hitherto, legislation had prevented the delegation of executive powers to a sub-committee but Section 101 now expressly enables this delegation to take place (with one exception not applicable to the present discourse). Section 102 concerns the cooption of non-elected members to committees and sub-committees and amends the Local Government Act 1972 by removing the restriction on the number of people who may be coopted on to sub-committees: 'It is only when these two sections of the 1972 Act are taken together that the radical potential of sub-committees as vehicles for the determination of local government policy by non-elected people became clear.'[8]

It may be that these new provisions are not implemented by local authorities. Time will tell, but the fact that it is now possible, if only in a small way, for non-elected members to actually make decisions is perhaps a sign of changing attitudes, somewhere, towards public involvement. It is, of course, quite possible for a determined local community to affect or change decisions. The movement to defeat the third London Airport at Stanstead is an adequate example. But it still requires a tremendous amount of effort on someone's part to organise a movement on that scale. The effort is all the more daunting without the surety that the voices will not only be heard, but will also carry the power to effect some change.

APPROACHES TO PARTICIPATION

Problems of size and a need to ensure that the interests of the public of some fourteen individual local authorities did not appear to be overlooked, led the Wigan Metropolitan Borough Council to introduce (in 1974) the concept of Leisure Advisory Committees. These took the form of open public meetings attended by members of the Recreation and Amenities Committees and senior officers of the Department of Leisure. Those of the public attending were invited to put their points of view or questions to the panel and any problem which could not be answered at the meeting was dealt with by correspondence. Each person attending the meeting received a copy of the minutes, which were also submitted to the Recreation and Amenities Committee, and was automatically invited to the next and subsequent meetings.

In an attempt to adequately cover the area, six Leisure Advisory Committees were set up, each meeting three times a year. There were times when the members and officials outnumbered the public, but many individuals and organisations undoubtedly found this a valuable forum to put their case across. From inception in May 1974 to January 1976, some thirty four Leisure Advisory Committees attracted nearly six hundred members of the public and raised or discussed two hundred and ninety points of concern or interest. This latter figure, however, does not include the numerous highway, housing, or other non-related matters which were raised and were referred to the appropriate department.

As the work of the Leisure Advisory Committees developed, there was an identifiable change in attitude from the public. At first the atmosphere was faintly hostile, each side unsure what the other intended, but then the true value of the meetings was perceived by some members of the public and the meetings put to good effect. Unfortunately, time does not permit research into the measure of benefit the public feel they derive from these Committees, but it is known that a few individuals at least appreciated the ability to pose questions about the authority's plans for recreation and to know that the Committees' principles ensured that they received an answer.

There has been one particularly outstanding success for the concept of Leisure Advisory Committees when, in response to the ubiquitous call for play areas, a survey of land availability in relation to play area provision indicated a location apparently quite suitable. It was with some surprise that the local Leisure Advisory Committee learned that the play area was not wanted by the local mothers because, simply, the site layout of the estate had effectively created a totally enclosed area of ground far more capable of supervision from kitchen windows than an authority provided play area a short distance away. In the normal course of events, that unwanted play area could have been constructed before local reaction had organised itself into writing to the department.

Leisure Advisory Committees have helped, too, in dealing with pressure groups and the 'club' reaction by providing a public opportunity to let off steam, to hear the local authority's points of view and reasoning, and to then discuss (initially a process of criticism and counter-criticism) the issue in question. The very fact that the public are able to speak directly to the members of the committee, the appropriate chief officer and his senior management staff, all of whom have gone to the public in their own locality and out of normal working hours, serves well, if nothing else, to break down the red tape, appointments and correspondence barriers which so often daunt a vast section of the population.

In the short time that these leisure committees have operated there have been no occasions when their existence has not helped. Indeed, the general principle of 'going to the people', whilst perhaps only part of a solution, has led to quite a number of meetings with select groups on such subjects as, for example, the development of allotment sites, horse and pony activities, and the use of the Department's new sports centres and their effects on nearby residents.

There have been many instances where participation has extended to no more than the alleviation of fears and anxieties, and this must surely be an indication that for many years to come much falls to be done in the way of publicity. Many people are content (for various reasons) to allow local authorities to continue unhindered with their plans for the development of community life and the elevation of the quality of life. For most people, concern is only generated when a local authority's proposals or actions have a direct effect and if, at this stage in the development of local self-government, all that the public ask is to be kept informed, is not that then the absolute minimum that ought to be undertaken by every authority?

Moving towards the higher reaches of Arnstein's[5] ladder, Wigan have prepared a Constitution for Community Centre Councils (see Appendix) which effectively gives the Centre Council a considerable amount of freedom to run the Centre for themselves and to organise their own programmes, etc. From Monday morning until Friday afternoon, the Community Centre Councils have absolute authority to organise the use of the Centre as they see fit. Applications for use are dealt with by the Centre Council and the local authority Council will not deal with any matter falling within the Centre Council's province. Indeed, there have been occasions to pointedly endorse the Centre Council's authority. Over the weekend periods the Centre is available for hire through the Department of Leisure in the same way as a public hall, but care is taken to ensure that weekend use does not operate to the detriment of the efforts of the Centre Council.

All the present weekday use of the Community Centres is understandably centred around local self-help principles, i.e. playgroups, aged persons activities, ballroom dancing, coffee mornings, bingo, etc. But all is not sweetness and light, and there have been occasions when disruption has been caused by clashes of personality. This, of course, is inevitable to some extent but, in one instance at least, the future of a Centre Council has been threatened by the severity of the clashes.

Each meeting of a Centre Council is attended by the appropriate chief officer in the Department, and although this creates a situation in which it is possible to influence the thinking of the Centre Council this generally does not occur and is not part of the chief officer's brief. He is there primarily to assist in a pseudo-secretarial and advisory capacity; to alleviate problems, which occur with any new project, and aid those not accustomed to the management responsibility of community facilities. He is, of course, a monitor of activities but it is conceivable that the need for anyone at all from the Department to attend will diminish as the Centre Council grows in stature and, more to the point, as the local authority perceives the developing success of what is still very much a new concept and a radical step forward.

CONCLUSION

It is difficult to assess just when and how far the public should be involved in decision making. Many decisions require no real involvement at all. For example, the facilities which each authority already has in the main only give rise to decisions affecting day-to-day running or general maintenance. If the true value of public involvement is to be realised then perhaps the exercise should only be implemented when major decisions are in the offing. In this way it is possible to 'write-in' public involvement stages in the programme and to ensure that this involvement is an ongoing aspect of each project on which the authority embarks. When this occurs, however, there is a coincidental change in emphrasis which may not be readily appreciated. It is the change from providing what the authority *thinks the public needs*, to providing what it *knows it wants*. And perhaps in reality this is the whole essence of public involvement: the removal of an arbitrary barrier which hitherto had prevented effective two-way communication. It is the resolution of the interface problem.

One final note of caution however. In the recreation and leisure field, the greatest problem, if one joins the 'involvement movement', is to separate the wants of the community from the wants of those who shout the loudest. This can only be effectively resolved by taking participation to the people, by asking and seeking advice and by willingly bearing the cross of involvement.

In less esoteric terms, this means recognising that one of the basic criticisms of public participation is that it is open to domination by pressure groups. The Leisure Advisory Committees, for example, have provided minority groups with the opportunity to make themselves appear to be a majority, creating the problem for management of ensuring that undue exclusivity of use does not occur. Human nature dictates that anyone who attends a public meeting is a minority person. He is one of the minority who are prepared to leave their television and warm fireside and tell someone what it is they require. There is danger in adopting the line, 'if people don't tell us what they want, they will have to take what we provide'. It is the majority who say little, if anything. But, in applying public participation principles, they are the people to be counselled. Pressure groups highlight certain deficiencies predominantly peculiar to their own needs. They may even claim to represent 'all the swimmers' in an area, but they could never claim to represent the people as a whole. They do, however, represent a body of users who provide part of the authority's income from facilities and to that extent they have a voice. But fully effective public participation means asking *all* the people of a catchment area. It means involving *all* of them and recognising pressure groups for what they are, a minority group of vested interests. No-one should make light of public participation, it requires tremendous involvement if it is to succeed.

The steps taken by Wigan are essentially in the nature of experiments. So far they have proved successful, although it is recognised that much still needs to be done. The Community Centre concept has much to commend it, in so far as it helps in the development of grass roots local self-government.

There may be many ways the experiments can be advanced, but until it is generally accepted that participation means just that, then experiments will remain such for some time to come. The power to involve the public in decision making by local authorities is there. It represents something of a departure from the traditional concept of democracy and from the way local authorities have been accustomed to working. But it is, nevertheless, a mutually beneficial change which will promote a much clearer and less autocratic view of the services local authorities provide. All that is needed now is the courage to implement it.

REFERENCES

1. The Report of the Royal Commission on Local Government in England (1966) *Local Government Reform*. (The Maud

Report). Cmnd 4039. H.M.S.O., London
2. Eddison, T. (1975) *Local Government: Management and Corporate Planning.* 2nd edn. Leonard Hill Books, London
3. Haworth, J. T. and Smith, M. A. (1975) *Work and Leisure: An Inter-disciplinary Study in Theory, Education and Planning.* Lepus Books, London
4. Eddison, T. (1975) Public involvement in local authority policy planning. In *Local Government: Management and Corporate Planning.* 2nd edn. Leonard Hill Books, London
5   Arnstein, S. (1969) A ladder of citizen participation. *Journal of the American Institute of Planning,* July
6. Rees, I. B. (1971) *Government by Community.* Charles Knight & Co. Ltd., Kent
7. Butterworth's Annotated Legislation Service (1973) *Introduction: Local Government Act 1972.* Butterworth & Co. Ltd., London
8. Richardson, A. (1976) Power to the co-opted. *Municipal and Public Services Journal,* 23 July

Appendix

RECOMMENDED CONSTITUTION FOR A COMMUNITY CENTRE

The Council shall be called 'The Community Centre Council'
Membership: The Council shall consist of:

a) The representatives appointed by constituent bodies and sections. Constituent bodies are such organisations as operate in the area of benefit and satisfy the Council that they are independent organisations or branches of independent national or other organisations. Sections shall be such groups as may, with the permission of the Council, be formed within the Centre among the individual members for the furtherance of a common activity.

b) Two elected representatives of the local authority's Recreation and Amenities Committee.

c) Such number of representatives of members to be elected from the community at the Annual General Meeting but not to be more than half the number of Council members appointed under Clause 1.

d) The honorary officers of the Centre and of the Council ex-officio.

HONORARY OFFICERS

The Annual General Meeting shall elect a President, a Treasurer and a Secretary and such other officers as it may from time to time determine.

e) The Director of Leisure (or his representative).

f) The Directors (or representatives of Social Services and Education Departments.

In addition the Council may coopt further members who shall be members of the Centre provided that the number of coopted members shall not exceed one third of the total number of members of the Council as defined above. All members of the Council shall retire annually, but shall be eligible to be re-appointed or coopted again. The Council shall have powers to appoint such committees as it may from time to time decide and may determine their powers and terms of reference.

DUTIES

The Council shall be responsible for the day-to-day management of the Centre and will advise the Recreation and Amenities Committee on all matters of finance and policy. It will be responsible for the development of clubs and societies associated with the Centre and attempt to maximise the use of the Centre in the interests of the local community. Decisions of the Council in relation to changes in finance or policy are subject to the approval of the Recreation and Amenities Committee.

3 COMMUNITY PARTICIPATION AND DEMOCRATIC CONTROL
A case study of a community college

by Arfon Jones

In August 1972, the Sidney Stringer School and Community College was opened in the Coventry districts of Hillfields and Foleshill. The institution was composed of 1600 pupils brought together from the amalgamation of two secondary modern schools and a language teaching unit. There were new buildings being built in the centre of the city to accommodate pupils, as well as two annexes (one nearby and the other a mile away). To service the institution was a teaching and community staff of 143, composed of the staff of the two secondary modern schools and newly appointed staff, some in senior positions, attracted to the new concept of community education.

Hillfields and Foleshill are densely populated areas with many new high rise flats or old Victorian terrace houses. The Hillfields area, in particular, had been the focus for a considerable amount of redevelopment for over twenty years. Residential property exists cheek by jowl with industrial premises and there is little open green space. In 1969 it was deemed a suitable area for a Community Development Project. The catchment area reflected roughly the school's population, which is approximately 50% Asian, 40% English and European and 10% West Indian.

Initially the project was seen as being a school with an element of dual use. Later the Local Authority rejected the concept of dual use of buildings with school finishing at 4.00 p.m. and the community taking over at 6.00 p.m. This was based upon their experience of management problems in dual use establishments, especially where the direction was not unified. It was decided that the school and all other activities would be under a single Head who would control an integrated staff. Emphasis on community education was helped by the appointment of a new Director of Education and the appointment of a working party on Youth and Community provision, which reported in 1969 to the Education Committee already concerned with the disruption in family life that 'positive action is required to reinforce family life. We have too a strong sense of the need in Coventry for development of a sense of community'.

Through the authority and the Community Development Project, a Community Education Project was initiated aimed at achieving links between schools and homes. As its leader stated, 'the whole process of community education is to raise the level of consciousness of the people who live in the area'. Aims and objectives were established by the new Head. What the enterprise aimed to do for the community was 'to be seen by the residents as an enterprise which is theirs, which has their interests at heart, to which they can turn for resources and advice, in which they feel welcome and secure. It aims to help residents to improve the quality of life in this area working alongside them and the other professional and political agencies . . . It aims to be a Community Centre managed by the residents for their own benefit with as little interference from the professionals as possible'.

It hoped for a 'complex integration of school activities on three sites' and the 'satisfaction of the real and priority needs of the people it serves rather than the personal satisfaction of the professionals.' The Head decided that Sidney Stringer, since it needed to be committed to innovation and was large and complex, needed the following organisational features: 'Organic-nonhierarchical-enabling multi-disciplinary teams of specialists to co-operate in projects or tasks. This would encourage initiative from younger staff and decentralise much of the detailed decision making.' Secondly, the institution would be 'project or product based, so that staff responsible for development of pupils and community members would have power to see that excellence is directed towards the needs of the people the college is servicing.' It was clear that many senior members of staff saw the institution as an agent of social change, though there would be fundamental disagreement among them concerning the nature of that change. They concentrated, to begin with, on the school.

The two secondary modern schools, which had been the major educational experience for most of the students and many staff, had been streamed, tightly knit, hierarchical closed institutions. They used, among other controls, corporal punishment as sanctions. Sidney Stringer reorganised teaching into mixed ability settings, with a team teaching an organic approach to the curriculum. In the first year corporal punishment, which had been used briefly, was abolished. The curriculum was given relevance and, in the first three years, a large amount of teaching time was given over to inter-disciplinary enquiry with individual resource based learning as its foundation.

The school emphasised CSE Mode 3 rather than 'O' levels and, as part of its common core in years four and five, students had to undertake a compulsory two year course in Social Studies which was to equip them to understand and analyse their environment, in particular that of their community. Contributions to the curriculum would come from adults living in the area. In its clearest form, Community Service was seen as paternalistic and regeneration would come from the students' new understanding and insights into social structure and relationships; the flesh and bones of Hillfields and Foleshill. Among certain staff there was a belief that this might lead the institution to take a critical stance in relation to the Local Authority and that this would be shown in the curriculum.

The first two years were very difficult. Many of the staff were apathetic or hostile to the community concept. Many were confused by the new structures and curriculum. Some of the newly appointed members, though conversant with the concepts of progressive education, lacked experience in basic classroom technique so that there was considerable suspicion and some intolerance between two large groups of staff. Initially, staff wished to be considered either as full-time teachers or full-time community workers. The senior management opposed this dual purpose concept, though at its inception, in terms of staff function, this was the reality. The present evolved system is based on the following:

1) All staff may volunteer for community work and for every hour spent in community work, time off in lieu is given, freeing them from teaching duties.

2) Community team members should have a teaching qualification and spend a percentage of their time on teaching duties.

We now have the following categories of staff:

1) Those who teach full-time.

2) Community workers who teach for a percentage of time.

3) Staff who spend 50% of their time teaching and 50% of their time in community work.

4) Staff who spend most of their time on teaching duties and some of their time in community work.

The distinction between traditional teaching roles and other roles have been deliberately clouded, but the nature of the institution has speeded up this process.

There were other problems as well. The new buildings were not ready and at one stage staff were trying to operate on four sites. There was a Gas Strike and the raising of the school leaving age. But most serious of all was violence, which at one stage took on a racial tone with whites and West Indians ganging up on Asians and with minor outbreaks of mugging. There was also large scale truancy for, in a confused new system, students found it easy to miss lessons. It may be argued that whenever two separate inner city schools are joined there may be problems similar to those one has described.

However, one feels too that the attempt to establish new techniques and norms exacerbated the problems. Today, the school has fewer than 1% truants and no violence at all in the classroom. There is the lowest rate of vandalism in any school in Coventry and an atmosphere that the many visitors describe as warm and happy. There are also excellent relationships between staff and pupils. The examination results are also good. There is a unified staff, nearly all showing various degrees of enthusiasm for community education.

While it is not possible to evaluate, in any statistical sense, causal relationships between any of the indices of progressive education and the present level of success, there is little doubt that the combination of those factors, within the context of community education, are its foundations. This success would not have been achieved if power and control had been passed to a staff body. In the first eighteen months, the majority of staff and parents would have voted for a return to established and traditional forms of education with an emphasis on strong discipline equated with corporal punishment. There would also have been decisions which would have divided school from community use of premises. Because power had been invested in a small number of senior staff, they were able, though not without much heart searching, to maintain allegiance to the established principles of community education combined with new educational strategies. Traditional structures would have, at least in my opinion, exaggerated racial tension and produced an atmosphere counterproductive to the involvement and participation of those members of the community least likely to take up activities. The following is a clear example of a total concept of community use which has repercussions in the short term for community development and in the longterm, perhaps, for weakening the cycle of deprivation.

One has to emphasise the school experience of children when attempting to understand strategies that lead to involvement by adults previously unwilling to participate. If the child experiences rejection, and if the structure is authoritarian, then it is extremely difficult to persuade the child, when he becomes an adult, to return to the institution, however well equipped or relevant the courses or activities might be.

Most Community Colleges have a mothers' group, but the Sidney Stringer group has certain differences. It is all white and was brought together in Sidney Stringer by the local Social Services Department. A community worker, who was also a qualified teacher of Home Economics, was attached to the group. They were given a 'space' in a project area where teaching in aspects of child care, in needlework and fashion for children of statutory school age also took place. A small creche was established for the preschool children, looked after initially by a rota of mothers and pupils involved in child care CSE courses. The mothers drank coffee and gossiped while gradually and with increasing confidence eavesdropped on lessons that went on simultaneously. The community worker, who had by this time gained their trust, then took certain lessons in child care and the teacher sat among the mums. The next step was to ask the mothers to exhibit some points of child rearing to the pupils, such as changing a nappy. Gradually discussion, informal and unstructured at first, started to take place which evolved to such a time as when the community worker with the teaching staff and outside help could start a formal structured adult education course in child rearing. Once mothers had confidence and security in education, the next stage was to disseminate their knowledge and new perceptions to other mums living in their neighbourhood. Mums, some of whom had rejected school, had experienced with confidence an adult education class where theory and practice, discussion and debate had been natural and acceptable aspects.

Some of the fifteen and sixteen year old girls would also have been a part of this group. Their future would be similar, in some instances, to the reality of the lives of the mothers. When they became mothers, perhaps at seventeen or eighteen, they too might face life in a high rise flat. It would not be sufficient to know that a playgroup existed at Stringer. It would be essential that the girl knew a welcome awaited her, that her response to school was positive and that she felt it to be a warm and caring atmosphere; that people she knew as teachers, whom she knew had cared for her, still existed and did not evoke hostile memories or threatened her hard earned and won adult status. There would be no possible way that such a girl would involve herself if she had spent most of her adolescence in the 'D' stream, forced to wear uniform and made to feel a failure. This is the reality of the total community concept. And what better person than an eighteen year old mother to talk to those girls, now fifteen and who remembered her as a pupil when they were twelve, about the realities of pregnancy and child rearing. The same principles underlined the approach to the involvement of Asian women.

The establishment of work with a particular group unused to the utilisation of leisure or informal adult education, demands the use of one worker to establish out of plant contact. This contact, in this case, was through the use of English as a Second Language and, because of the formalised end product, acquired the full support of the Asian community. However the real benefit accrued in socialisation and an examination of Western concepts of play and language development in both mother tongue and a second language. On a simple level, many women found this to be their major social outlet and rescue from loneliness in an alien community.

For the involvement of the vast majority of adults, who normally do not take up adult education, the following criteria must apply:

1) One or two staff solely concerned with establishing relationships and leading groups, which may be in the first instance small in size, into the new and perhaps forbidding environment.

2) The gradual introduction of teaching staff who are first seen as small parts of the group and not as teachers of pupils.

3) That the content of courses become specific only when the group have reached a consensus as to the nature of the problem, which may be anything from child development of the adolescent to the demands of unskilled work in a factory environment with no union protection.

4) That when the educational process has reached a certain level of competence the mothers, in this case, become further agents of change and take their conceptual knowledge of their initial problem and their verbal power over their previous conditions into their own neighbourhood, undertaking the informal adult role and passing on their new knowledge. Here again the community worker welcomes and establishes the new clients, but also backs and supports her first contacts: all this in a warm and caring atmosphere.

In a multi-racial setting it has proved clear that it is important to treat ethnic groups separately. It is not useful to start a multi-racial group because through a variety of motives the major group will become dominant. It is more important for all groups to establish their identity on their own. A meeting can be arranged, perhaps once a term, where all groups can see the benefits of cooperation or even amalgamation. In the first instance, a community organised rummage sale. In the second, the establishment of a common multi-racial creche.

It was always the intention at Sidney Stringer that the management of the institution would eventually pass into the hands of the community. In other words it was insufficient that participation was being achieved, at various levels of intensity, from formalised badminton classes to informal education, with groups who have previously rejected education structures and values. It was felt that democratic control and decision making should be eventually fundamental to the management and accountability of Sidney Stringer.

Accordingly, a Sidney Stringer School & Community Association with its own constitution (Appendix A), developed in consultation with the Local Education Authority, was set up. In essence, it was open to all people who lived in the catchment area and was an attempt to widen responsibility for decision making. The basis of the Association was the Council which debated and voted upon major issues. It in turn set up sub-committees composed of parents, users, students and staff examining in detail various aspects of the institution; Education-school sub-committee, Resources and Finance, Youth, Leisure and Sports. These sub-committees were financed on the basis of application from the monies received by the Council. The intention was that each sub-committee would play a major part in policy initiation and also in helping to administrate various activities. While the Head was ex-officio on each committee, the relationship between his powers, as laid out in the instrument and articles of government and that of the Association, was never made clear.

The direct link between the Association and the Board of Government (Appendix B) was established by election of individuals from specified categories of membership of the Association. It was felt that a large number of individuals elected by the Association was to be able to safeguard its interests and allocate funds to its development. Difficulties arose between those who saw themselves as accountable representatives of the Association and others who saw themselves as governors with a wider brief than the Association. Others saw the Association not as the integral basis of the institution, but rather as a useful subsidiary analogous to a Parents Teachers Association. It would seem that a two tier system of democratic decision making in the government of the college was being set up. At all levels there was a two tier system of accountability. In the case of staff representatives, from staff to Council staff representatives to Staff Board of Governors. The constitution was confused in two areas, though in themselves they need not have been major problems. The first was concerned with the control of cash and decisions about expenditure created by various activities; whether the control remained with the professional staff, with the Association, or with the Board of Governors. The second area was the relationship and power of the Head in relation to both the Association and the Governors. However, even if clarification was available, there was a more fundamental error which was the failure to perceive the relationship between power and democratic control.

The Local Authority, in its genuine attempt to set up a democratic structure, perceived the Sidney Stringer Centre as fulfilling the needs of the area of benefit and felt it necessary to give power to the community. But what was clear from the previous liberal attempts of the Community Development Project to devolve power was that one was passing power not to the participating masses, but to those who were clearly adroit at using, for instance, committee work and constitutionalism. In the often humdrum details of committee work, it was a particular type of person who maintained sufficient enthusiasm to develop control. The majority of people in the catchment area were unused to the ethos of committee work or were bored or made insecure by the genuine manipulation of procedures. Community staff may have found themselves in the position of having brought carefully nurtured members to committees only to see their proteges' insecurity heightened or their own close relationship demeaned by the genuine but complex formal structure of decision making. A person who enjoys committee work (even for the greater good) is not typical of the majority, especially in an inner city area. Sidney Stringer Council became dominated by staff and its racial balance did not adequately reflect its catchment area. Attempts to increase members and participation failed because the structure, albeit democratic, inhibited involvement.

The Local Authority also had the desire that excess monies should be used for the benefit of the people of the catchment area. Profits made from the bar should return not to the Education Authority, or even to the bar itself, but rather to the individuals and groups in the community. While it was seen that the Board of Government would recognise broad areas of financial policy, the actual specific expenditure would remain in the control of the Finance Committee of the Council. However, the Council was small groups of individuals motivated by various aspects of the human personality; from genuine desire to help to a desire for political control and political financing.

G. D. H. Cole[1] argued that it was only in the participation at the local groups and associations that the individual could 'learn democracy':

> Over the vast mechanism of modern politics the individual has no control, not because the state is too big, but because he is given no chance of learning the rudiments of self-government within a smaller unit.

What actually happens is that individuals gain control by the support of other small groups and maintain that support through the use of power. A kind of working class bureaucracy is established, whose major impetus follows closely certain aspects of Weber's analysis; not so much in the disciplined subordination to a hierarchy of command, but rather in presenting a barrier in which even the willing local citizen has difficulty in participating and in perpetuating its own existence. And when the committee has also the power to give out cash grants, the action of the Local Authority, in transferring parts of its financial control to the local community, is not democracy but the passing of power to a smaller group who desire to do good from the limited perception of a detailed knowledge of a small segment of a community or neighbourhood. And this perception, though not thankfully at Stringer, could be racist, prejudiced or ideologically motivated.

Very little education in democracy takes place since the elements of control and power are already well understood. Liberals and radicals who advocate the power of association and neighbourhood groups must be clearly aware that they are not handing over power to the people, but to small networks of hardworking persevering individuals whose actions and involvement in constitutional and democratic frameworks are often a major barrier to participation by larger groups of individuals. There is a specific danger clearly outlined by D. P. Moynihan[2] in his criticism of the American poverty programme, which the Stringer experience could not to date refute. To guide groups into participation in an attempt based on a tenuous theory about the alienation of the poor and the evils of powerlessness, and attempt to produce widespread democratic control and participation, is really to pass power to yet another group and perhaps deny those in most need from the benefits of an enterprise set up to satisfy those needs.

The second danger is the use by ideologically motivated professionals of the structure of a democratic institution and their own verbal power to gain control or to put their own spokesmen into positions of control. Teachers do not have a political constituency, but association constitutions allow them to decide the course of political action. It is often the young hardworking committed teacher, often single, who is able and willing to spend much of his leisure pursuits in committee work and the aims of the institution. The more senior teacher, because of curriculum demands or indeed family commitment, may not wish to engage in such action and is thereby often denied the opportunity to have his attitude and perception of the educational and social process recognised, and acted upon, even when they are in the majority. Professionalism can be seen as either a set of actions described by linguistically determined orders of meaning that separate and mystifies the amateur, or it can be seen as a body of skills and layers of meaning and experience that supports an individual engaged in an activity, however ill-defined that activity and its associated values might be.

At Sidney Stringer, the democratic structure of the Association allowed informal control and, in the instances of some committees, formal control to be passed to groups of staff who had no accountability for their actions. They acted as individuals, making decisions or supporting arguments without any reference to any named and debated objective specified by the institution. Though a paid professional, his leisure time was spent in action that reinforced or opposed his professional duties. A member of the Community Team, for instance, has to debate and declare his action as part of a general policy agreed and accepted by the Head and the Board of Governors. As a member of the Association, the same member of staff had accountability only to his own conscience, or ideology, even though his actions were similar to that of his paid duties In most instances he was perceived and listened to by members of the Association as a member of staff. These criticisms are easy and the errors obvious even to the inarticulate. Alternatives are even more tenuous, but they must be looked at.

One of the most powerful groups at Sidney Stringer is the professional. Immersed in and committed to his task, he has such command of techniques and details that it takes a particularly courageous or boorish layman to object to the principles of an institution upon which so much hard cash and effort is spent; especially in open debate. It would be more difficult still for an immigrant with little confidence in his command of English to contradict the expert. Obviously, there must be major checks on the scope of the professional as recent events in Tyndale School so clearly show us. But the professional worker, whether teacher or community worker or, as in the case of Sidney Stringer, a combination of both roles, has, through his training, the organisation of the institution and the new roles that he is asked to develop, as well as a constant contact and reappraisal to make of both his own educational philosophy and those of his colleagues. Whatever democratic structures are laid upon him, by the very fact that he undergoes training and is immersed in detail, he is paid to interfere in people's lives. In one sense, the act of successfully motivating a child from a non-academic family will in some fundamental way change the structure of that family. By involving parents in differing child rearing practices, the professional influences community life (e.g. by educating a black child in this country to fit into two differing cultures he changes and interferes and intervenes).

Only the exceptional laymen is able to compete with his expertise and, in an institution of 1600 students, 2000 adult students, of 250 full- and part-time staff, issues and decisions must be informed ones. Decisions have to be justified but, with all the recognised dangers of elitism, paternalism and tokenism, the professionals' extra power in a democratic structure must be recognised and understood. Evidence from other institutions suggests that by retaining power in the hands of the professional, the motivation of people to participate in change is weakened. For instance, when parental response is ignored or shunned and is seen as a threat.

We have learnt at least two lessons from Sidney Stringer:

1) To ignore the formal and informal power of the professional is to falsify the analysis. It may lead to situations where the structures for establishing democracy and participation are illusions where the majority of people are denied the human resources available to them.

2) Openly, the professional must justify his use of power to the people he serves. If he is honest, discusses problems and disagreements openly, establishes a close and frequent contact at both the institution and the home, then, in the experience of Stringer, he receives an open and supportive response. He must not deny his professional skills and experience, neither his responsibility to those in his care and his accountability to the Local Education Authority.

In the Stringer experience, it would appear that participation is greatest not necessarily within democratically established structures, but where the professional, as part of a team attached to that institution, exhibits his professionalism and lays bare the content of his method to the resident or parent. A major example of this may be seen in Neighbourhood Group Work (Appendix C). The basis of this work lies in the first activities initiated at Sidney Stringer. Because buildings were unavailable, staff worked with small groups of individuals who normally would not join other clubs or associations. The staff followed conventional community development approaches and were successful in articulating needs. They established playgroups, a newspaper called Foleshill Roots, and a Residents' Group. In most instances, attempts to involve residents in organisation and transferring direct control resulted in either the sudden demise of the activity or its gradual decay.

The radical ethos of the late 1960s made staff particularly sensitive to accusations of paternalism, or tokenism, leading to errors. For instance, Foleshill Roots, which gave a valuable service as a local newspaper involved in local issues where interviews with local residents helped to articulate demands and attitudes, was sold directly to the public and thus, surviving without subsidy, died because control and technique was made the responsibility of local residents, many of whom wanted little to do with organisation, but valued and supported the newspaper. Nevertheless, the value of local street based contact, if only for establishing means for contact between institution and people, was seen as crucial in establishing participatory structures. Accordingly, the catchment area was divided into specific areas, though the boundaries often owed as much to convenience as to knowledge of community feeling. As part of their professional duties, staff were allocated to each area with the initial brief of establishing contact, to seek and to hear needs, and to see where and how the institution could react to those needs.

In 1976, one area team developed to the stage of the following objectives of (a) assisting residents' groups in application for planning permission for a playsite and its development if successful. Play is considered an important issue in the area and is to be pursued whether planning permission is successful or not; (b) exploration and development of Neighbourhood tutor group work; and (c) establishment of tenant groups to take up tenants' problems and other issues that might arise. The members of staff involved here are a Scale 2 teacher of Heavy Craft, and a member of the Senior Executive Team.

In another area, a Scale 1 Mathematician and a Scale 2 Social Studies teacher, who is also a staff governor, alongside a part-time playleader who is not attached to Sidney Stringer, is attempting the continuation of work with parents on educational issues and play; the establishment of Saturday morning 'play time' and 'junior' (7–11 years) youth club; and the extension of contacts to non-Stringer parents. In another area, a community worker, who also teaches alongside a drama specialist, is attempting increased links with the Residents' Association and improvement of their play provision; the development of family language tuition and increased educational support for non-English speaking families; and the development of group discussion sessions for Asian teenagers. It is crucial that the work is reported and discussed at an appropriate institute team. There must be continual feedback to help sensitise the institution to the articulated needs of the community it serves.

One further important development is that each area now elects its parents onto the Council of the Community Association from which, as parents, two are elected onto the Board of Governors. Here we have a clear line of participation from small local neighbourhood groups to the Council of the Association and onto the Board of Governors, though again it should be stressed that the parent so involved passes many tests and demands many qualities, especially endurance.

It is the role of the professional to support, guide and in some instances select the parent, the student, or the adult users, who need to be represented. To hand over to those who can easily speak, is a reneging of responsibility by those paid to protect the majority. The cake is never sufficient to fill all bellies. Therefore, the crucial role of the professional is to protect those unable or unwilling to demand a slice. In the case of Stringer, this might mean those without English or specific immigrant women or single parent families. And they are protected on the Council or Committees by paid officers so that the cash or human resources available are directed towards those in most need. And to determine this, democracy is, in a sense, irrelevant, though participation is not.

It is thus perfectly possible for the two groups mentioned (the white women's groups and the Asian non-English speaking mothers) to have their views adequately and strongly presented at council meetings. These issues have to be discussed, if necessary by a professional in their own secure groups, who has the onerous and difficult task of presenting the issues and indeed to guide people's thinking. In other words, in a fashion similar to the teaching process. But he does this not as an individual elected onto a particular committee, but as a professional and a part of a professional team with specific objectives and aims fully discussed within the structure of organisation laid down for professional workers. The politician with a political constituency must not be ignored and must not lose confidence in his right to question, promote and dismiss those paid to help the needs of his constituents. Often his confidence has been undermined by criticism from the far Left about the unrepresentative nature of his vote, and also by his desire to support his paid officials when, in many instances through his political party, he has major contact with his constituents and their feelings.

In a Community College which aims to integrate school and community, the parent becomes a key client. Many schools in inner city areas express dismay at the 'lack of interest' shown by parents in school and education, especially at parents meetings. The Stringer experience contradicts this in great measure though to begin with staff outnumbered parents at meetings. The parent is interested in Sidney Stringer because his child attends, but he is also interested in leisure in his own right as someone living in the catchment area.

In our very early days we insisted that the House Head, who was responsible for the academic and social development of 120 pupils for five years from the year they arrived until the year they left school, was charged with making at least one annual contact at the home of the child. Despite initial difficulties and fears by House Heads worried about visits to homes, this became an established practice. There are obvious beneficial results in motivating children. However, the crucial result was the involvement of the House Head in the family. At best, and we stressed that the visits should be positive and that the House Head should visit not because Johnny was in trouble but because he was doing well, the House Head became immersed in the family. Once a relationship has been developed, the House Head would ask the parent to attend important meetings, including those discussing the curriculum. In some instances, the families' problems would be discussed. The House Head acted as a lever to any excess flights of curriculum fancy by his more ambitious colleagues and was able to assess the tempo of community feeling, not only about the feelings of parents, but that of adults as well, and this he could feed back into the organisation of the College. He could involve parents because his role was easily recognised and trusted. The 'pure' community worker will have great difficulty until he too disguises himself as a teacher, or someone concerned with adult education.

At its most extreme, or at best, the teacher's role widens and he can become teacher, social worker, friend and community action politician, though this is extremely demanding and few can manage more than two functions. But, at the very least, the member of staff's knowledge and experience of the community gives greater depth to his analysis and understanding of the needs of his pupils to the relevance of the curriculum and to the attempts to communicate the value of education to parents and residents. He also widens his outlook to see himself as part of a multi-professional team; a team composed of social workers, community workers, teachers from junior and infant schools, as well as his own colleagues with different functions in his institution.

An illustration of the role in its more pure form is that funded by the Gulbenkian Foundation where a Young Persons Development Adviser was established with the specific task of raising the educational horizons and expectations of a particular deprived area. Working closely with other agencies, he has shown that a concentrated multi-professional approach can create major responses from parental involvement, on the one hand, to a proper concentration of support and treatment to individuals and families in great difficulty, on the other. His work suggests new roles and functions for adult education tutors operating often, at present, with groups who are most able to help themselves. At Stringer we have found that meaningful participation is closely related to the professional worker who, in this context, acquires immense responsibility analogous to the process of teaching where guidance is a central concept. We have found that the participation of adults, too often rejected by the educational system as being uninterested, is closely related to the ethos and values of the school and their school experience.

We have found that democratic structures help to alienate the very people to whom liberals and radical authorities have attempted to transfer power. In some instances, if given guidance by professional workers, many groups that are normally classified as non-participants may raise their consciousness and perhaps demand a say in running an institution.

REFERENCES

1. Cole, G. D. H. (1919) *Self Government in Industry*. G. Bell &
    Sons, London
2. Moynihan, D. P. (1969) *Maximum Feasible Misunderstanding*.
    New York Free Press

Appendix A

COMMUNITY ASSOCIATION CONSTITUTION

The major categories are as follows:

Individual Membership: shall be open, irrespective of political
party, nationality, religious opinion, race or colour, to:

a) All persons aged eighteen and over who live in the area of
benefit or who are registered pupils aged eighteen and over in full
time education at the College, all parents of registered pupils in full
time education at the College and all teaching and non-teaching
staff of the College, who shall be called Full Members

b) All persons under the age of eighteen who live in the area of
benefit or who are registered pupils under the age of eighteen in full-
time education at the College, who shall be called Junior Members.
Junior Members shall not have the right to vote at members' meetings
but may have representatives on the Council of the Association
(hereinafter called 'The Council') elected in accordance with Clause
8 (d) and (g) who shall each have the right to vote as if they were.

Full Members: Well wishers anywhere who shall be called
Association Members. Any application for Associate Membership
must be approved by the Council of the Association. Associate
Members shall not have the right to vote at members meetings but
may elect representatives to the Council in accordance with Clause 8
(h), (i), and (j), who shall have the right to vote as if full Members.

Group Membership:

(a) Constituent Bodies shall be such voluntary organisations as
operate in the area of benefit and satisfy the Council that they are
independent organisations or branches of independent national or
other organisations

b) Sections shall be such groups as may, with the permission of the
Council, be formed within the Association among the individual
members for the furtherance of a common activity.

These groups would then vote and elect members of representatives to become full voting members of the Council of the
Association, who subject to the limitation set out in Clause 10 hereof,
the policy and general management of the affairs of the Association,
shall be directed by a Council (hereinafter referred to as 'The
Council') which shall meet not less than three times a year.

The Council shall consist of:

a) Four representatives from the teaching staff of Sidney Stringer School and Community College elected from and by themselves.

b) Two representatives from the non-teaching staff of Sidney Stringer School and Community College elected from and by themselves.

c) One representative from the Community staff of Sidney Stringer School and Community College elected from and by themselves.

d) Seven pupils in full-time education at Sidney Stringer School and Community College elected from and by themselves.

e) Eight representatives of community associations or similar bodies active in the area of benefit, to be selected in such manner as the Council may determine annually, (such representatives to be excluded from voting on this annual selection).

f) Twelve parents of pupils in· full-time education at Sidney Stringer School and Community College elected from and by themselves.

g) Four users of the youth facilities, who are Junior Members elected from and by themselves.

h) Four adult users of the Sports facilities, not more than one of whom shall be an Association Member, elected from and by themselves.

i) Four adult users, other than staff of Sidney Stringer School and Community College, other than of the sports facilities, during school hours, not more than one of whom shall be an Associate Member, elected from and by themselves.

j) Four adult users, other than of the sports facilities, outside of school hours, not more than one of whom shall be an Associate Member, elected from and by themselves.

Appendix B

BOARD OF GOVERNORS

The Board of Governors would consist of:

a) Fourteen persons nominated by the Local Education Authority of whom:

(i) four shall be members of the Local Education Authority and also members of the Education Committee of the Local Education Authority;

(ii) four shall be members of the Local Education Authority;

(iii) six shall be persons with knowledge and experience of the local community, selected in such manner as the Local Education Authority shall determine.

b) Ten persons being members of the Council of the Association and elected by the said Council for nomination as Governors of whom:

   (i) two shall be parents of registered pupils in full-time education at the School and Community College;

   (ii) one shall be a member of the academic staff of the School and Community College mainly engaged in daytime teaching;

   (iii) one shall be a member of the academic staff of the School and Community College mainly engaged in other than daytime teaching;

   (iv) one shall be a member of the non-academic staff of the School and Community College;

   (v) two shall be registered pupils in full-time education at the School and Community College;

   (vi) three shall be persons to act as the common representative of constituent bodies and sections of the Association.

Appendix 3

NEIGHBOURHOOD GROUP WORK

It is intended that wherever possible the staff involved should co-operate with and assist and ask assistance from House Staff, senior faculty staff and other members of the Community Team. This should evolve naturally with a greater degree of communication.

The School and Community Association hopes to add to the limited resources already made available, to find and establish new or one-off activities.

It should also be noted that the programme outlined is not an absolute one, but will vary according to the different needs and demands discovered within the various areas.

GENERAL TASKS FOR ALL GROUPS

a) Having elected a parent representative to the Council of the School and Community Association to assist them in effectively representing the views and interests of others in the area.

b) To improve communication between the School and Community Association and Neighbourhood Groups.

c) To arrange for the distribution and help develop the Newsletter 'WHEN'.

d) To encourage and establish Neighbourhood sports competitions and other activities, e.g. Christmas concert, five-a-side football.

e) To promote facilities available at Sidney Stringer, both on and off site and to encourage the development of new activities.

f) Following up last years school leavers with a view to giving personal advice and assistance where needed, plus appropriate general action if found applicable.

g) To establish a small planning/reference group of residents to discuss and refer points to and help direct Association representatives.

h) To develop a greater sensitivity on personal problems and issues requiring action and better communication with House Heads, Social Services.

4 COMMUNITY CENTRES
A case study of community involvement

by John T. Haworth and Tim Mason

Community centres can be very varied. There can be widespread differences in facilities, activities and methods of organisation. Some centres may be linked with other institutions such as schools. But whatever the differences may be they have in general the rather diffuse aim of trying to cater for the needs of the community. In following this aim some centres show considerable ingenuity in involving individuals in the organisation of their own activities and experiences, in other words, in decision making.

The centre examined in this chapter is one example. It was opened in 1974 and proclaimed as 'A new idea in community provision'. Located in a working class area it combined facilities which are the joint responsibility of the Borough Recreation Department and the County Education Department. As an information leaflet stated: 'The centre is not simply an extension of the school but has been designed to provide a wealth of facilities to cater for the needs of all members of the community'. The facilities consist of a sports hall, gymnasium, swimming pool, squash courts, library, creche, lounge bar, restaurant, coffee lounge, general activities area, spectator galleries, rooms and equipment for further education, all weather floodlit playing areas and outdoor sports areas. Yet the claim to innovation, in so far as it is justified, is not so much in the facilities as in the philosophy and rationale chosen for the centre. Integrated rather than dual use was to be the mode of operation. Adults were to be able to use the facilities alongside school children. Integration of the generations was an aim. A policy of open access was adopted, the centre being open to everyone, with no entrance charge and only a nominal membership fee. It was hoped that eventually opportunities would be provided for everyone in the surrounding community.

Central to the concept of open access, and in fact to the whole philosophy of the centre, was the policy that individuals should be given the opportunity to organise their own activities and experiences. The two main methods adopted to achieve this were, firstly, the formation of self-programming groups in which individuals could come together and organise and programme their own activities, obtaining help from the staff if required; and, secondly, the formation of a Users' Advisory Committee. Since these methods could be used in most community centres, this chapter looks at the experience of them in practice.

SELF-PROGRAMMING GROUPS

A considerable number of self-programming groups have now become established at the centre. Many have started at the request of individuals, or small groups of people, who wanted to use the centre as a base and meeting place for their pursuit, whether it was fishing, caving, chess or general social activities. All of these groups work closely with the Users' Advisory Committee, but have their own committees which plan, publicise and run their own events. They are autonomous groups which use the centre as a base, although their moneys are audited by the Users' Committee.

Golden Years Group.   One of the first groups to form, and one which is still highly successful, is the Golden Years Group. The success of this group illustrates the capacity of local people to be involved in decision making at this level, particularly if they can obtain sensitive assistance in the early stages of formation of the group. The group was formed in consequence of an attempt by the community staff at the centre to try to assess the needs of people in the immediate locality, which consists of a council estate, a group of deck access flats and three blocks of multi-storey flats. Housing departments' decisions in the past meant that many of the people living in the multi-storey flats were old age pensioners or couples whose families had now left them. Of the deck access flats, one in four were for single people, mainly old age pensioners. The other flats were for families with children. Since social and community provision in the locality was minimal, the possibility existed that there was a need for some form of new community groups. The problem was how to make contact with the local population in a way which would provide confidence and understanding; to reach groups of people whose normal contacts with social agencies had invariably been on the level of complaints and negative approaches.

To overcome this problem, adults who used the centre's facilities and who lived on the deck access flats were asked to deliver and collect a questionnaire. The use of local people had a threefold function. Initially it helped to rid the respondent of the suspicion of a 'prying' authority. Secondly, it gave the worker an opportunity to meet more people in the flats through introductions. Thirdly, these approaches were much more confidence inspiring for the people than simply having a stranger knocking at the door and introducing himself. The questionnaire results concerning older people indicated that there could well be a need for new activities. In view of this, the Adult Education Tutor and the Community Worker visited the older people who had replied to the questionnaire and invited them to a social meeting to discuss what provision could be made for them at the centre. The first meeting was very informal, with a tour of the facilities followed by tea and biscuits and a discussion of what they wanted.

A small committee of ten (from the people who attended) was formed at the meeting to help construct a programme of activities for an initial period of six weeks on one night per week. The programme was prepared mainly by the Adult Education Tutor and the Community Worker who then submitted it to the committee for approval, which was received. They then organised the publicity for the programme by using local radio, press and distributing 1000 leaflets in the local community through shops, laundrettes, doctors' surgeries, as well as distribution to local old people's homes. The first six weeks were very successful, more people arriving with each week. Another six week programme was worked out by the Adult Education Tutor and the Community Worker in conjunction with the committee. Publicity leaflets were distributed, with the committee assisting. The second six week period was again highly successful. After this, the committee made the subsequent programmes using the Adult Education Tutor and Community Worker for help and assistance with the printing and distribution of the programme and for obtaining equipment in the centre.

The group has now been running for two and a half years, meeting regularly on Thursday nights. They have also instituted a Monday morning session and a Tuesday afternoon session for small games and a chat. Their evening session has a very varied programme from slides to bingo; singing and concerts to running their own shows; dancing, and trips to places of interest. Besides planning and organising their own programme of events they also successfully undertake fund raising to help finance activities.

Preschool playgroup. Although the formation of the Golden Years Group was a success, the history of another group, the Preschool Playgroup, illustrates the problems which can arise if the planning is not right.

The survey of the deck access flats had supported the intuitive feeling of the Community Worker that there was a need for some preschool provision within the area. However, it presented a very difficult problem since the creche facilities at the centre were in continual use by the users of the facilities. The initial step was to find some premises where provision could be made and some way of funding this. The Community Worker based at the centre organised meetings with the social services and housing departments, both departments being aware of and concerned about the situation. The group decided that there were two possible solutions to the provision of preschool activities. The local authority could establish a preschool playgroup and then enlist community support, or they could encourage and support the mothers on the estate in forming and running their own playgroup. The latter was chosen since it was felt that there was almost as much need on the deck access flats for some form of participation by the mothers as there was for the playgroup itself. It was also thought that a playleader should only be brought in from outside if one did not emerge from the mothers' group. After much discussion about premises, it was decided that the social services department should approach the housing department about the use of a room in the deck access flats. A date was fixed for the next meeting and the mothers who had replied to the questionnaire were invited. However, only two mothers turned up, and both said that a more informal meeting would probably be more effective, and one of them volunteered the use of her flat on an afternoon.

The Social Worker and Community Worker, along with the two mothers, visited all the people who had replied to the questionnaire and gave them a personal invitation to the next meeting. This was attended by ten mothers who set up a committee. The committee elected a playleader and officers, drew up a system for supervision of the children and decided on the categories of children who could attend. They proposed various events to raise money and suggested that in many cases their husbands would be able to help with alterations to the premises.

This meeting took place early in the July of that year, but by October, the money for the necessary alterations was not forth-coming and the mothers' interest was quite decidedly on the wane. The local authority representatives were still fighting their way through the newly reorganised local authority system, although representatives from the social services felt confident that the money would be forthcoming.

The committee, now dwindling in numbers, agreed to run another census of the deck access flats to draw up a list of children who would want to attend the group and to see which mothers would be prepared to help. They also decided to open a bank account and approach local firms for donations and to contact local nursery schools for assistance with furnishings and toys. The census showed that in the deck access flats there was even more interest in the playgroup. The officers were now in a difficult position with regard to the mothers and the slow way in which local authority systems work. There was virtually no progress for the next few months until the social services department allocated the money for the work to be done on the room. During this time the vast majority of mothers totally lost interest and resentment towards local councils was reestablished and hardened. Only four of the mothers stuck it out until the money came through.

The playgroup finally opened the following September for five days a week both morning and afternoon. It employed a playleader full-time. However, difficulties were experienced. Only a small number of children attended and there were only four mothers helping on a regular basis. Often the playleader found herself totally on her own. After a few months the group was running out of money and the electricity bills had not been paid. There was still no more interest from the mothers of the deck access flats. However, some mothers from the local estate began to show interest and bring their children along. It was therefore decided that the group should be cut down to two days a week, mornings and afternoons. The playleader left and one of the mothers took her place. The mothers had a strenuous period of fund raising to pay off the group's debts. The group got on an even keel and had eight or nine children attending each play session, but there were still problems. The mothers from the deck access flats resented the increasing numbers of children coming from the council estate.

Since January 1977 a waiting list for places has been built up. Interest in the playgroup has been fostered by a community worker working solely on the deck access flats in conjunction with a new community worker from the centre who lives in one of the flats. The future for the playgroup looks secure, at least until the present mothers who are active drop out as their children reach school age.

Challenge Club.   A final group to be looked at, and one which is highly successful and has become a registered charity, is the Challenge Club. The history of this group and its aims are significantly different from the others. It is a group set up to challenge physically handicapped young people between the age of six and eighteen. It has a formalised and functional constitution necessary because it is a registered charity.

From opening the centre had a two hour session for disabled swimmers in the swimming pool. This session was quite extensively used by up to twenty five disabled people of all ages with volunteer able-bodied swimmers assisting in the pool. In June 1975, the centre held the 'Disabled Games' for the region. The games created a lot of interest among both members of the public and the staff at the centre. They also provoked the question as to why no team was entered from the town. Many of the users of the centre's bar and social facilities watched the games and expressed an interest in helping a group of this sort get off the ground. In September 1975, interest was still high and the Community Worker and the Sports Organiser investigated the possibilities of setting up a challenge club. A public meeting was called at which a demonstration of disabled sports was presented. After discussion the club was formed. A steering committee was elected which met regularly until the next public meeting. During this time the committee endeavoured to find premises suitable for the activities of the club. Eventually it was agreed with the school at the centre that the school hall could be used each Wednesday evening. This meant that the young people could continue with their swimming lessons.

In April 1976, the second public meeting was called. The constitution was passed and a full committee was established to run the affairs of the group. The Community Worker did not become a member of the committee, but actively supported all the group functions and committee meetings, as well as coordinating the registration of the club as a charity. The group has been highly successful. It takes part in regional and national games for disabled people, as well as running its weekly group night. It has over fifty disabled people as members whom it transports each week to the centre. It is hoping to acquire its own mini-bus.

Although the group is probably the most successful self-programming group at the centre, it is possibly helped by the nature of its members. People are much more willing to help both financially and with their time for something which is quite obviously benefiting young people who are definitely disadvantaged. It therefore has a quite significant start on other groups at the centre, particularly with regard to fund raising. A study of programming groups at the centre indicates that the potential for involving people in decision making is almost limitless, providing that groups are allowed to develop slowly and in their own autonomous way. Probably the most important single factor is that they should be allowed to build up and keep their own identity. This means that, to a certain extent, they must be financially independent and be able to take their own decisions about their future.

Perhaps the most crucial factor to be taken into account by the professional worker is the role he or she should play in the group, and the type of support to give to it. Too much support and the group becomes just another activity provided by the centre. Too little or ineffectual support and the group collapses, as almost happened in the case of the playgroup. Many management decisions which are taken can affect the groups. They are prone to failure if the facilities which they want are not available in the same place at the same time each week. The volunteers who run the groups quickly become disillusioned if they have to become too involved in the bureaucracy which exists in both the centre and local government. The job of the professional is to help the groups when and where they need it, but also to make them as self-sufficient as possible, thereby freeing himself for other functions such as giving assistance with the formation of other self-programming groups.

THE USERS' ADVISORY COMMITTEE

The committee consists of a majority of users that are elected annually. Working class members make up a significant proportion. The centre staff, Borough Recreation Committee and the local Authority Department of Recreation send representatives, and similar provision is made for the County Education Authority. The committee has a set of formally stated objectives drawn up primarily by local authority officials although approved by a Users' Steering Committee and ratified by a public meeting. A consideration of the part played by the Users' Committee in decision making, in relation to these objectives, and the role of officials and councillors is instructive. The objectives of the Committee are:

1) To represent the users of the centre and other interested sections of the community and provide a vehicle of expression for their opinions to the appropriate local authority.

2) To collect information and suggestions and to advise the officers on the programming of activities and other aspects of operating the centre.

3) To consider conflicting claims for the use of facilities and to recommend fair solutions.

4) To explore ways and means of extending and, where necessary, improving the facilities so as to meet more fully the needs of the community.

5) To assist in the smooth running of the centre.

In connection with these interrelated objectives the Committee has played a useful role in developing the social activities of the centre. It has made a number of useful suggestions concerning new activities and facilities, and has helped with their organisation. Some of these suggestions have been collected from users and other members of the community. For example, bar football and table games are now available and in much demand. Dances and socials are very popular. An old people's party is run annually. Some help is given with a children's party. The physically disabled are encouraged to use the centre. Provision is made for patients from nearby mental hospitals and the committee takes an active interest in their welfare. Archery is a thriving activity and was adopted by the centre after requests were made to the Committee by members of the community. The Committee has been involved in the organisation of open day activities. Although restricted initially, the Committee now undertakes fund raising. It runs a tote and holds events such as jumble sales. As a result it is able to give some financial support to a number of self-programming groups at the centre.

The Committee has had partially successful discussions with the Transport Department of the Borough to improve bus services to the centre, and discussions with the social services regarding transport for the disabled. In playing this positive role in decision making, the Committee has been greatly helped by the work of the principal and staff responsible for social and community matters. In some cases the staff have acted as enablers. They have helped the Committee achieve its objectives by providing valuable information or by making contact with departments in the local authority. They provide support in many small, but crucial ways. By being present in the building when events by users were first organised, they were able to help with last minute organisational hitches such as room keys not being available. They have not been afraid to join in with the mundane work and lead by example. Help of this type has been most appreciated by the Users' Committee.

At other times, staff have been able to point to unforeseen difficulties associated with a course of action. In many cases this has been done in a constructive way by encouraging action with cognizance of difficulties. Problems have not been used as excuses to avoid action, or even to induce apathy or disbandment of the committee. Of course, the enthusiasm of the staff has not always been well placed. For one event, which the Committee were planning, the staff organised the whole programme and presented it to the Committee for formal approval. This was not appreciated. Neither have the staff and users always had the same priority of objectives. At one time some of the staff considered that the Committee had become too involved in organising dances. They queried whether this should be an important objective of the Committee. In general, however, the staff have not dominated the proceedings or used them just to further their own ideas.

The involvement of the Committee in decision making could have been much greater had there not been differences of opinion with the Recreation Department and its committee. A look at these differences is instructive since it illustrates that the conceptions, attitudes and values of local authority officers and councillors can have a significant effect on community involvement. It also indicates that

while a local authority department may have community involvement in decision making as an objective, this is not a guarantee
that it will be given a high priority in practice.

At an early stage in the development of the centre, a number of
users asked for the formation of sub-committees for social activities,
sport and further education. The desire for a social sub-committee
was particularly emphasised. The Users' Committee reported the
opinion of some users that the centre was becoming a glorified youth
and sports base. They stated that not everyone wanted to participate
in sport. Many did not want to come to the centre to be active after a
'hard day's graft', so chess, whist drives, dances and films were
suggested as alternatives.

The request for these sub-committees was discussed fairly
frequently at meetings. Various reasons against the idea were given
by the Chairman of the Recreation Committee and the Director of
the Recreation Department.

1) That the presence of different sub-committees might be
divisive, or that pressure groups would form.

2) That sub-committees could put too many obligations on staff as
each would have to be serviced by the Recreation Department.

3) That a representative from the Recreation Department would
need to be on each sub-committee to ensure that things ran correctly
and were kept in order. This would make it too expensive in staff
time since the Leisure Department might have to deal with many
centres.

4) That each sub-committee would have to report back and this
would clog the machinery of government.

In any case, it was considered that sub-committees spend too much
time on trivia and the Chairman of the Recreation Committee was
genuinely concerned that the centre should not become a collection
of self-interested groups. So much so that no clubs were allowed to
form and all groups had to be open to all members. The Director of
Recreation was equally concerned with the quality of life in the
Borough, but, perhaps naturally, he took an administrator's view.
The centre was viewed as potentially one of many. Concern was with
precedents which might be set and the effect of these if replicated
many times. Plans for action had to be canalised through the
recreation department so that it could coordinate. Users' Committees
had to be discouraged from taking unilateral decisions and, at times,
reminded that they were advisory. The formation of sub-committees
was postponed.

Whatever the intention of the Recreation Department, their policy
produced considerable apathy amongst many of the members of the
Users' Committee. They did not feel involved. One member said that

he did not now speak at meetings because he had spoken many times previously but to no avail. The Committee was forced into the position of dealing with very detailed matters on many issues, such as the type of spot prizes required for a dance and the number of doormen needed. While some members enjoyed this, others did not. One committee member indicated that the prospect of dealing with what for him were 'trivia' had almost prevented him from coming to meetings. Attendance at meetings did decline.

Another area of contention between the Users' Committee and the Recreation Department was the question of fund raising. From virtually the inception of the centre the Users' Committee had wished to undertake fund raising activities. It was obvious to them that there would always be a shortage of money. The Recreation Officials, however, again raised a number of objections. The Chairman of the Recreation Committee feared that the activity would come to dominate the work of the Committee. The activity, it was suggested, could build up a sort of exclusivity by the people closely involved; caste systems could develop. The officials claimed that the activity would be offensive to many people in the centre and that in any case the activity would result in local authority committees shirking their financial responsibilities, especially if the users were successful. As a new department trying to establish a baseline for their estimates, the representatives were concerned that this could be effected adversly. They considered including in the estimates a sum of approximately £1000 for the Users' Committee to spend. Whether this would have been approved by the Recreation Committee, however, is an open question. The 'squeeze' came and the estimates were slashed.

Many of the points put forward by the Chairman of the Recreation Committee and its Officials were sincere attempts to do the best for the centre and the Borough as a whole. But they were based on conceptions, attitudes and values which clashed with the different ideas and perceptions of the users on the Committee. At one stage, for example, a dress making class was forbidden to hold a sale of work to raise funds for a Christmas party. Eventually fund raising did get going, but not before many members of the Users' Committee had become further disillusioned with their role. While only small to moderate sums have been handled, this has been done responsibly and usefully. Most of the worries of the Chairman of the Recreation Committee and the Director of the Department have not materialised, although opinion has been voiced by some members of the Users' Committee that perhaps too much time has been devoted to fund raising at the expense of other objectives. Certainly much more could be done by the Committee to try to communicate with users and non-users in the community, an area at which they realise they have not been successful.

While it is recognised that the Recreation Department and its committee has to be in a position to influence (to ensure, for instance, that non-articulate groups are not left out and that conflicting claims between different groups can be settled), if public participation in decision making is an aim, it would seem necessary that the work of the Recreation Department should be conducted with considerable delegation of decision making power with the groups within the community. The Leisure Department may usefully give advice to groups, but the tendency towards increasing administrative efficiency at headquarters, at the expense of local flexibility, should be resisted.

A look at another aspect of the work of the Users' Committee can also be taken as giving some support to this conclusion, or at least not negating it. The Committee has been very active in considering conflicting claims for the use of facilities and in attempting to assist in the smooth running of the centre, one of its formulated objectives. Particular attention has been given to the unattached youth problem. While the committee has not been able to produce satisfactory solutions, which is not unexpected in this very difficult sphere, it has taken as reasonable an approach to the subject as the professionals.

In the area surrounding the centre, there are many young people. The Youth Service based at the centre provides for the fourteen to twenty year olds. National Education Policy does not allow it to cater for the under fourteen year olds, although it has tried to do this to some extent. With a policy of open access at the centre the social areas are often swamped by youngsters aged eight to fourteen year olds. Many of them wish simply to sit in the centre and have coffee. Others are naturally noisy and untidy. Families feel excluded.

Many suggestions concerning the problem have been made by users at Committee meetings, although not all are in agreement. Table games were suggested and provided. A time limit on length of stay for unattached children was tried. Some children, however, maintained that their family was in other parts of the centre and the staff did not always have the time to check on this, even if they suspected otherwise. Volunteers have worked with the children. An 'under-fourteen' youth club was run and a quiet room with a television was staffed for a while. More use of school rooms was proposed and ways were investigated of making them more attractive. The use of one of the rooms in the main centre was suggested. This was eventually taken up by the youth service for the non-joiners, but there were difficulties in finding ways to use the money available to pay the temporary staff. In any case the main social areas were still open to the non-joiners since the Recreation Committee policy for the centre was to integrate generations. A proposal to have a separate night in the main centre for non-joiners was also vetoed on those grounds. Some users on the Committee have suggested that non-joining youths should not be allowed in the centre, but others, however, proposed that they should have the same rights as adults. As a result of a change of political power occurring in the Borough, a new Chairman was elected to the Recreation Committee. It voted to institute an admission fee in order to try to keep down the number of non-joiners and make the centre more attractive for family use.

A final area, in which the Users' Committee has played a key role, is in meeting its objective to provide a vehicle for the expression of the views of those users and sections of the community who are actively interested in the centre to the appropriate local authority. It is in trying to fulfil this that perhaps the crucial importance of having users involved in decision making becomes most readily apparent. While the discussion so far partially illustrates the work of the Committee in meeting this objective of representing views, particularly on the level of individual activities, recent developments at the centre illustrate the need for the users to be involved in broad policy issues.

The local Government elections of 1976 produced a working majority for the Conservative Party in the Borough. Their manifesto promised unspecified changes at the community centre. The party was not in agreement with the community policy, as practised. Some of the progressive educational ideas did not find favour and rates were being spent on activities at the centre which could be viewed as suspiciously like social welfare for the working class area. At the same time, the Borough Recreation Department was very disenchanted with the County Education Department. Cooperation on the financing and management of the centre had not been possible. In line with the requirement of the Labour Government to curtail rate increases, the Recreation Committee commissioned a management services document to see what financial savings could be made at the centre. The document indicated that if the centre changed from integrated to dual use, with the public having access primarily in the evenings and at weekends, there could be considerable potential savings. However, the document did not discuss the purpose of the centre, although it did claim that some parts were not well used during the day.

A report calling for this change was passed by the Recreation Committee without discussion with the Users' Advisory Committee, despite the fact that this was called for by the labour councillors. The proposals in the report included closing the bar during the day and increasing the prices in the evening; stopping lunches in the cafe, not making facilities at the centre available to the public during the day apart from access to the swimming pool and the squash courts at lunch time; instituting an entrance fee; dispensing with membership requirements and operating the centre the same way as other facilities controlled by the Recreation Department, such as baths; dispensing with the need for a management committee; staff cuts; and a review of user charges.

The Users' Committee recognised the need for economies at the centre since most departments in the authority were having to cut their budgets. But they objected to the changes in philosophy, policy and practice which were being introduced under an economic umbrella without any open discussion. The centre it was felt was being moved away from combining social and informal leisure provision with recreation to becoming a sports centre. In dual use, virtually no provision was to be made for shift-workers who used the centre, for mothers who came to courses and activities during the day and who in many cases used the creche facilities, for patients from the nearby hospital who used the social facilities during the day. Daytime facilities also would no longer be available for the Golden Years Group. Lunch and bar facilities would not be available to local workers. And the youth problem was being tackled by trying to keep them out.

Labour councillors on the Users' Committee provided information indicating that the hypothetical savings to be made at the centre were only a small proportion of the budget of the Recreation Department. It was also clear that much of the 'savings' were to be made by transferring staff from the centre to the Recreation Department. Information was made available which showed that figures used in the management services document relating to bar profits were out of date. The bar was making considerably more profit than had been indicated. And, many of the proposed savings would require capital expenditure on the building. The Users' Committee considered there were alternative ways of making economies which had not been discussed. They believed that, rather than cutting services and increasing prices, the potential of the centre for daytime use could be profitably exploited, a course of action which had been previously neglected. The Users' Committee asked the Chairman of the Recreation Committee for consultations, but they were informed that they would be consulted after the Full Council had considered the management services document. The Chairman of the Recreation Committee was emphatic that it was the Council that made policy. The Council ratified the document.

The Users' Committee produced a document drawing on information presented by councillors and others. It emphasised a number of points, including the fact that the Users' Committee was properly constituted and elected in consequence of a Council directive and that it was there to advise the Council. It requested that full cognizance be given to the concept of the centre, as outlined in the rationale, and that the centre had not been allowed to develop its full potential for community use, particularly with regard to daytime activities.

The document pointed out that the bar lunch service had been very successful, until stopped by the Recreation Department, and that its reintroduction could prove popular and profitable. Daytime use of squash and badminton facilities could, it was suggested, be furthered by a revision of advanced booking policies; recreation facilities could be offered to the seven day cover services such as fire, police and hospital services. With imaginative planning it was proposed that it could be possible to sell available services at the centre, rather than cut them in half and then charge considerably enhanced prices for the use of what was left. It was also noted that capital expenses on locker systems, which would be introduced to save on staff, did not include the high costs of maintenance. The document also stated that membership at the centre should not only be maintained, but should be developed in order to make people aware that it was their centre, to encourage them to put something in as well as take something out. Membership charges could remain minimal, while income would be modest, if membership were coupled with a few rules it could help with the youth problem. Finally, a management committee was deemed to be crucial.

The Users' Committee met representatives of the Recreation Committee and officers of the Leisure Department, but the meeting was not a success from the users' point of view. Little notice was taken of their alternative proposals and the Recreation Committee implemented its own. The only concession was that admission charges were less than originally proposed. As far as the Users' Committee was concerned, the limitations to the concept of responsibility without power was obvious.

To round off this section on the Users' Committee, a number of points may be summarised. A users' committee can play a useful part in helping a centre realise its objectives. It can help, for instance, with representing the views of users and the community, by collecting information and suggestions and considering conflicting claims for use, exploring ways of extending facilities to meet more fully the needs of the community and assisting in the smooth running of the centre. Another equally significant part it can play is to make its presence felt on the broader issues of policy. It can challenge the unfounded assumptions and value judgements of local government officials and committees when these occur. It can widen debate so that problems are not considered solely from one viewpoint, such as finance. In the short term, of course, it may not be particularly effective. But in the longer term it could influence events.

A users' committee's effectiveness in meeting these objectives is obviously influenced by many factors. Like any other organisation, the users' committee is made up of individuals with diverse interests. Some members may prefer the minutae of a centre's work, such as the type of spot prizes required at a dance, but others prefer to consider broader issues. If a committee is to remain operational and as representative as possible, each meeting must take account of its members interests and abilities. A committee must also periodically review its work and its objectives. Not all objectives automatically receive equal attention. New objectives may come to the fore im-perceptibly, such as the pre-eminence of organising dances. Conflicts of interest can also develop. For instance, not all proposed solutions to the youth problem were based on similar interests. Access to in-formation is important for a committee and the role of the councillor can be crucial in this area. But perhaps of greatest importance is the influence of the conceptions, attitudes, values and commitment of the staff and elected members in local authority and at the centre. They can significantly facilitate or hinder the work of the users' committee in meeting its required objectives. They can determine whether or not there is in effect the power necessary to make decisions to go with the responsibility for meeting objectives.

REPRESENTATION

One problem which can be common to both self-programming groups and users' committees is that of representation. When users' committees are established, considerable care is often taken to try to ensure that they are representative of the interests they are to serve. The constitution is carefully planned and members may be elected at an annual general meeting. But, of course, it is well known that this may not produce a committee which is representative of the com-munity. And even if it goes a considerable way towards this, there is no guarantee that the committee will retain its balance. Members drop out: 'The people who end up ruling the roost may be the stickers and the stayers: the knot of self selected persons who like planning and plotting things'.[1] This also applies, of course, when committees are elected by self-programming groups to run their affairs.

Recognising this, however, is not to imply that committees should not be established or that power should be the sole prerogative of officials and councillors. As this study has illustrated, their views on community provision can be coloured by their values, attitudes and conceptions. They may not always be in the best interests of the users or the community and, although a committee may be based on a narrow section of the community, this is not necessarily a valid criticism in itself. As Hill[2] indicates, what is important is the aim of the committee and the success or failure of its contribution. However, in order that a committee may have appropriate aims and actions it should obviously be encouraged to undertake self-appraisal.

Committees should check to see that as far as possible their procedure and language, as well as the agenda, do not prevent members from attending. They should recognise that their knowledge of the views of their constituents is limited and attempt to remedy this as far as possible. Contact with users is obviously essential. In addition, for a centre users' committee, it may be advantageous for it to include in its membership a representative from each self-programming group and one from each area of the community.

Other methods of enhancing communication may also be explored. A self-programming group may run a community newspaper, possibly in conjunction with the users' committee. Community video can be experimented with and carnivals and happenings can be tried. Information can be exchanged in meeting places in the community, such as clubs and pubs, shops and offices, and other work places. In short, an attempt must be made to establish a continuing dialogue with the community. This way representation will be tested in the community. The role of the staff and the councillors on the committee will be crucial in supporting these endeavours.

Perhaps however there is an even more fundamental aspect to representation. Not all members of the public have set opinions on what opportunities they would like to see available and they may not be aware of some which are. As such, representation may involve a two-way exchange of information. A centre and its representatives may have to extend a warm welcome to people to 'taste its wares'. But, if the dignity and value of each individual is to be preserved, this must be done with emphasis on the fundamental opportunity. The opportunity for the individual to decide on his own activities.

CONCLUSION

The following points, concerning community centres and public involvement in decision making, can be made in conclusion:

1) The concept of self-programming groups is viable providing they are allowed to develop slowly and autonomously.

2) Users' committees can be valuable, but likewise they must be given some authentic decision making power.

3) For the concept of involvement to be effective, the commitment of centre staff and policy makers in local government is essential.

4) The danger, however, is that in local government authentic public involvement in decision making will be sacrificed on the altar of administrative efficiency.

REFERENCES

1. Finer, S. E. (1977) *New Society*. January, p. 73–74
2. Hill, D. M. (1970) *Participating in Local Affairs*. Pelican Original, London

5 THE PEMBROKESHIRE COUNTRYSIDE UNIT
An experiment in participation

by John Barrett

My story starts in 1966. It is a simple story and has nothing whatever to do with formal committee decision making. Further, it is concerned with increasing participation through sharing knowledge. It is no more than a personal initiative in response to what turned out to be a bigger need than I, at first, appreciated.

I had been running the Dale Fort Field Centre for the Field Studies Council since we established it in 1947. Through the years more and more people on holiday to the Pembrokeshire coast came out to the Fort in search of answers to questions: 'Can you tell me if this is a fossil?' 'I picked up these shells and can't find out what they are?' 'I've seen a little brown bird . . .?', and so on. Just by supplying answers, I realised we were adding to the pleasure of those holidays. In any case I had always believed that, for most people, the enjoyment of the scenery was greater the more you understood how and from what it was made.

Meanwhile, the number of questioners increased and so, in 1966, I tried my first experiments. Firstly, I displayed in local pubs and car parks, and beside tactical paths, a simple poster saying that if anybody cared to turn up on the appointed days and times to the five rendezvous listed I would try to show them whatever it might be that was advertised. So it was, on the first of those days (it was a Tuesday afternoon in August), that I made my way to the bottom of the Red Cliff path wondering if anybody would want to be told about the rocks along Marloes Sands. It had not occurred to me that well over a hundred would turn up. On the Thursday following, 140 people in fortyfour cars rallied at a cross roads to be shown something of the antiquities on the Preseli Hills. The other three occasions were on that same scale and the five days put together gave me a lot to think about.

The second 1966 experiment was to prepare what I called 'A Plain Man's Guide to the Path round the Dale Peninsula'. The route was some six miles long and thirtynine points were discreetly marked along it. This was not a soft option 'nature trail'. The Guide contains notes on history, geology and geography more than on plants and animals which are all too often not there when needed. The

questions raised are not answered at their first appearing. The user
has to think why whatever he sees is how he sees it, to compare one
view with another and to make notes about the differences. He is
encouraged to make a land-use survey on the $3\frac{1}{2}''$ to a one mile map
attached to the text, using the outline categories that I listed for him.
In short, to get his money's worth, the user has to do much of the
work for himself. Sales were immediately (and continue to be)
substantial. A family may, and does, occupy a whole day in observation and argument. Their gratitude continues to be reported to
me that things like earth movements, intrusive quartz, wave-cut
platforms and glacial activities were explained in words they can
understand and 'Why has nobody done this for us before?'.

In 1967 I extended the experiments to include evening talks about
the general background against which a particular case would be
demonstrated in the field next day—obvious titles like 'The Rocks
and Landscape of Pembrokeshire' or 'Prehistoric Man in Pembrokeshire' or 'The Tides: Their Rhythms and How They Work'. At
the end of that year I found myself writing in my report to the Field
Studies Council:

> Five lectures in Dale, repeated in St David's, were listened to by an
> aggregate of 775 people. Even more attended the eight field excursions.
> Who would have thought that pouring rain would not daunt eighty
> people from being shown the geology of the Little Haven section? All these
> people came only because they were interested; family parties would come
> several times. Teaching, for it was teaching, in this atmosphere is far
> more rewarding than teaching some of our resident courses. When hungry
> sheep look up, they must be fed; those who live in Centres can so easily act
> the shepherd. After this summer's enlarged experiments, I see an im-
> mense opportunity to provide a service to the community and thereby to
> enhance the status of the Council.

That largely fell on deaf ears, but luckily I noticed in paragraph 11
of the White Paper *Leisure in the Countryside* (Cmnd 2928) that 'A
major task (of the about to be formed Countryside Commission) will
be to stimulate and coordinate education in the need to conserve the
unique features of the countryside'.

At that time I already knew that I ought to move on from Dale
Fort. Where we had set out to stimulate an interest in natural history
and to give to urban adults and school children some understanding
of the origins of their being and experience of the beauties and the
forces of nature, times had so changed that the new fangled fashion
of 'ecology' was all the rage. Sixth form geographers solemnly spent
all day measuring angles of slope or the size of pebbles; botanists
counted all day with a 5 m quadrat; if animals did not respond to the
X^2 test for statistical significance they did not exist. I believed it

was wrong (and I still do), not to say silly, that some parties went
home at the end of a week unable to write a sensible paragraph on
the general constitution of the peninsula.

So in 1968, with the evidence of my continuing experiments, I
persuaded the Countryside Commission to pay my wages to the Field
Studies Council and so allow me to develop full time the work I was
doing for Everyman, both he who lived in Pembrokeshire and he who
came to us on holiday, looking for that kind of guidance I have
described. In the October of that year I finally left the Fort and
became the Pembrokeshire Countryside Unit.

To begin with I had not thought that I would need a building. The
writing and guiding could all be done from home where I had my
own books and reference material. The work of planning a field
excursion takes just about as much time as writing a full scale
scientific paper. Searching the map for a possible circuit along
rights-of-way (without a legal right to be there, the whole day is
in jeopardy from some dog that was not under control causing the
withdrawal of permission to pass that way, no matter how readily,
even enthusiastically, that permission had originally been given);
walking the chosen circuit to see that the rights-of-way were 'goable';
getting them cut out if they were not, and that probably means doing
it yourself; surveying the places where up to, say, forty cars could
stop without interfering with the traffic, and 'traffic' includes (in
season) the milk lorry and the combine.

Then all the reading up to ensure the important features along
that route, whatever they might be, were presented in a coherent,
accurate, up-to-date and intelligible way. The superficial, worse still
the evasive, answer will not do. You never know who is in the
audience. Once, having been thanked for putting in a good word for
the Saints, my response that they were marvellous men was cut short
by 'Oh, I know. You see, when I haven't my shorts on, I'm paid to say
so too. I'm the Bishop of Liverpool'. On another day, somewhat
uncertain of the oxides of silica, a senior physical chemist in
Pilkington's, the glass makers, put me right—silica was meat and
drink for him.

Thus the series of field excursions widened and lengthened. Some
lasted all day and were based on the general natural history of the
route which was often along the clifftop path that by now ran all
round the 168 miles of the Pembrokeshire coast. Other all day series
laid an emphasis on a particular feature—the New Stone Age burial
chambers, for instance, or the Pre-Industrial Revolution Sea
Trading from Cleddau quays. Some were all walking, covering up to
seven miles, while some were car-borne and involved a minimum of
exercise. Half-days were usually devoted to more particular themes,

but never to the exclusion of whatever chanced to appear. While looking at the rocks of a cliff section, it would be crazy to ignore Gannets or Porpoises offshore or Vernal Squills or Violet Oil Beetles along the way. The passing cloud formations often told a weather story easily explained by anybody with a basic understanding of their sequence but yet completely mysterious to (or, more likely, unconsidered by) nearly everybody else.

I then did some quite specialised half-days, carefully labelled in the programme so that nobody would be misled (always provided they read what I printed). A series of 'lessons' in bird identification was quickly booked up. For those lessons I had to limit the number to ten otherwise everybody would have seen and heard nothing. I conducted them tightly and laid a particular emphasis on identification by ear, which is after all how at least three-quarters of the birds are identified in the field. It proved that this disciplined, 'serious' work was just what the participants wanted. Most of them were prepared to do the homework needed to become proficient in spotting at least the commoner birds around them and, of course, there is no short cut or alternative to hard work.

Likewise with the identification of the cliff flowers, people want to know how to tell which is which and they are eager to absorb practical lessons in the use of a flora and of simple keys. If the 'teacher' can add notes on the natural history of the individual species as he goes along so much the better, but hard application for a couple of hours was what was wanted. To come upon a family two days later struggling with the relevant Field Guide, and getting answers, was among my greater rewards.

When the tides were right we had sessions on the natural history of the shore. Again I had to limit numbers. You simply cannot show details of pattern and colour to more than about a dozen others. The programme notes warned that a hand-lens would be useful. Surprising (or is it?) how few people have ever used a lens. Time was well spent in teaching them how to do so. Only the tiny number who habitually carry a lens (far, far more useful than a pound note) are able to enjoy the flashing lights from a Blue-rayed Limpet or the 'perforations' in the leaves of a St John's wort.

I learned the trap of numbers on the shore early and in the hard way. I had included an afternoon in August for children only. Our youngest son and a pal of his, who is also good on the shore, came to help me. Even so, we were seriously outnumbered by the 120 or more kids who turned up! A dear person came from the crowd, 'You need help. I'm a biology teacher'. I never knew her name, but the four of us did what we could, not least in preventing the tinies from being drowned in the pools by the bursting throng. What an afternoon that was, but impossible not to believe that some impression of excitement and wonder did rub off on almost all those kids and on the phalanx of anxious parents standing back on the rocks half enclosing our endeavours. Above all here was positive proof of how much families on holiday wanted to know about these things. Nobody has to engender interest, it is all around all the time just waiting to be shown a way out.

Anything I put into the programme produced a response. A Christmas Treasure Hunt to see sixtyfive species of birds and find fifty species of plant in flower during four of the eight days immediately after Christmas was enjoyed by as many as forty on each day—families in their holiday houses who had got over the excitement of presents and 'pud' and had nothing special left to do. I treasure the memory of the day when, walking the seven miles round the edge of the Llys-y-fran reservoir, we sheltered under a bank from driving snow while eating our sandwiches. Most of those with me had never considered even the possibility that they might one day enjoy sandwiches in a snowstorm. That picnic still counts among them as high adventure. This was Scott on his way to the pole!

We all take too much for granted. When time was up with a gang of kids on the shore I said, 'We can't go back the way we came; so it's up the cliff we go'. And up they all went except one—a serious little boy who had his specimens tidily organised in polythene bags, cross-referenced to his notes. I hung about pretending to be looking at the lichens as he painfully inched up. Then, as he seemed to be quite stuck, I encouraged with: 'Come on; nothing to it; let me take your specimens. Look, the others are all halfway home'. 'It's all very well for you', he said, 'but if you had lived all your life in Ealing it wouldn't look so easy.'

No doubt at all, the essence of my work was (is) in these field excursions. The reality of the countryside, the touching, the smelling, the beauty of what is all around and the first understanding of the unity of Creation—eyes which before had never seen now began to open. Soon, though, I began to consider how much more I could do if I did have a building. The Countryside Commission found the £5000 needed; the erstwhile Pembrokeshire National Park Committee gave us a good site close to the sea by a car park in Broad Haven. I then assumed the label The Pembrokeshire Countryside Unit and hoped it would be appropriate.

A minimum collection of reference and text books enabled us to answer a wide range of questions. When a boy brought to us a collection of shells we could, of course, simply have named them for him, but, before he was out of the door, he would have forgotten half of them and muddled up the rest. In any case a name, just as a name, tells you nothing about the organism. Much better, then, to sit him down at a table, give him a simple mounted bull's-eye lens through which to see some detail and show him how to use the book most suited to his age and experience. Then leave him to try to find the names for himself. Watch him covertly; as soon as he is stuck I would happen by and start him off again. In this way he produced for himself the answers to his original questions and he would be able to get more answers to more questions if only he had a copy of the book to take away with him.

So we stocked as large a range of books for sale as we could afford. The flow of natural history books bemuses the public which has no ready way of distinguishing good from bad; less still can they identify exactly what best meets a particular need. We therefore sieved, from the flow, what we knew to be good of their kind; from Ladybirds to New Naturalists, from Field Guides to Linnean Synopses and FBA keys. We stocked all kinds of local material, wall charts and a range of maps and, of course, we had to become registered booksellers. This way, we could say to the boy with the shells 'This is the best book; you know now how it works. Christmas is coming. If you want to go on finding more shells, what about putting an idea into dad's head? If it's a no go, then by all means'come back here as often as you like and use our copy'. In that simple way we might have stimulated an interest that would develop and delight him all his days. The joys of natural history are unending. Could a joyful boy ever be a bad citizen?

In the Unit's annual programme I listed two periods a week under 'Can I help you?' when I guaranteed I would be in the building (you will understand how much I was away in the field doing this and that). Students galore came in during those times needing help with their 'projects'. I have no space here to elaborate on the inadequacy of the far too many teachers at all levels who authorised these things. All I could do was to reshape some impossible theme to the local practicabilities. We would have biology teachers who were 'rubbing up the red seaweeds' but did not quite know how to set about it. Parents came in with sons who wanted to know how best to plan for a job in the open air or which university was good for oceanography. Leaders of youth clubs and scouters were planning next year's camp: Where should they go? What ought they to see? Would I do a day for them? Would I talk one evening? And so on. All kinds of organised parties, students mostly, wanted special talks to meet their particular needs. The static display and exhibition in our one public room had to be made telescopic to accommodate this demand on our resources.

Outside the building we ran a simple weather station—Stevenson screen, max., and min., wet and dry, rain gauge, sunshine recorder.

Most people have no idea how meteorological data are accumulated and have never seen a maximum thermometer or how a rain gauge works. So simply from questions prompted by the instruments, the chance came time and time again to explain fronts, wind circulation and so on: 'Oh, that's what they mean on the telly!' Nice to cause pennies to drop.

We had a notice board and on one side the meteorological readings for the last seven days were posted. The current synoptic situation (derived from the BBC and the morning paper) was summarised on one panel and a local forecast for eight hours ahead and ten miles radius was written on another. In no time, people came just to read our forecast, almost as many as came into the building — a solemn responsibility if ever I had one! The questions and comments were another opportunity to explain and demonstrate from the passing clouds. It is then that you find out that most people have no idea where north is. On the other side of the board we had the tide times and range for seven days ahead, and it is amazing the extraordinary non-understanding about tides: 'Do you mean they come in and out *every* day? Well, what about night time?' 'Why does the tide stop when it gets to the top?' — try answering that one!

Another panel on the notice board was headed Country Diary. Here, I wrote up a few simple things I happened to have seen. 'First, chiffchaff song. Kidney-vetch, seapinks in full flower; scurvygrass past its best. Young ravens hatched. Small tortoise-shells flying in warm corners.' or, in August maybe, 'Basking shark off Newgale y'day. Fulmars leaving nest sites. Painted Ladies and Red Admirals scarce. First Parasols along cliff edge.' Virtually every item was news to most people. Very, very few had ever thought they might note a butterfly: 'How can I tell them apart?' 'Have you seen the wall chart inside?' 'No.' 'Well, have a look at it. I think it will help.' Of course it did and the enquirer would buy a copy and, from then on, it was looking to see if the Large Whites were of the spring or summer generation. Very simple stuff, but we all have to start from the beginning. Any number of people are much more interested than they themselves may realise if only somebody will take the trouble to show them how the world spins round in words they can understand.

In 1972, my last full year before retirement, over 10 000 people visited the Unit building; at the busiest more than 350 people a day passed through in August; far too many with whom to make useful contact. Altogether 2352 (1618 adults and 734 children) attended on the eighty field excursions I conducted, despite the dreadful weather of that May and June. The nineteen evening talks drew 573 adults and 185 children.

Those who prefer to spend their holidays among the splendours of

Pembrokeshire are, anyhow to that extent, different from those who prefer the gregarious and mechanical opportunities at Rhyl. But I am in no position to conclude that this is something to do with 'class' (whatever 'class' may be). While all sorts and conditions of men and women have been out with me, I do note that the response in the relatively uncaravanned north of Pembrokeshire far exceeds that in the over-caravanned south of the county. I leave others versed in class distinctions to draw what conclusions they will. My conviction could not be shaken that very few people have not within them an interest in the natural world. That interest may be masked by layers of urban ignorance and prejudice, but it is nearly always responsive to a simple demonstration and explanation of the way the natural world spins round.

An unconscious return to the origin and mainspring of their being, prompts the participation of so many who come out with me. This return may be even deeply unconscious in those whose lives have been bleakly grey and pressed by poverty. Their eventual metamorphosis into conscious understanding is none the less genuine, naive maybe, but sometimes transcendental. Rich man, poor man, beggar man, thief, all may be brought to lift up their eyes unto the hills and so accede to a strength they never knew they had.

My report that year goes: 'The sales of books, maps and charts increased to show a healthy profit and, together with the amount taken for outings and lectures' (which was 15p per adult and 10p for those at school), 'we have reached the stage where we are self-supporting in all but wages. This is something I always believed we might do.' Self-supporting means what it says. My colleague, Ieuan Griffiths, and I swept the floor, washed the windows and cut the grass for ourselves. The income from sales, outings and lectures paid for all our maintenance and materials, electricity, postage, printing, mini-van running and insurance, literally everything except our wages. I retired in July 1973 and there my story comes to an end, except to add that I still contribute to the walks and talks programme that is now the responsibility of the Pembrokeshire National Park Authority.

In retrospect I know now how great was my advantage when I came to deal with the public, of having had to teach for twenty years all the kinds of students that came to us at Dale Fort for field courses in anything that could be sensibly studied out of doors. In those early days no warden could say 'I'm a zoologist and so I don't know anything about the rocks'. In those early days we were no more than old-fashioned, on-all-fours naturalists imbued with the notion that our joy and limited understanding of the natural world should be shared with anybody who wanted to learn. We knew within ourselves how much joy there was in knowing a little and finding out more, and we wanted to show others how to catch their opportunity. When specialists came to the Centre, we carried their jam-jars and no student learnt as fast as we did. Those academics teased us as 'jacks of all trades'. Our riposte was that we were becoming masters of the workings of the parish of Dale and, in less particular, of Pembrokeshire. Geography, geology, botany, zoology, climate, history, prehistory, in fact anything that pertained to the peninsula, was grist to our mill. This was surely the best possible training, and far more useful than a PhD, for the work that was to come from the Countryside Unit. Alas, that kind of twenty years' experience is available only to a lucky few.

Its component parts are, however, not so scarce. In any area, inquiry will soon discover who the knowledgeable naturalists are who have the ability to communicate that knowledge. If a man knows only about flowering plants, have him understand how many are eager to learn about flowers from him. An expertise limited to local architecture will find a ready response provided that expertise can be communicated. Those who are invited to share in a teaching programme will have been so only because they can teach whatever it is they know. To accept offers of help from any volunteer leads to disaster if that volunteer, no matter how much he may fancy himself, turns out not to be securely grounded in his subject or if he lacks the good teacher's knack of communication. Some kind of testing and training must often precede the acceptance of an offer and there will be many whose offer has to be declined altogether, no matter how great the embarrassment.

This equally applies to the information desk, as in the field. An Information Officer is almost useless if he cannot distinguish between rock- and meadow-pipits or between tormentil and cinquefoil. Not to know the location and course of the local Civil War battles, or the larger geological structures underlying the area, is to be disqualified. Not to keep up to date by reading the most relevant publications and journals is to perpetrate a fraud on the public. This kind of countryside information service belongs much more to the teaching profession than to public relations. A school's museum service contains much that applies. The warden of a bird observatory even more. A good sixth form biology or geography teacher may be best of all since, being good, he or she will quickly add to what he already knows about his surroundings. Accepting an applicant who has never before studied the area is to admit you expect little service from him for a couple of years while he learns his way around. Being able to identify the local workings of general principles and stories (down to the gate to go through to find it, or the course of the stream that contains it) are the hallmark of a worthwhile information officer.

The notion of 'guided walks', call them what you will, has now been taken up elsewhere, notably by National Park Authorities. They have never achieved the fashionable status given in their day to Nature Trails and now to Country Parks, partly perhaps because those who do the funding have not yet understood what kind of guide is needed to realise the potential. The staff in field centres should be pre-eminently the best equipped to do this job but, I fear, they think that Everyman on holiday with his family is beneath their academic dignity. They who involve themselves embark on a missionary journey. To transmit understanding and excitement is at the heart of the secret of good teaching. Good teachers are not uncommon. Is this not just the right time to enrol those who have organised splendid field courses for their classes and ask them if they would like to transfer for a few years to whole-time work out-of-doors, preaching and teaching in their own way to those who only wish they knew whatever it is being laid open for them? Let no man, who has not himself fully demonstrated his own ability in the field, start telling these teachers how or what to do. This is a matter of personal, even idiosyncratic touch.

This touch can be applied throughout the land: 'Oh, Mr. Barrett, we live in such a dull district. Nothing has ever happened there. We don't even have any birds', is the voice of a very hungry sheep. The run-of-the-mill towns, the least glamorous landscapes, all have their treasures which their inhabitants would delight in if only somebody would tell their stories.

Likewise, inside the building, no amount of circuitary, multi-lingual stethoscopes or automatic lecturettes is a substitute for a well informed staff. This gimmickry itself becomes almost competitive between proprietors: 'Our electric bees buzz louder. Our primrose aerosol lasts longer. No wet shoes, no soiled hands. Experience the mountain in five throbbing minutes'. Too many of these expensive peepshows are interposed between the visitor and the reality only just outside. I have watched bus loads disgorge, storm into the tunnel of nature, press all the tits, see the colours flash, not hear the stereophonic water gurgling, and splurge out at the far end looking only for the icecreams.

What kind of understanding does this generate? It is only one step from an elaborate drive-in cinema. All the effects could be plugged into the car; no need to get out at all into that damp fresh air. Why not stay at home and see it there, so saving money on petrol? But, in fact, if such a display was carefully placed under tight educational supervision in a shopping centre or museum courtyard, it might stimulate a visit to the real thing. However, in a National Park, or any real countryside, money (and it is a lot of money) would be better spent in selecting and training competent staff to show off the wonder, beauty and mystery of the real thing.

Expensive proprietal gimmickry too often masks an inadequate understanding of the essence of the reality. The reality far transcends all mechanical immitation. The short cut, the easy way out leads to the slippery slope of self-deception by provider and consumer. Getting and spending, we lay waste our powers.

Participation is service and personal acceptance. It is to leave with others a share of the reality and an understanding (no matter how new, small or fragile) of the beautiful wholeness of the natural world. It is to open eyes which have never thought to look before and be the cause of an acceptance in others of man's responsibility for the wellbeing of Creation.

6 ADVENTURE PLAYGROUNDS AND COMMUNITY INVOLVEMENT

by Paul Soames

Inner city areas in Britain are dominated by deprivation, inferior housing, schools and facilities, and declining industry. Estates, old and new, have failed to provide an answer to these problems. Indeed, they have created more questions, bad access and provision, no play space, and highly concentrated populations. Even 'New Towns', the panacea of many a housing problem in the 1950s and 1960s, are developing into modern slums and creating as many problems as they are solving. Who are the sufferers caught in the middle of this trap? The people who live there. And who are the most vulnerable people? The children, and so it is they who suffer the most.

Play and the development of play facilities, then, begin to assume great importance in such areas where space and opportunities are at a premium, but where energy, creativity, frustration and aggression are at a peak. What is being done and what can be done? Inevitably, different organisations and authorities have sprung up all over the country to try and tackle 'play' and its provision. Also, many of those groups have come up with different ideas, strategies and interpretations. As a result, confusion and misunderstanding often abound between, say, local authorities and voluntary play associations. The ultimate sufferers in such circumstances are often the children for whom both are trying to provide.

How a group interprets the word 'play' will decide how it tackles its provision. Some people are satisfied, or so it seems, to provide concrete or tarmac play areas for children, areas which are dull and unimaginative and often dangerous. A Design Council survey, issued in May 1976, estimated that twenty thousand accidents a year, many of them bad, some fatal, occurred on such playgrounds. Iron frames and immovable concrete pipes are no stimulation; any fun to be had on them is over in five minutes. Or there are the novelty items, steam engines and tractors which have all the moveable, interesting bits stripped off so you just sit there and wonder what happens next. This type of provision kills creative play stone dead. They might look nice, but they serve no real purpose or value as far as the children are concerned.

Others see play as an activity that must be highly organised, structured and within limits, with adults controlling the environment and the process of playing and the children learning exclusively from the adults instead of from themselves. Sports and competitions often abound and indeed make up the programme for such organisations, and they become 'leader' orientated thus giving the children the role of followers. I am not suggesting sports or competitions are wrong or undesirable. They are often eminently desirable and useful, but to make them a centre piece and not part of other activities, and to have adults organising, planning and leading, seems to me to be too much like school and not a lot like play. Besides, organisations such as scouts, guides and army cadets provide and cater for such activities; and very well they often do it, though they could hardly be called organisations involved in play and its development.

Play is a natural and spontaneous activity which has limits one minute and none the next, which is made up of fantasies and adventures but which above all incorporates joy and fun. It is not an activity that can or should be contained or structured. As Lady Allen of Hurtwood, who pioneered adventure playgrounds in this country, said: 'Every child is an individual marvel, gifted with unique capacities'.[1] Are we to deny them the opportunity to develop these capacities? We will if we limit their horizons by providing what we feel they need all the time and without letting them have a say. What then is the answer? Well, one of them is certainly the adventure playground, the concept of adventure play, free play, experimental play, the opportunity for the child to find out for itself what can or cannot be done, what does or does not exist. In short, an interesting well supported adventure playground has more to offer children and community as a whole than many other types of play or community facilities that are at present provided.

WHAT IS AN ADVENTURE PLAYGROUND?

An adventure playground is a place of discovery, experiment, enjoyment and freedom. Geographically it is an area that is often found in the middle of estates, on street corners, on old derelict building sites, bomb sites and public parks, with sizes ranging from a quarter of an acre to two acres. A playground must offer activities ranging from the completely unstructured and free to the relatively structured and organised, because children enjoy and must have the fullest range of experiences that they can possibly get. As R. D. Laing points out in his 'Politics of Experience': 'The two most important human needs are experience and control over one's own experience'.[2]

Materials and space to use those materials imaginatively and constructively are essential. Opportunity and atmosphere are also necessary to stimulate the child into activity. This is where the role of the worker on the playground is so vital to the playground's success.

A playground worker needs to be committed, sensitive and aware. His art is to be a good communicator and, basically, his role is one of friendship with the children and adults he meets. Sometimes he is a teacher, when showing how or why a certain thing is done, sometimes a parent when he protects and advises, other times a mentor when he listens and sympathises. Perhaps, however, most of all he is someone who children turn to when parent, school or friend has rejected them either temporarily or for longer.

When working in a play environment a constant problem, or rather a challenge to the worker is the decision whether to interfere, participate or supervise.[3] Professor Sorenson, a Danish architect who along with Marjory Allen pioneered the cause of adventure playgrounds, put it this way:

> When contemplating an adventure playground, it is opportune to warn against too much supervision and too many arrangements for the children. It is my opinion that children ought to be free and by themselves to the greatest possible extent. A certain supervision and guidance will of course be necessary, but I am firmly convinced that one ought to be exceedingly careful when interfering in the lives and activities of children. The object must be to give the children of the city a substitute for the rich possibilities for play which children in the country possess.

'A certain supervision and guidance' is necessary from the workers. It is, for instance, better to intervene with a group of children who are building a hut and have come to a halt over a particular problem, and are losing interest because of that problem, and advise them what to do, even show them, so that they can continue, instead of walking off frustrated or thwarted. I also believe that if a child is modelling, say out of wood, it is better to go and give a helping hand and help to get a finished product that works or stays together than leave him to finish a model that falls apart at first touch and leaves him annoyed and confused. However, it would be wrong to interfere with a group of children who are play acting a home or school scene as they so often do. Such activities are often sacrosanct and any adult interference or involvement, unless asked for, often destroys the game. The worker then has to be aware of what is happening and where, and then decide what action he should take if, indeed, any is necessary at all.

Often the workers must initiate projects themselves and then withdraw or participate as the situation demands. Projects ranging from the building of huts, forts, tree houses and tunnels, to cooking, painting, climbing, digging, dressing up, to group games, camping, outings and visits. In other words, a good playground offers a whole range of opportunities. Let us take one example, painting, to show the scope the playground can offer. A child's ideas and vision of painting is usually limited to the piece of paper and water paint on the desk in front of him, or the sight of his father painting their home. A playground can offer a child the opportunity to paint a piece of paper or a brick wall, or a climbing structure, or the side of a hut, or indeed the opportunity to decorate the play hut itself, and there is not just water paint but emulsion, 'grown ups' paint to be used with 'grown ups' brushes. In this instance, the child is experimenting with different textures, tools and materials to gain the widest possible comprehension and use of them, stretching their minds to meet the challenge that is offered. Where else could he experiment in such a way?

As a playground develops and becomes recognised, a mutual trust develops between child and worker. Both feel that something positive and good is happening and so constructive activities continue and mutual benefit is reaped:

> What kept the thing running happily was a feeling that all our efforts were in a common direction, towards something we all wanted. This situation cannot be forced. As one project follows another a mutual trust gradually emerges. It is an integral part of the atmosphere of the playground'.[4]

THE PLAYGROUND AND THE COMMUNITY

An adventure playground is usually based within a local area or community and therefore serves the children in that area. Consequently, to thrive and prosper it needs the support of the people around it. However, for different reasons, playgrounds are often seen as anti-social, sometimes because of their physical appearance, often because they represent apparent disorder or are seen as anti-authority because they do not seem to fit into society's orderly patterns and rules. Indeed, they do not and should not and this often worries people. It is here that the role of the worker comes in because the playground is responsible to the community around it as well as to itself. The workers must justify the playground's existence. Hence, contact with parents, schools and social services is essential so that a dialogue of information and explanation can be set up. Fears about the playground must be calmed and rationalised, its positive aspects emphasised to the extent that a working relationship is built up with the community around. Local businesses are another potential area of support, support in the form of materials and goods for the playground, and perhaps financial, if they can be persuaded that a playground is a worthwhile enterprise. The aim of this is to get the playground accepted as an integral part of the community and this depends on the worker's ability to communicate well with people.

This process of acceptance is often long, especially if the

playground has been 'planted' in an area, but the struggle for recognition is worth it. Notting Hill adventure playground, in London, one of the first and longest surviving playgrounds, has developed activities outside of its original play function as it has grown and been accepted by the people around. There is an old age pensioners' club, a preschool playgroup, a parents' club and also a youth club; all responses to local needs. A number of playgrounds up and down the country can boast such developments, developments that indicate that the playgrounds concerned are becoming part of, or are part of, community life.

The so called 'unattached' often find their way to adventure playgrounds, being attracted by the 'open' door policy most playgrounds operate.[5] They are often seen as problems or threats by parents and children alike, and often by youth workers as well. Indeed, they will create problems if they are viewed and know they are seen as such. Many of them require someone to talk to or are crying out for some kind of help. The playground worker can offer some support and advice. Perhaps he can enlist their help on the playground, especially with construction work. Many playgrounds are understaffed and, with his knowledge of the area and the services, he can perhaps act as an adviser or investigator for them. Perhaps he can just sit and listen to them over a cup of coffee because so many young people are alienated and, as a result, never have anyone with whom they can sit and talk, especially someone who is sympathetic. Yes, this is extending the adventure playground worker's role into youth work and encroaching on youth service territory, but the youth service is failing to attract these young people. Only one in three young people who have access to the youth service actually uses it. That leaves an awful lot of uncatered for young people. So the playground worker often finds that he is becoming involved with youth work with the young people in the surrounding community as well as working on the playground with the younger children.

Playgrounds, then, often develop other services and facilities for the community. A crude comparison can be drawn with a tree. For a tree to thrive it needs good roots in the surrounding earth and a supply of water to nourish it. If it has these requirements, it grows and flourishes and develops new branches. If it is denied support, it has weak roots and a poor water supply, it withers and dies and is no use to anyone. Adventure playgrounds have often earned bad reputations in the past, often justifiably so because they have been badly run and managed. This is sad because it colours peoples' attitudes to future projects and makes them wary when people talk of play or playgrounds. Certainly a badly run playground is an eye sore and has a destructive effect on workers and children alike. It demands hard work and commitment for a playground to be a success with everybody.

What causes a bad playground? In the main it is bad leadership from the workers, often allied with bad management committees. A playleader's job is, in many respects, impossible to do. He is an educator, social worker, innovator, confidant, semi-parent, a kind of Robin Hood in fact. This all demands skill, energy and commitment; not all play workers have this. Playgrounds have sprung up all over the country. Many have employed people who are frankly unsuitable for the work; people who have felt that working on adventure playgrounds is an easy option from other jobs; people who have lacked dedication and imagination. Such workers are often found sipping endless cups of coffee, sitting in their office while the children outside are getting bored and frustrated because there is no stimulation of action, there is no sense of involvement or achievement on their part. They want a bit of advice, or tools and materials to help in constructing a hut, but it is not forthcoming. They drift away and come back later disillusioned and show it by perhaps vandalising the site. These people often do not last for long. The turnover rate in London several years ago was quite incredible. At one time it was estimated that eight months was the average time a worker spent on a playground. Unfortunately, a number of these workers have also damaged the idea of adventure playgrounds in the eyes of the community, to the extent that people are reluctant to lend their support to future projects and developments.

This therefore calls for careful selection of workers by committees and not just taking the first choice that *seems* suitable. Even if it takes several sets of interviews, it is worth it to find the right group of people. This is a very important consideration as the future of the project depends on this selection. This choice obviously depends on having an aware management. Bad management will employ bad workers, whilst good management will employ good workers and give them good support thereafter. An important recipe for success.

PLANNING AND MANAGEMENT

It is only recently, it seems, that planners and architects have realised that it is important to make room for play areas and open spaces when designing new housing areas. Mercifully, the idea of high rise conurbations as homes for people is declining and more thought is going into what surrounds communities and their appearance. However, a great deal still needs to be done in this field. We could perhaps take a 'leaf' from Denmark, where adequate space and facilities are required by law when new housing is being developed. For many, however, this trend and thought in planning was too late and they are left in the hideous housing estates of yesteryear. What can they do?

Certainly more public participation is necessary in the planning of new estates and towns. This participation must start at the very beginning of the planning process before plans are drawn and contracts sought, i.e. What type of housing is desirable? What community facilities are necessary? What kind of transport and road system is desirable? How accessible are the shops? And so on. Perhaps, as far as children are concerned, it would be an idea for architects and planners to study (while training) childhood environments and needs so that when it comes to designing they have an idea who they are designing for. Many architects have never lived in or experienced working class communities. They have different outlooks and expectations and perhaps lack of understanding is one reason why so many problems and mistakes have been made in the past.

To those who live in relatively new housing complexes where participation in planning was unheard of, and indeed for those who live in much older housing stock, the concept of participation can still apply. Space and provision for play is inevitably lacking and therefore work has to be done to remedy this. Often, in older housing areas, pressure groups have grown up to combat the lack of facilities. It is the job of the authorities concerned to listen to these groups and work alongside them in planning and providing new facilities. As Lady Allen, a landscape designer herself, points out:

> The fact has to be faced that modern civilisation interferes with a hard and heavy hand in the spontaneous play of children. The use made of land around buildings is still almost always totally unsuitable for children. Most of the vast building schemes in many countries are horrible places, planned without love or understanding. This arrogance, this paucity of invention, this disregard of the worth and scale of the individual represents a world wide disease and is one of the tragedies of affluence. The designer must devise new means for establishing a connection between the buildings he creates and the people on the ground. [1]

If planning is about thought and involvement then so too is the management of playgrounds. The two are very closely linked. Basically there are two different types of management, voluntary and statutory. When adventure playgrounds first started they were almost always run by voluntary, charitable groups. It was not until they became recognised as worthwhile projects that local authorities decided they ought to get in on the act. Indeed the people who set up one of the first playgrounds in Lollard Street, London, in the early 1950s were condemned by many people, in and out of authority, as communists and their project to be subversive and anarchic! I hope attitudes have come a long way since then.

Many local authorities now have Playleadership Departments or have Playleadership sections within their Recreational Departments. The Greater London Council has a Playleadership Department which employs some three hundred people full and part-time. Many local authorities run schemes which have no management committee at all. Playground workers are responsible to a local authority officer, often termed a 'field officer', who is in turn responsible to his Head of Department, so there is a straight ladder of authority up and down. The workers on the playground are in this case local authority employees. One obvious disadvantage here is that with no management committee, made up of local people to whom the playground is responsible, there is the possibility of alienation from the community and a feeling of being imposed upon by the local authority, although this can be alleviated if the workers realise that they are responsible to the community and carry out the tasks mentioned earlier. Often such playgrounds have higher staff ratios than voluntary run schemes. This is certainly true in London where better conditions of service and also a better choice of goods and materials are available basically because they are local authority employees with access to council services.

Local boroughs and authorities often support the various groups and organisations that spring up which aim to provide playgrounds and play opportunities for children, support in the form of grants for equipment and personnel and sites for use as play centres. It would be impossible to number the different organisations and small groups up and down the country that run playgrounds but they range from the London Adventure Playground Association to the Pitsea Adventure Playschemes Association from the Swansea Adventure Playground Association to the Glasgow Play Association, and so on, down to tenants groups and community groups that run just one playground. The constitution of a typical organisation runs: 'Either alone, or in conjunction with other voluntary and statutory bodies, to further the provision of adequate play facilities for children of all ages, by the establishment of a properly staffed adventure playground, and by the extension, improvement and provision of such other play facilities as may be deemed right from time to time.' (Pitsea Adventure Playground Association).

These groups often develop as a result of a successful summer playscheme which people feel needs to be carried on all year round and expanded to cater for more children, or they grow up as a result of unrest because of a lack of facilities. Alternatively they form to bring together various groups within a Borough or area who are concerned with play and its provision and need an umbrella organisation to coordinate their ideas. Most of these organisations run on shoe-string budgets and cannot afford to employ as many workers as they would like, especially in the economic climate of today with its rising costs and spending cuts, a topic to be returned to. Many of these groups also fail to offer sufficient support to the workers on the playground, which is often disastrous because if a playground cannot turn to its management committee for finance and moral and physical backing it can so easily collapse. The workers cannot and must not be expected to do all the administrative, financial and supportive work for the playground, they must have a good secretary, chairperson and treasurer to back them. Strong management is essential for these voluntary groups if they are to survive.

Most management committees are made up of volunteers, often with full time community workers, teachers, social workers coopted on to them to inject advice and experience. Committees should not be too large or unwieldy, but at the same time reflect as wide a range of interests as possible. The key job on the Committee is that of the Secretary, for it is that person's job to liase as closely as possible with the workers and the management. This job is the vital link. The Secretary provides the administrative skills, whether it is letter writing, day-to-day cash dealings for equipment, supplies or petty cash or the promotion of the playground in the community, press and other related meetings. The Secretary must be backed by a good chairperson and treasurer and the other members of the committee, for there are always jobs to be done, for example, the ever present problem of fund raising. It is essential that the management understand the workings of the playground. If they know the purpose of a playground and what the workers' tasks are, they will know (as we found out earlier) what kind of staff to employ and how to back them up, what kind of people to approach for support and money and what the problems of working and running a playground are.

The obvious and best way for management to understand is for them to try and spend some time on the playsite with the workers and children. To actively involve themselves in organising particular events like barbecues, fetes, discotheques, and so on. This cooperation between management committees and workers is so important for the future development and support of playgrounds. Without it, frustration develops between the playleader and their committees, both feeling that they are being misunderstood and, as a result, friction often develops to the ultimate detriment of the children, for whom both are, in fact, working. This must be avoided. This type of participation, however, does involve great time and effort, particularly on the Secretary's part. This must be realised when the job is taken on, but it is important for other committee members to realise this as well and help share the load of work. Involvement of as many people as possible is very important, especially in a community run enterprise.

Many playgrounds and play organisations realise the importance of this communication and actively encourage it. The Handicapped Adventure Playground Association, for instance, place great importance on committee involvement on the playground, with five management members working on a regular weekly basis on their Chelsea playground. There is a danger though of involvement that leads to interference or the undermining of the playleader's role. This is a situation that must be steered clear of and committee members made aware of. The playleaders have been employed to do a job and their role must not be usurped by management members. Each must be aware of their role in the organisation of things, but at the same time keep a flow of information, help and advice going between them.

An idea put forward recently by a playground in London, to help overcome the problem of weak management, money worries and contacts, was that of a playground 'integrator'. His role would be 'an amalgam of executive offices, community worker, playground administrator, association manager and work co-ordinator'. He would be employed alongside the playground workers and based at the playground, he would work closely with the management committee and link up with other voluntary and statutory bodies, recruit volunteers and negotiate placements from training and educational institutions, find resources, research into the possibility of new playground projects and build up an information service at the playground. This seems an eminently sensible and logical step to take and is one possible solution to the problem of management, and certainly one worth pursuing further. Local authorities could help a great deal here by supporting such initiatives and encouraging the growth and development of local organisations and associations.

Let us not forget a sector of the community that is often disregarded or left out when we talk about community provision, and that is the handicapped person. Play and play opportunities are just as important for them, indeed more so. It is important for groups to work towards the integration of handicapped children into the community and one of the first levels it can start at is in the playgroup, playscheme and playground. All it requires is a little extra thought and planning on behalf of the workers concerned and perhaps some research by the playground 'integrator' we have mentioned. Perhaps groups and associations could approach local children's hospitals, subnormality hospitals, children's homes, special schools, with the support of the local authority, and see if any work can be done in providing play facilities for the pupils and patients. This kind of work is being pioneered by the Handicapped Adventure Playground Association, another creation of Lady Allen. There are four playgrounds in the London area for handicapped children, and they also disseminate information and advice to groups interested in setting up similar projects. They are, however, only scratching the surface. A lot more needs to be done by other groups both statutory and voluntary if the play needs of the handicapped are to be adequately met.

There are a number of organisations that exist to promote the idea of play and playgrounds, but do not actually manage them. They provide information and support, with personnel who can advise groups what to do, who to approach and where to go. Perhaps two of the most well known of these organisations are the National Playing Fields Association and, more recently, the Fair Play for Children Campaign. The former has been in existence for many years and was a pioneer organisation as far as the promotion of adventure playgrounds was concerned. Its Playleadership Department employs field officers who are assigned particular areas of the country to cover. Their job is basically to encourage the provision of play facilities in those areas, but a frequent criticism of this Association is its remoteness from the grass roots of play, its only contacts coming from its field officers who cover vast areas — seven cover the whole of England and so cannot hope to do all that is necessary. While they do this, the rest of the Association sits in offices in London away from the reality of day-to-day activities. Some of this criticism is perhaps justified, but with its limited resources can it do more? The National Playing Fields Association has provided a valuable publicity service for play and they do perform a valuable function in bringing groups together, in the form of Play Councils in particular areas, and en-couraging individual groups to start projects. They also provide a forum for discussion of playleadership on a national basis, as well as encouraging and supporting training programmes. However many active playground workers do feel alienated and are uninterested in such organisations. They feel that there is no proper understanding of playground work and the problems that exist on playgrounds, and view such groups as bureaucratic animals. This is unfortunate as it tends to split people who are essentially working for the same goal and so cause additional problems. Lack of communication between the two groups seems apparent, it is a lack that should be remedied.

The National Playing Fields Association can take most of the credit for the starting of a nationwide campaign called the Fair Play for

Children Campaign. It was they who financially supported the campaign for its first two years and saw it off the ground. This campaign started as a result of a letter the Bishop of Stepney sent to The Times in 1972 which deplored the death and injury of children who were forced to play in the street because there was nowhere else for them to play. Since then, the campaign has spread into a national one with full-time staff being employed, groups affiliating and action being taken with the aim: 'To encourage and stimulate the provision of facilities for children to play'. The campaign works on three levels with regional and neighbourhood groups, with national organisations, and finally with central government. It has a big job to perform and, being a 'campaign', it has to be dynamic and progressive which it often has been, but which it will lose if money is cut and ideas falter and stagnation sets in. The measure of support it has got from organisations, statutory and voluntary, indicates the goodwill behind its aims which will hopefully make for success. Both the National Playing Fields Association and the Fair Play Campaign complement and overlap one another in their work, but they do provide valuable support and encouragement to groups all around the country who are struggling to make children's lot a better one. They should have enthusiastic backing.

VALUES—GOOD OR BAD?

As has been mentioned before, playgrounds are often seen as subversive or permissive places. Indeed they do not conform with many of society's rules and provisions, and they should not do so. A playground offers a child an environment of his own where he has control and the freedom to use his instincts and grant his wishes. There are very few places in our society where children are allowed to do this. But some people are afraid to give children this amount of freedom and say in their own lives. Why? Well that is a question only they can really answer, but perhaps it lies in the fact that adults do not like to have their own values questioned, especially by those younger than themselves, and see any move to have them questioned as a threat to their security and power. Playgrounds seek to breakdown barriers, question the established facts and challenge accepted rules, after all that is what play is all about—questioning, searching, experimenting. In so far as this is permissive and subversive then, yes, playgrounds are exactly that.

However, it is the positive side of concepts and ideas that the playground promotes, not the negative destructive side. The role of the worker is to stimulate positive action and involvement to get the child to challenge constructively, to question constructively so that he is not left in a void, he knows there is an answer to his problem or his experiment. It is not permissive to encourage this kind of mental and physical activity, it is only right that they should be faced with such challenges. The children of today have to face the problems of tomorrow which we are giving them. To make a good job of it, they must be aware of what is happening to them as well as being aware of their own abilities, skills, limits and barriers. The adventure playground concept can only have a positive effect on them, as Jack Lambert found out when he toured Denmark: 'They seem to realise instinctively that these playgrounds offer something that is of fundamental importance to the children, and they positively want to give their children opportunities to be constructive. Beyond this it seems to me that they have a higher regard for the instincts and wishes of children than we have, which makes them more ready to provide what the children themselves ask for: the British are more inclined to take the view that adults know best.'[4]

It is possible, though, for badly run playgrounds to have negative, even destructive, values. If the workers are not sufficiently committed or dedicated, if the management committee is weak and ineffective, then the playground will rapidly run downhill with vandalism, destruction and abuse becoming rife and only negative attitudes being expressed. In such circumstances, the playground must shut as soon as possible, until such time as it can be successfully reopened. The running of a playground must never be approached in a half hearted way, better to have no playground than an apology for one.

The values a playground transmits are closely linked with the values a school transmits to its pupils. Indeed, play and education are very closely related. Froebel realised this some 150 years ago and his stress on the importance of play in learning now plays an important part of preschool and primary education in this country. It would seem therefore that people involved in education and people involved in playgrounds have something to offer one another in terms of advice and expertise which would be of ultimate benefit to the community around. Many comprehensive and secondary schools are turning towards community work and involvement. Perhaps playgrounds have something to offer here in the way of advice and support. Why shouldn't a local school design and build a playground in its neighbourhood that many of the school pupils would use? Perhaps too some of the ideas that children have, and the way in which children play on playgrounds, could influence the way teachers think and act in their job, that would surely be to the children's and the school's benefit.[6]

When talking about values, we have to look closely at the role of the playworker and the influence he has in his work. A playground worker is an enabler, that is he furnishes the children with the materials, authority and ability to carry out a project or scheme, he enables them to do it. Could he also be a 'conditioner', that is could or does the worker create an environment, both physical and mental, that conditions a child's actions and responses?[7, 8] Most adults find that children come into contact with have some kind of 'conditioning' power over them. Parents and relations condition the child into family life values; teachers educate and so determine children's ideas, aspirations and abilities; doctors condition and control children's health; policemen condition a child's attitude to the law, and so on. All these adults have a control over how the child develops. Many of them overlap and complement each other and people will argue that some of these controls and conditions are good (e.g. the role of the doctor and parent), others that some of the controls are bad (policemen's attitudes, for instance). The point I am making here, though, is not whether these particular controls are good or bad, though this needs to be followed up and discussed, but that these controls and conditions *do* exist, always have done and that they exist for adults as well as for children. Most adults in a child's life are conditioners of one sort or another and so they determine radically the child's development with the child having little or no say in the matter.

The essence of an adventure playground, as has been discussed earlier, is the freedom of opportunity to experiment, explore, discover, to be able to decide for oneself what is desirable and what is not; whether to play by oneself, or with peers, to enjoy oneself. The enabler (playworker) is thus creating with the children an environment where this can happen. It would be naive to think that in creating such an environment certain conditions would not exist. The site, for instance, is one control that has to be obeyed. It is no good building a swing on the pavement outside the fence! Also, the fact that workers are employed means that certain conditions have to be abided by. Obviously the playworkers themselves have their own standards of discipline, morality and approach and they will apply these, and perhaps modify them, in the course of their work on the playground. Their work will, in other words, reflect the way that they have been conditioned to certain standards of discipline.

Other controls will exist. The relationship between the community and the playground will, for instance, affect the way the site works. The parents will expect a responsible, mature attitude from the workers, while the workers will expect a trustful respectful attitude from the parents. This involves communication of ideas and thoughts which will condition the way the staff work and think. Another example could be the use of four different children wanting to use one piece of equipment that only one can use. A solution has to be found. That one piece of equipment and its availability conditions the way the four children will react, but here lies the beauty of the adventure playground for there is an alternative. There are other pieces of equipment and there are also materials available to construct more. The child has got a choice, a choice he can make. A final example could be the interference by one group of children on another group, to the extent that activity stops and hostility begins. The worker then has to decide when, how and if he should involve himself. To avoid the situation getting right out of control he will probably intervene and help to solve the problem. The way he approaches this will control the children's reaction and condition their response to him and the environment as a whole.

The enabler, therefore, does have a framework and certain conditions to work within, which he transmits in his work with the children. Without a structure, the project would collapse, but he also acts as a deconditioner. That is, he leaves or stimulates the children to take the initiative and find out for themselves what they can do and what they cannot and where barriers exist or do not. They do this within the loose framework provided. In other words, they are given the conditions and environment to challenge and explore and rethink the controls and environment they live and play in. They are given the chance to decondition. An adventure playground is unique in the fact that the conditions it provides in terms of staff and surroundings are far less rigid and disciplined than most other childhood environments, thus allowing the child as much scope as possible to plan *his* own environment and life and not have it done for him. This is at the crux of the whole concept of adventure playgrounds, if we lose sight of this then adventure playgrounds will die.

DANGERS

As I see it, at the moment, there are two dangers to the adventure playground movement in this country. One is more immediate, the other more longterm. The first threat, the immediate one, is that of public spending cuts. Over the next couple of years, and perhaps for longer if there is a change of government, cuts are going to be made and social services, education and community provisions are going to be hit. Adventure playgrounds are often viewed, especially in areas where the concept is new, as being on the fringe of social services and community provisions, a luxury that can perhaps be done without, or given less of a priority. They will therefore be vulnerable when authorities look at their budgets and pick out what to do away with. What could happen?

Running and maintenance grants will be cut back to local

authority and voluntary run schemes, salaries stopped or cut back, workers not replaced when they leave, equipment grants halved, or even stopped, and playgrounds shutting because authorities can no longer afford to run them or pay the staff. Other smaller scale projects, such as playgrounds and holiday playschemes, may be affected too. It is a grim picture, but a picture that could well become familiar over the country as authorities tighten their belts. In short, play provision could be pushed back years if serious cuts are planned and approved. These cuts would be false economies. Without playgrounds, play space and playworkers, children will be forced to play on the streets with all its attendant dangers, delinquency will increase and cost the state money in repairs, prosecutions and detentions. The children will become mentally and physically stagnant because of the lack of facilities for them, and apathy and boredom will reign more than it does now. As a Fair Play slogan puts it: 'Prevent effectively rather than repair expensively'. What people must do is to organise themselves to fight any such cuts. Organise themselves around their playground, their play association, their play council. Playworkers in London, for example, have formed a branch within the National Union of Public Employees. One of its tasks in the future will be to act against cuts in play provision in that city. Other groups must act in similar ways before it is too late. This is rather a sad picture, but it is a picture that will not occur if sufficient pressure, feeling and support is gathered behind those who care about play provision for children in this country.

The other danger to the playground movement is the progressive professionalisation of play. Play and its provision is for the children of our town and city communities, the children belong to the adults in those communities and it is essential for these adults to participate in the provision and distribution of play facilities. It seems to me that, increasingly, the opportunity for public participation and involvement is decreasing. Local authorities are creating their own departments to deal with the provision of play and seem to be getting further and further away from the concept of helping the people decide what they want and where. The danger lies in the formation of another youth service where the emphasis is on professional people and expert help. Where civil servants, or their like, hand out reports concerning the plight of our youth (but do very little else) while the people who they are meant to be working with become increasingly alienated. This is a generalisation, but it goes to serve my point that play and its provision could, and in some cases is, slipping out of the hands and control of the people it is meant for and being taken over by bureaucrats. This often happens quite unconsciously on the part of the authorities and the people.

One example of how this is happening is in the appointment of playground workers. One often sees adverts for qualified playleaders, or qualified playleaders preferred. This automatically cuts out a whole range of people who might fill the post admirably but whose qualification is experience, not degrees or diplomas. They might be residents in the town or city the job is advertised in, but they are put off by the word 'qualified'. They are being alienated. Another example, as we have seen earlier, is in the 'planting' of playgrounds or play ideas on communities by professional planners and architects without consulting the people their projects are meant for. One example will go to serve the point of lack of participation and thought by these people: Kensington and Chelsea Council in London gave the go ahead to build and, in fact did build, what they termed an 'adventure playground' on a new housing estate in North Kensington. The playground was just a concreted surface with a play hut which occupies the bottom of two floors of a high rise block. The children play directly underneath and beside the blocks of flats with all the resultant noise and dangers for both children and the people in the flats above. There was no equipment, so all the children had was barren concrete to play on. Is this an adventure playground? Where was the participation and involvement here? Fortunately, work is now being done by the local Play Association and the playground playleaders to rectify the situation. But what did the people of Lancaster Road West Estate feel about the playground that was meant for their children? No-one knew because no-one asked until it was too late. In other words, local people are not being encouraged to work on or to participate in a project or scheme that is for them. Professional help is being drafted in to run and plan projects for them. Yet another move away from participation being made.

The solution to this trend lies in the communication between the relevant authorities and the people, represented by community groups and associations. Perhaps part-time training schemes can be set up to help local people who are interested in running schemes, or grants and cooperation given to groups for research into play provisions to be done. Representatives of the relevant authority and relevant community groups should sit down in each other's meetings and discussions. There are examples of such cooperation and they are ones that should be followed up and explored. In Islington, London, for instance, the Council ran a training scheme specifically for voluntary management committees of playgrounds and playschemes. This course gave advice and described the skills necessary for the management of projects. An extremely valuable exercise for people who perhaps felt inadequate and lost in this role, but who in the end finished up confident enough to go back and form a management committee from their own community to run a project? Wandsworth Council in London organise parent workshops before the summer play projects start in the Borough. These again offer skills, advice and information for the parents so that they are able to approach their particular projects positively and with an awareness of what to avoid and what to encourage.

On a larger scale, we have the Westminster Play Association[8] which is a voluntary organisation that coordinates play provision in Westminster. It is supported both in terms of finance and equipment by Westminster City Council and 'exists to bring together and to support local people who care about the needs for children's play in their area and who want to do something to alleviate these needs'.[9] In other words, the Council is giving the resources to the community to work out their own programme and not imposing a programme upon them. It must be added, though, that the Westminster Play Association has been a victim of spending cuts with its grant being reduced from the Council. A negative move.

All this serves to break down barriers and get a two-way flow of information going which can only be to the benefit of all parties concerned. Community participation must not be sacrificed for what may seem to be the streamlining and professionalisation of play provision.

This survey of playgrounds, their functions and management is of necessity short. It is impossible in one chapter to go into too much detail. For example, a whole chapter could be devoted to the kind of values play and playgrounds in particular transmit. So things have been left out and generalisations made. The chapter is written from practical experience, not from an administrator's or sociologists's point of view. As such it may be simple in its presentation. I have, however, tried to explain why playgrounds exist and why they serve a useful purpose, how they are managed, the importance of participation and why it is vital that playgrounds must be allowed to develop and so enhance the lives and future of our children.

REFERENCES

1. Lady Allen of Hurtwood (1968) *Planning for Play*. Thames & Hudson, London
2. Laing, R. D. (1977) *Politics of Experience*. Penguin, Middlesex
3. Millar, S. (1968) *The Psychology of Play*. Penguin, Middlesex
4. Lambert, J. & Pearson, J. (1974) *Adventure Playgrounds*. Penguin, Middlesex
5. Benjamin, J. (1961) *In Search of Adventure*. National Council of Social Services

6. Ball, C. (1973) *Education for a Change*. Penguin, Middlesex
7. Hott, J. (1964) *How Children Fail*. Pitman, London
8. Hott, J. (1964) *How Children Learn*. Pitman, London
9. Westminster Play Association (1976) *Snakes and Ladders*. (A directory of play, education and leisure activities for children and their parents.) Compiled by the WPA, London

COMMUNITY INVOLVEMENT
IN DESIGN

This section looks at involvement in the design process and begins with a general consideration by Professor Eggleston of the contemporary concept of community and the role of education for participation in design for living. Eggleston argues that the modern concept of community, involving the public in decision making, is fundamentally different from the traditional. He also argues that it is in leisure where this new concept is coming to life and that this is closely paralleled by contemporary changes in education. He illustrates this with some of the work of a school design and craft education project of which he was director.

The author of Chapter 8—David Harding, a town artist—has considerable experience of involving school children and other members of the public in the design process, particularly in relation to the environment. He discusses this and other projects, noting that changes in the approach to design and a loosening of planning controls will be necessary to create opportunities for people to make the creative contribution of which they are capable.

One region which Harding advocates as crucial for community involvement is housing and Chapter 9 by Rod Hackney, architect, tackles this area. He discusses the self-help rehabilitation projects, in which he has been involved, and stresses the opportunities for participation that are still not being exploited but which the 1974 Housing Act affords. Hackney emphasises the importance of sensitivity and awareness in the project leader in helping to shape decision making for the benefit of the whole community.

In the final chapter of this section, Michael Tempest, a county council architect, discusses the experiences of public participation in the design of education and leisure facilities. While there are, currently, limits to this process he sees the development of school-based leisure centres as important for involving the public in the design of future building and other programmes in the community.

Collectively, these chapters illustrate the enormous potential which exists for involving the public in design.

7 COMMUNITY DESIGN AND EDUCATION

by John Eggleston

The concept of community is not only ancient, but also surrounded by nostalgia. 'Let us recapture the spirit of community' is a reliable rallying cry for all who campaign for any kind of social reform. It evokes a concept of a small intimate society in which man can live his life wholly and satisfyingly, in close mutually supportive relationships with his fellow man and enhance the quality of both his own life and theirs. It is seen to be a society in which the needs of the individual are fully satisfied from its own resources, where his rights and duties are not only properly balanced but fairly shared. Leisure, like work, family, religion and all other aspects of life are closely related.

Though the content of community embraces the whole of human life and not solely its educational arrangements, it is nonetheless a concept of central importance to educationalists. Yet to talk of the development of community education alerts us at once to an important distinction between community in a 'traditional' society and a community in a contemporary western European context. In earlier societies, community was the only form of social organisation available to man. Membership of the urban or rural community was inescapable and exclusion from it removed virtually all protection from physical attack, hunger, disease and other perils. Man was born into a community, lived and died within it and knew no other form of life or indeed, for the most part, any other form of community.

Conversely, in modern societies there is no inevitability about living in a community. Indeed, its fullest form is the exception rather than the norm. To achieve a community life style requires conscious decision and often considerable effort on the part of the individual and the corporate organisations of modern societies (church, state and business and above all educational institutions). Community does not spring spontaneously, it has to be worked for by teachers, youth leaders, welfare workers, community centre wardens, town planners, personnel officers and other members of the army of specialist agents of contemporary society. New towns and suburbs do not become communities as part of a divine order, but they may be helped to do so by skilful planning and guidance.

The change from a society wherein individuals are obliged to become members of a community to one in which they have a choice is of course the change from *Gemeinschaft* to *Gesellschaft* (from community to association) that was analysed by one of the greatest European social scientists, Ferdinand Tonnies.[1] For over a century the dichotomy first explored by this writer has formed a central basis for the discussions of sociologists, social psychologists, economists and other social scientists. This discussion has been particularly concerned with the development of the contractual relationships which have come to form the dominant pattern of human affairs following the decline of community. It is a pattern of specific contracts for specific purposes. Most notably these are to be seen in work where the worker commits his skills, strengths and brainpower to produce a specific product or service in return for an agreed reward. But beyond the exercise of that contract he is free to be a different person in family, leisure, religion and elsewhere. Instead of the multi-purpose member of a community, he becomes a series of different people in different social contexts of modern society.

Yet, however great is our nostalgia for community, it is an inescapable fact that decision making in most known communities in history has been anything but democratic. The vast majority of the inhabitants of the medieval communities lived a life in which most decisions on leisure, as well as almost all other aspects of life, were made for them by a small elite group. Decision making, though indeed located within the community, was exercised by the few rather than the many.

REDEFINITION OF COMMUNITY

It is the argument of this chapter that the concept of community, involving mass decision making by its members, is a fundamentally different concept from the traditional one. Moreover it is argued that it is substantially in the exercise of leisure, defined in its widest sense, that this new definition is being brought about and that contemporary changes in education closely reflect this process of redefinition.

The longstanding patterns of education have faithfully reflected the traditional concept of community — that a few take decisions and the majority be educated to follow them. Let us take, as an example, the ways in which people are educated to use recreational space and indeed their own 'territory' in modern society. For a quarter of a century, schools have reinforced the role of the 'expert' in town and country planning, recreation, social services, housing and many other categories of human activity. The concept of the expert is that of a person whose training and experience allow him to make the right decisions for the majority. The first task of the school has been seen to be one of selecting a small group of young people who have the capacity to undertake appropriate training so that they themselves become experts. The second task has been to ensure that the others will be able to respond to the expertise of the experts and above all to see their role as necessary and legitimate. Often teachers, who are committed to helping young people to maximise their creative and expressive potential, still play a major part in bringing about a suitable deference to the experts. A recent case in the writer's experience may serve as an example.

In a comprehensive school, a lively and enthusiastic art teacher was running a highly successful course of study for the 'leavers' class. With them he was exploring ways in which they could express themselves in designing and producing their own distinctive living space through creating furnishing, decoration and personal equipment of all kinds. The emphasis was strongly on decision making and personal expression. Yet the culmination of the course was a visit to the London Design Centre where the group of students were shown the kind of interiors that were really recommended by the experts. The Design Centre approved items that they should purchase. They were also told of the approved sources where these items could be obtained. In short, the culmination of the course was, in a quite remarkable way, a statement of the superior expertise of the Design Council and its assessors.

Yet, though schools have persisted with such approaches for many years, it is increasingly clear that they are by no means effective in achieving their ends. A vast majority of products bought for the home and for leisure are not those approved by the Design Council. Leisure activities by young people are by and large only infrequently those taught and approved by the schools. The dress and other personal decoration worn by young people is only infrequently that recommended and endorsed by the teachers of home economics and art and craft. On a more widespread scale, even after a quarter of a century of town and country planning, we are faced with spectacular problems of conservation, environmental preservation and pollution.

COMMUNITY AND EXPERIENCE

At the heart of the matter there seems to be a determined desire on the part of individuals to make their own decisions about their dress, their possessions, their property, their land, their use of leisure and a wide range of other aspects of their personal life. Recently the writer was travelling by train and was looking at the succession of back gardens of a modern and obviously 'well planned' housing estate. The houses were unquestionably well designed and constructed and had an 'appropriate degree of variation that a wise planning authority had seen fit to incorporate in order to avoid monotony and repetitiousness. Yet this degree of variation was obviously quite insufficient for the residents. In the back gardens there was a flowering of individuality of a kind that would bring distress to most planning offices. The gardens were sprouting with sheds, lean-tos, terraces, patios, concrete gnomes and much else. Not only was the variety remarkable, but the human effort that had been put into the work was striking.

In leisure the same diversity was clearly visible. The move from mass spectator sport to individualised participation sport is well documented. It has even been noted that in the remaining sports such as Association Football the amount of individual expression among the followers is remarkable. If one visits one of the new style sporting events one can marvel at the extent of individual decision making that has taken place. At an amateur, as opposed to professional, motor race meeting one is impressed not only at the variety of technological expression of a high order to be seen in the vehicles, but also at the aesthetic expression to be seen in the colour and the styling of the vehicles. Much the same may be seen at a Karting Meet or at a Land Yachting gathering. This individual expression, or 'customisation' as Tom Wolfe puts it, is not of course confined to race meetings. It may be seen in the way in which people of all ages and social groups express themselves and make their own decisions about how their cars and other personal equipment looks. A glance through the pages of Custom Car magazine indicates how widespread this experience of decision making through leisure is. Rayher Banham[2] has reminded us how the very young with their Chopper bikes are involved in a very similar process.

So far we have emphasised the powerful incidence of individual decision making in leisure in contemporary society. Yet it is important to emphasise that, although apparently idiosyncratic, it has an important collective effect. Unquestionably it is the widespread and extensive exercise of decision making in this way that is the real determinant of the human environment in which we live. Increasingly, the architects, town planners, housing managers and building developers are coming to realise the essential truth of this. Recently one of our most eminent planning consultants conceded that in his future development schemes he would have to take cognisance of the insatiable desire of people of all class and age groups to extend, modify and individualise their homes. The theme is developed further by Jameson in his article 'Thirty Wasted Years'.[3] Increasingly too there is evidence, in certain situations, that the powerful desire of individuals to determine their human environment takes on a new powerful, collective voice. Such an example arose after a disaster in the Ronan Point tower blocks in London where an explosion severely damaged the accommodation of many of the residents. The result was the development of a powerful challenge to the experts by the residents who, for the first time, found themselves able to communicate with the experts to articulate and express an argument with confidence and conviction.

THE EXERCISE OF POWER

There is considerable evidence of a latent but unquestionable enthusiasm throughout modern society to be able to challenge the experts, to make one's own decisions about leisure and, much else, to get 'off the receiving end' and 'contract into' decision making. Impressive evidence of this arose in a study on the Youth Service in England and Wales conducted by the author.[4] In extensive discussions with young people there was clear indication that one of the most fundamental desires was to 'count for something' in society. Respondents were clearly aware of an education that had unambiguously put them on the receiving end of the foreman, the social security officer and the whole gamut of experts in modern society. They wanted to reach the situation where they were able to engage in activity in which they counted for something and were accepted as doing so by adults. They searched for leisure opportunities where this chance was seen to exist. The remarkable popularity of leisure devoted to community service organisations such as Shelter, Child Poverty Action, Release and a variety of other national and local bodies could only be explained in these terms. These organisations often provided activities that, in a different context, would have been perceived as drudgery or tedium. Yet they helped young people to feel a sense of involvement in decision making, participating in a collective challenge to the decision makers and being helped to obtain the words with which to make a point and the confidence with which to use them. Yet it was important to recognise that the desire of these young people to get off the receiving end was in no sense a revolutionary fervour. Most were emphatic that they wished to count for something or at least have the chance to do so in a society similar to the present one; not a radically different one. The call was for a wider distribution of power rather than a new distribution.

In reaching the concept of power we have perhaps reached the heart of the move to decision making in the community. Unless the individual feels he has the power to shape his own life, his actions and his surroundings then not only is he unfulfilled but also he can have no concept of community in its contemporary sense. Indeed he may make the situation negative, adopting a not uncommon attempt to count for something by engaging in disruptive and destructive activities in the community on the terraces, the public loos and in other 'no man's land situations'.

THE ROLE OF EDUCATION

The picture we have painted so far is one in which there is considerable evidence of individuals making their leisure decisions in a modern community. It is one in which they can be seen to be striving for some kind of personal power with varying degrees of success. If we now turn to the changing educational arrangements of modern communities we can see small but perceptible signs of a response to these demands. We can see this in the curriculum of physical education where emphasis is laid increasingly upon opportunities for participation in minority sports as well as in the team games and athletics that have for so long dominated the curriculum in secondary schools. Similarly, emphases on dance and movement have augmented much of the traditional gymnastic curriculum. Parallel emphases occur widely through the so-called academic curriculum as well, where more and more attention is devoted to creativity, individualism and decision making. Here sound economic reasoning reinforces the concern for individual decision making. In the past the main economic function of the school has been to produce armies of young people with a capacity to undertake remembered skills and to reproduce remembered knowledge. They have provided the main bulk of the labour force in factory and office. Increasingly, computerisation and automation of various kinds have provided more effective alternatives to human labour. Even where they have not, the escalating costs of employing a large number of individuals to perform repetitive tasks has forced 'labour intensive' industries into decline; the recent history of the Post Office and the Railways offers abundant testimony.

If human beings are to obtain employment in modern communities they are increasingly called upon to undertake activities that are distinctively human — the development of new ideas and the adaptation of existing ones. These roles are not confined to executives and technologists, but exist far more widely. One of the key occupational roles for many school leavers is that of maintenance engineer or service technician. It is his job to diagnose faults in the vast array of equipment in home, office, farm and factory that characterises modern society; to identify faults, to make decisions as to whether it is feasible to repair or to replace the equipment, to undertake the necessary work, to organise a supply of spare parts and often to be responsible for accounting, collecting cash and arranging a work schedule in a variety of locations. In short, it is his task to make decisions.

It is a recognition of the economic as well as the social necessity of educating human beings to make decisions that characterises the current developments in Nuffield Science, the new mathematics and even the new humanities curriculum. Indeed it is in the Humanities' Project that some of the most interesting preparation for decision making in work and in leisure has been attempted. In this project, students in school are given experience in making decisions on important moral issues that they are likely to encounter in their communities. Issues such as labour relationships, race, sex and many other fundamental areas are considered. In each, students are presented with a wide range of material on the topic in question, i.e. newspaper cuttings, extracts from books, newsreels, pictures, propaganda leaflets and much else. After reading them or examining them they are called upon to express their own views on these issues..The teacher's role is that of a 'neutral chairman'. It is his task not to say what are the right or wrong attitudes but rather to say to children who express a view 'why do you think that?', or 'what are your reasons?'. In this way, students are being obliged to think out their decisions so that faced with decision making opportunities in adult life they will be equipped to make reasoned judgements and, perhaps even more importantly, to be able to defend them.

COMMUNITY DECISION MAKING IN THE SCHOOL

An example of a similar approach, closely related to preparation for leisure, occurred in the Design and Craft Education Project directed by the author.[5] The project was concerned with the design and execution of a wide range of three dimensional work which was conceived as a decision making activity in which students, individually or collectively, were called upon to diagnose problems such as a need for leisure facilities or equipment. Then, through a series of explorations, trials and evaluations could reach a solution that was not only satisfactory but could be justified as being so. This went far beyond the normal goals of craft competence. A typical example of one of the project activities could be the designing of a leisure area that aimed to involve its students more fully in the community in which they live, to give them the experience of responsibility, decision making and participation in local affairs. Let us assume that the school serves a large and somewhat under-privileged housing estate in an industrial city. As in many similar situations the school is attempting to improve the facilities of the neighbourhood as part of the project. An often needed facility is play equipment for younger children in their leisure time.

The designing of such equipment would almost certainly be seen to be a major responsibility of the design department of the school. How would this be done? The teacher and his students would already have a preliminary knowledge of the problem and an understanding of the human purposes at issue. These would, however, require some further exploration. How large is the relevant child population of the area? What is its age distribution? Is the birth rate rising, falling or remaining steady? Information of this kind, which could be sought from the Education and Social Service Departments of the local authority, would give some indication of the demand for facilities and the existence of any play facilities in the neighbourhood which, unknown to the school, were in fact being used. Are there special reasons, such as traffic hazard or violence, that would make mothers of young children unwilling to use such facilities even though they did exist? Questions such as these may call for survey work by the students in and around their own homes, for visits to the parents of young children, the police and other civic authorities. In this way, a precise profile of the nature and extent of the need for play facilities may be reached.

With such a profile compiled, further preliminary work would be called for in which the restraints and resources available could be considered in detail. As with all design processes it is important to explore the experience of the past. Were there previous attempts to provide play facilities and, if so, why did they fail? Are there problems in their design that, with hindsight, could be remedied or are there inherent difficulties that call for an entirely new approach? What of the likely location of the play facilities? Are they to be indoor or outdoor or both? If indoor, who will provide the premises? If outdoor, who will provide the land and ensure that it is suitably enclosed? Are the locations available feasible from the point of view of access or do they require parents to bring their children long distances or risk crossing busy main routes? Would the location be supervised when in use? If so, by whom? Would this be undertaken by senior students at the school or would there be regulations that required the presence of at least one trained adult? If the latter, who would be responsible for the recruitment and possible payment of such an adult? If supervision was essential could the location be effectively closed off from use when such supervision was not provided? Would it be necessary to ensure supporting facilities such as first aid equipment and toilets?

All these indepth questions concerning constraints and resources are essential preliminaries to the designing and construction of the play equipment itself. Only if the answers to such questions are satisfactory is there any prospect that the equipment, once provided, can and will be used in the manner envisaged. All of the enquiries are within the scope of a cooperating group of students and teachers. All of them have a relevance far beyond the specific issue at stake, a relevance that is likely to have meaning in the later lives of the students in this or other communities.

Having undertaken this still preliminary work, detailed consideration of the facilities to be provided may be undertaken. Some kinds of facility will already have been readily eliminated such as, for example, soft toys if the location is to be an outdoor one. The next step is to consider precisely what will be provided. Let us assume that the preliminary enquiries have failed to throw up the possibility of an indoor location or adult supervision, but that a sector of a local park is to be made available and surrounded by 'child-proof' fencing by the park authority. It is, however, unlikely to be 'vandal-proof'. In such a situation the equipment to be constructed will need to be permanent, non-portable and capable of withstanding weather and possible physical violence, as well as normal usage by the young children.

Narrowed down in this way, the design process can take on a sharper focus. What sort of equipment, satisfying these criteria, do young children enjoy? Students may well visit play facilities beyond the community or in schools where they are provided and study children at play, noticing what equipment is popular and the use to which it is put. Detailed measurements may be taken not only of the equipment but also perhaps of the sizes of the children themselves. What are the financial resources available? Can the school raise funds to purchase suitable supplies of, say, metal tubing to produce climbing equipment, hardwood, new or second hand, to provide benches, concrete and concrete tubes to make tunnels and obstacles?

DESIGN EDUCATION: WHAT IT IS AND WHAT IT DOES?

Possibly the local authority will have funds available for equipment or a community association may make a donation, or it may even be possible to arrange a sale of work or jumble to raise funds. But what of the skills available? Does the teacher have competence in the use of concrete? If not, is it possible for him to attend a course of the kind run by the Concrete Development Association, or can assistance be obtained from a local builder or contractor who may even be able to arrange for the loan of a concrete-mixer for a short period? Is welding equipment available for the construction of tubular climbing frames? Can the school's circular saw cope with thick sections of hardwood? What contribution can the art teacher make concerning the colour combination of the proposed equipment? Can the home economics teacher advise, from her knowledge of the physical development of young children, or the more beneficial kinds of equipment that may be provided? And outside the design department, to what extent can the other departments of the school (social studies, language, mathematics and science) provide resources both of understanding and expertise? Can the project

benefit these other departments in turn? Is there perhaps the opportunity for an interesting study by the English teacher and his
students of the way in which language is used during play in the
formulation of rules?

Considerations of this kind will have led to a specification of
objects of play equipment to be constructed within the design
department that take into account as fully as possible the needs and
capacities of the users, the resources and competences of the school
and its personnel, the nature and properties of the materials envisaged and, perhaps most importantly, the creative capacity of the
participants to devise new solutions that go beyond modifications of
existing ones. With such a specification, possible solutions may now
be explored. Mock-ups of envisaged equipment can be constructed;
children of the appropriate age groups can be invited to try them out
and their responses recorded; the equipment can be modified and
rearranged on site and the responses compared with those to previous
arrangements; the aesthetic consequences of various groupings of
equipment can be appraised. This part of the process may occupy an
extended period of intense activity as step-by-step modifications and
improvements to the original solutions are formulated.

Meanwhile, there may be further detailed consideration of the
resources of the school for production. Do the workshops or studios
need modification? Is new material or equipment to be ordered and
assembled? Are production-line arrangements needed and, if so, how
can they best be planned in order not only to ensure sound
production arrangements but also to give students the opportunity of
experiencing how such arrangements may be optimised through
rational discussion? Are there likely to be bottle necks in certain
aspects of the production? If so, how may they be eliminated or at
least minimised? How may individuals be trained to undertake
specific tasks with which they may be unfamiliar? Is a rigid division
of labour likely to be the best solution, or will some members of the
production group become bored by being involved in more repetitive
tasks? If so, does there need to be some system of job rotation? How
will quality control be maintained? Will there be need for safety
testing of the individual components of the swings, climbing frames
and other facilities before they are finally assembled?

Eventually, when the design is finalised and the production
arrangements are confirmed, the actual manufacture of the
equipment can begin. But the design process is by no means over, for
not only has the manufacture to be completed successfully but the
equipment has also to be installed effectively, and possibly some of
the construction work has to take place on the actual location itself.
It is then necessary to ensure that the facilities are satisfactory in use,

to undertake post-delivery checks and maintenance over a period. Ultimately, the knowledge gained in the post-production period becomes the raw material for further design processes in the future.

It is important to emphasise that not all aspects of a full design process have been mentioned in this example. Notably the whole question of market research, sales promotion, marketing and accounting, items that form essential components of the design process in a normal industrial company, have not had to be taken account of fully here. But there is no reason why in suitable projects these activities too should not form part of the total process of education that is experienced by the students; they too are important components of the industrialised community in which they will spend their adult lives. It must also be emphasised that no one example can be representative of the many schools throughout Britain where community oriented design processes are taking place and wherein participation by members of the local community are a regular feature. Recent issues of the magazine Studies in Design Education and Craft have featured accounts of such projects in Aberdeen, Belfast, Leeds, Leicester, Oxfordshire, London and many other parts of Britain. Other examples are described in detail by the author.[5] A notable example in a recent issue of Studies in Design Education and Craft is the Front Door Project conducted at Pimlico School.[6]

One of the important features of these and other preparations for community decision making is that they relate to the student's present condition. Community decision making is not an abstract process; it must relate to real issues and have suitable urgency. The history of school projects is all too often one in which the students participate actively within the context of the school, yet there is not a visible relationship between the work in the school and their every day lives. As we have mentioned earlier, the dresses the girls make in the needlework period are often not the ones they wish to wear in their leisure hours. Yet the effort they are prepared to invest in their leisure wear may be altogether greater than they are prepared to invest in their school activities. All too often the social realities perceived by the teacher in the school are quite different from the social realities of the student's community in which his real decisions are being made. The willingness of many students to 'please teacher' often masks the dissonance.

A good example of this occurred in a youth club visited by the author. Like many other youth leaders, the warden of this club was under considerable pressure to add a specifically educational component to his programme. He had not found this easy. Members turned up enthusiastically on disco nights but their educational aspirations seemed to be minimal. On one evening, however, the leader was enthusiastic. He explained that the girls had asked for a course on good grooming. He had immediately telephoned the area youth officer and in no time at all it had been arranged that a home economics teacher with a special interest in this subject would run a course. The author attended the club during the third session of this course and it was already clear that things were not going well. The initial group of girls had declined from twelve to six. The response of those who remained was unmistakably one of boredom and antipathy. It was not hard to see why. The girls were, by most contemporary standards, already well able to handle make-up and had obviously progressed a long way in their capacity to achieve the image they sought. The teacher however, seemed quite oblivious of this and was presenting a basic grooming course that had unmistakable connotations of the early 1950s. Much of what she was saying was of enduring importance but, though it was coherently and enthusiastically presented, it made little impact upon the girls. For them she was 'out of touch'. She failed totally to recognise the signals that the girls presented to her as clearly as they could. As one of the girls said at the coffee bar afterwards: 'The trouble with that teacher is that she makes us feel so inferior'.

This example is not intended to suggest that in helping young people to make decisions we should 'sell out' to them, accepting their view of society as being the only one or even the most important one. Rather it is that we must start where the student is if we are to move forward with him in achieving decision making, whether it be on leisure or any other aspect of life. To paraphrase Bernstein 'if the consciousness of the teacher is to be in the minds of the student then first of all the consciousness of the student must be in the mind of the teacher.'

POWER AND DECISION MAKING IN THE COMMUNITY

Yet the concept of democratic participation in preparing for decision making in democratic society involves rather more difficulties than we have as yet addressed ourselves to. We must return to the concept that was introduced earlier in this chapter, that of power. Let us consider a community project in decision making in a rather run-down housing estate that constitutes a school's catchment area. The older students may well have a local reputation for indifferent or even anti-social behaviour. Yet with an enthusiastic design education teacher they may come to participate fully in a series of activities in the community, i.e. creating and running playgroups, redecorating old people's homes, helping the handicapped. As a result of this the students will not only gain a 'design experience' but also achieve recognition from the community at large. The local newspaper will probably print their photographs and comment favourably on their work. Civic leaders may come to meet them and congratulate them. Instead of feeling outsiders in the community they will come to feel like insiders.

But where do events lead from here? It is quite probable that the students and their teacher will soon reach the limit of what may be done for the old people by digging their gardens, decorating their homes and helping with their meals. But they may well realise that the old people have other and more fundamental difficulties that cannot be solved by direct action alone. They may have leaky roofs or blocked drains and find that the local authority or corporation that provides their homes is tardy about necessary maintenance. There may be difficulties in the provision of the subsidised public transport to which they are entitled. At this stage the students may plan and execute other equally creative activities to solve these further problems. They may write letters to the local newspaper, petition the members of the local housing committee, seek interviews with the officers of the local authority. In so doing they may find that response to their actions may be different. The local newspaper may redefine them as a group of teenage trouble-makers led by a 'radical' teacher. The local councillors, especially if they are also members of the education committee or the school board, may well complain to the school that this is an inappropriate activity for its teachers and its students.

Here we have reached one of the fundamental issues of community education. It is to help young people to reach a perceptive appraisal of their environment, to make decisions and to express themselves, to identify their needs and argue them effectively. It is, then, equipping them to claim and exercise personal power in society. Yet as the example makes clear, such a claim, to be effective, may need to challenge those who already hold power in community and society. At such a moment the teacher and those who run the schools must keep their head and not run for cover. The evidence of the Youth Service Project was very clear. Young people wished to count for something or at least have the chance to do so in a society similar to the present one, not a radically different one. The call was for a wider distribution of power rather than for a new distribution. Certainly it is arguable that in the power structure of most industrial societies redistribution is possible without fundamental change. It is not difficult, for example, to envisage many more people playing a part in the considerable power exercised by worker unions and local government bodies. Some schools have reported that a number of young people who learned decision making responsibility through community projects in school have already found opportunities for active participation in the affairs of their union or local government.

There are, of course, other problems that may confront the teacher. A characteristic one is the availability of resources, material and non-material. Yet many teachers have found that activities of the kind that have been discussed make less demand on resources than more conventional ones. Moreover, the resources of the community are often made available in a very full way for soundly based community projects. There are also many examples of the beneficial effects of creating situations in which informal even unstructured participation can be effective in community activities. Nicholson[7] has suggested that the more successfully designers create a 'non participant environment' in the community in which members can only make decisions but cannot in any way make their mark upon their environment so people will more zealously attempt to establish their individual presence in it even to the extent of behaviour which is labelled as vandalism. 'The structural modifications' that take place in waiting rooms and public conveniences help to make Nicholson's point. He advocates an alternative concept for the provision of community amenities in which the opportunity to participate is built in, even into the architecture of the community. The argument emphasises that, not only formally but informally, an education designed to inculcate respect and to put people into a received environment gradually gives way, in the face of growing desires and expectations of community participation in decision making, to one in which individuals become active rather than passive members.

In this final example we have perhaps reached the fundamental issue of decision making for leisure and life in general in the modern society, a feature that is essentially not only for the individual but also for society itself. It is that the very concept of the modern community and life within it becomes unattainable unless the individual has a chance to express himself fully and that the wide ranging field of leisure provides a major part of his opportunity to do so. In the past, individuals have for the most part achieved personal expression marginally, covertly or by challenging the regime of the expert. The argument of this chapter has been that through education and the full experience of leisure a new state of affairs arises in which universal decision making characterises the communities of a modern democratic society.

REFERENCES AND NOTES

1. Tonnies, F. (1955) *Community and Association* (trans. C. P. Loomis). Routledge and Kegan Paul, London

2.   Banham, R. (1971) Had I the wheels of an angel. *New Society*, 12 (August)

3.   Jameson, C. (1971) Thirty wasted years: British architecture since the war. *Sunday Times Magazine*, 6 February

4.   Eggleston, J. (1976) *Adolescence and Community*. Edward Arnold, London

5.   Eggleston, J. (1976) *New Developments in Design Education*. Open Books, London

     (This volume contains an overview of the Design and Craft Education Project and other contemporary research and development in design education. The full range of publications of the Design and Craft Education Project are available from Edward Arnold, Woodlands Park, Maidenhead, England. A further source of information are the twice yearly issues of *Studies in Design Education and Craft* obtainable from *Studies in Education Ltd*, Nafferton, Driffield, N. Humberside.)

6.   Adams, E. The front door project. *Studies in Design Education and Craft*, 9.1

7.   Nicholson, S. (1972) The theory of loose parts. *Studies in Design Education and Craft*, Vol 4, No 2

8 PLANNING, BUILDING AND PARTICIPATION

by David Harding

My awareness of the necessity to develop opportunities for the involvement and participation of people in contributing to their own environment grew initially from my work in murals. The works had to relate in some way to the group for whom and by whom they had been commissioned. I could not simply be an instrument of external unrelated imposition. An illustration of this was the making, in 1962, of a mural for the Hebridean Island of South Uist, which bore only a token relationship with that community. When being given the opportunity five years later to make another mural, the need to relate the work to the community was much stronger. Local slate and pebbles were used, words in Gaelic became a more powerful part of the concept, and I looked for opportunities to discuss the work with local groups. Though this was not yet involvement in decision making, there was a degree of participation and to that extent my attitude evolved in that direction.

In the intervening years I had been developing an arts section at a College of Education in Northern Nigeria. It was a fairly remote situation and the community was residential. The arts were believed to be the basis of education and, in this rare situation, I was able to fully utilise activities in the visual arts. It became starkly evident, however, that I could not impose my European culture and tradition on the people with whom I worked, but rather adopt the role of enabler. I taught skills but, in all else, tried only to be the instrument through which these people developed their own creative ability based on their own cultures and traditions. Painting activities were developed to murals and patterns on the inside and outside of compound buildings. In so doing, I became conscious of the fact that the visual arts offered the opportunity to people to make a very direct and dramatic contribution to their own environment. In 1968, I went to Glenrothes to become what is now known as 'Town Artist'. Here, my belief that I should not be the only person with the privilege of making visual statements on the external built environment has been confirmed. Opportunities should also be created for other members of the community to do so.

MURALS

The first project I initiated was with primary school children. The aim was to get individual children to make a personal and permanent contribution to the external built environment of the town. The medium I chose was terra cotta clay which, when fired to vitrification, will withstand external exposure. Each child in a class formed a piece of clay into a roughly rectangular tile, while modelling on the surface a design of their choice. When finished the children signed their names on the front surface. When the tiles had been fired, the whole class assembled at a site in their neighbourhood and each child cemented their own tile onto a wall. Ten groups of tiles have so far been done and therefore around three hundred children have made their own small, though significant mark on the town. This kind of ongoing project could be continued extensively as in new housing developments there are large wall areas needing life brought to them. As more groups of tiles are added to the original group, the whole wall will eventually become covered in ceramic relief.

Wall paintings are being done by secondary school youths. The procedure here involves the art teachers in the schools. To begin with, an elevation drawing of a particular wall is given to two or three classes. The site is visited and then each child works out their own ideas for the wall. The selection of which idea is to be executed is done by the class members voting for the one they want. The selected design is then painted by a group assisted by the Town Artists.

In one project, a class of male youths described as 'unteachable' worked on designs for two underpass walls. The group, numbering thirteen, voted on a combination of two of the designs and one week was allowed to paint the murals. Working hard, and taking short lunch breaks, the work was completed on the Thursday of that week. Having a day left over, we painted a nearby concrete sculpture thus improving the visual quality of the badly weathered concrete. Though it would be wrong to exaggerate the longterm fruitful results of this project, it was reported to me that in the ensuing weeks this group had become more responsive to work in the school. Those pupils who had normally been unresponsive due to boredom and feelings of inadequacy were, for a time, stimulated and as it were 'walked tall'. In fact, two or three pupils, who were a constant source of trouble, began to organise projects in an art class similar to the mural activity. How long these responsive attitudes lasted I do not accurately know, but the fact that they did exist was reported to me by several teachers. More than two years after the project, the headmaster of the school confirmed this change in the pupils' attitude.

Another secondary school has a continuing commitment to paint murals on the gable ends of two shops. Every two years new murals are painted. To date, each shop has its third mural and in this way different groups have had the opportunity to become involved in the work. A new pedestrian underpass to be built near this school had one class working on ideas for painting the two walls of the underpass tunnel. Meanwhile, the class visited my workshop to see the preparation of moulds for the external concrete walls, having seen the construction drawings for all the site works and been on site to watch one of the concrete walls being poured. The group has therefore, to that extent, become familiar with the work process which their murals will eventually complete. And yet another pedestrian underpass being built had pupils from another secondary school designing panels which have been enlarged to form plastic moulds. These moulds will create patterned reliefs on the concrete walls of the underpass.

All these foregoing projects were organised through the aegis of the school system and, naturally, I wanted to extend the opportunity to others outside. This involved, in the first instance, locating youths on their own territory—the street. This was made easier by the setting up of a temporary adventure playground and the cooperation of the playleader. In this neighbourhood there is an ugly little building called a 'Gas Governor House' which seemed to be in need of improvement. It had already been extensively sprayed with graffiti and so, in this instance, it was decided to use an aerosol spray for the work. To begin with, however, no one was keen to become involved in the project and it emerged that this was partly due to the fear that while engaged in the spraying, they would be 'lifted' by the police. After many assurances that this would not happen they agreed to do the work. Two of the group came to my workshop and worked out an idea based on several sketches done by other members of the group. When the execution of the mural began on site the police did arrive, along with gas officials and a postman. The latter had passed by earlier in the day and had immediately telephoned the police to report that, 'two men with beards and six youths were spraying graffiti on a wall'. I had had prior discussions with the police and they had decided not to give the project their blessing, claiming that to promote an activity like this would encourage the spread of more graffiti. It was later admitted that this in fact had not happened. The local gas board officials had not been informed that I had obtained permission from their headquarters to use the wall and so the incident passed off with no repercussions. No further graffiti appeared on the wall for some months, but when it did it turned out to be a repetition of a piece that had been covered over. It was someone's nickname, but this time the person had fitted the graffiti into the form of the design!

Having given a talk to a 'young wives group' in Glenrothes about the work of the Town Artist, one of the members asked if I could paint a mural on a wall near her house. I suggested that if she felt the wall needed a mural then she and her friends should design and execute it. This suggestion provoked a response typical of a society that has been schooled and not educated, 'we have no ideas' and 'we can't draw'. However, some months later the group did come forward with an idea and nine women and their children painted the wall. In an attempt to extend this kind of activity further I intimated in the local press that if anyone was keen to paint a mural I would try to arrange it. One mural that was done was adjacent to a block of flats that had become unsightly due to the weathering of the cement-based surface render. This fact became so obvious after the mural was completed that it became a matter of urgency to have the whole flat block repainted. Apart from assistance by the artists in the organising and the execution of these works they are the designs of either individuals or groups.

In the mural movement which has swept the USA since 1967, there is a school of muralists who work towards the making of community murals. The artists and the community work together from the beginning. The theme and design evolve from a consensus of the group and the execution is carried out by the group. The concluding act is the dedication of the mural which takes the form of a street festival. This form of approach to murals has begun to develop in the UK, spearheaded by Carol Kenna and Stephen Lobb who founded the Greenwich Mural Workshop. Out of the USA movement there has grown a whole variety of art workshops dedicated to the creation of a public art manifesting the social, cultural and political aspirations of the people: 'What is needed is to return art to the people as a means of expression of their lives. The people have been robbed of this — the power to formulate their own views of the world, including the power to give visual form to the world'.[1] The Public Art Workshop, founded in 1972 on Chicago's West side, is a store front mural and photo workshop, mural resource centre and a community art centre. Similar descriptions could be given to City Arts Workshop of New York and City Wide Murals of Los Angeles.

HOUSING

The regular maintenance of external paintwork of council houses includes the painting of house doors. Since I was involved in assisting in the general external environmental improvements in an area of Glenrothes, I was asked to propose a colour scheme for the front doors of all the houses. My response to this was to call at every house with a batch of colour samples and ask the householders to choose their own colours. Almost without exception there was a quick and positive decision, emphasising that most people have strong personal preferences about colour. Some related the choice of colour to things like the hall, the porch or something in the garden, but all seemed to derive a genuine satisfaction from being given this opportunity. This is a simple yet positive example of direct decision making and should be a universally accepted procedure in local authority housing. Unfortunately, housing management attitudes and bonus systems for tradesmen play obstructive roles in this kind of activity.

A sympathetic attitude to such activities has been adopted by the Director of Architecture and Planning of Glenrothes, John L. Coghill, with some interesting results. When the recent selling of council houses was in full swing it was astonishing to witness the rapidity with which new owners identified their own houses. This came in a whole assortment of ways, ranging from painting the outsides in unusual colours to the introduction of trellises and wrought iron gates with original designs. Greater freedom for self-expression on the outside of the council house should be permitted. Yet restrictions on tenants often go even further. I read in one town's tenants' handbook, in the section devoted to advice on interior decoration, that tenants were cautioned not to use dark or exotic colours!

At present the greatest area of freedom that exists for council house tenants is where they have a garden. Here some have made unique idiosyncratic statements defining their territory and creating personal identity. For many people there is a strong need to do this and encouraging the extension of these activities to the house itself would add immeasurably to the breaking up of what is usually a visually monotonous outlook. Applications to build extensions, balconies, verandas, patios, etc., should be encouraged since this would afford opportunities for the making of permanent personal statements which would in turn add visual interest and variety. However, most planners and architects do not wish to see their uniformly planned housing areas broken up in this way. These areas are so often seen as an overall composition and any intrusion, be it of colour or structure, is rigorously excluded. Changes in the approach to design and a loosening up of planning controls is necessary to create the opportunities needed to produce a latent contribution in skills and imagination that could be made by people to the built environment. A unique example of what people can do from scratch is to be found in the Pitsea/Laindon area of Basildon where a group of owner built holidays huts and houses were allowed to remain and eventually develop into solid permanent homes.

In France, Bernard Lassus, Professor of Architecture at L'Ecole de

Beaux Arts in Paris has, for some years now, been recording and studying the activities and results of what he describes as *Les habitants-Paysagistes* (literally: dweller-landscapers). His observations have been conducted mainly in rural town or village situation, not in council housing areas. He has found a great wealth of individual creativity covering the walls of houses — patterns made with shells, stones, tesserae, broken ceramic, etc., the filling of front and back yards and gardens with sculptural forms and the decorative painting of walls and fences. Too many of these 'professional' activities are written-off as the 'wishing-well and gnome' culture of suburban semis, but I hold that they have a deep psychological significance. In Los Angeles, the Watts Towers of Simon Rodia is an example of this kind of activity in one of its greatest flowerings, and for this they are justly famous. The towers were built over a period of many years by Rodia in his backyard. Using strips of scrap metal, he formed a group of towers ranging in height from 15–75 feet. He covered the towers and the walls of the backyard with mosaic made from broken dishes and bottles. Like Ivan Illich, I believe that 'People do not only need to obtain things. I think they need above all, freedom to make things, things among which they can live. To give shape to them, according to their own feelings, their own tastes, and their own imagination. And to put them to use in caring for each other and about each other.'

BUILDING SITES

Another element which has guided my activities in Glenrothes has been the relationship between myself, the work and the workers on the building site. The spaces and forms are conceived during the planning and design stage of the building development. By deciding to use the materials of the building site as far as possible, I also try to conceive works in such a way that their execution and finishing demand the skills of the site worker. The works therefore, to that extent, become group activities out of which is extracted the maximum amount of skill and creativity.

Many of the opportunities for craftsmanship and imagination have been lost to builders through the introduction of building systems and also through, again, bonus systems. Bricklayers can earn large bonuses, but very often at the expense of the quality of the work. The artist working with the building team can create opportunities for craftsmanship to be demonstrated. The chance to test oneself, to do something unique with care and precision, has evoked responses of real pride and satisfaction to the completed work. In one area of Glenrothes, we proposed several projecting brick patterns. One could sense from the comments and jokes on the site that each bricklayer appointed to do these patterns was chosen because of the skill each had already displayed.

Time and care was taken by each to do the very best job they could. Years later one of these bricklayers approached me in a pub and recalled that he had done the very first brick pattern on that site. He spent some time telling the whole pub about it! Two men, Archie Speed and Bob Lumsden, have set out some excellent areas of granite setts, one of which is a very complicated spiral formation. Another difficult banked area had to be done and the job architect, Jan Miezitis, suggested that the two men work out their own solution to the problem of how to lay out and pattern the work. This they did with excellent results. This approach has been continued with other men on other sites with satisfying results and I see no reason why it should not have a universal application.

WORKING IN PUBLIC

Hugh Graham, an artist who is presently working a two year period with me, believes essentially in sharing his creativity, skills and working process with other people. He had begun to consider the making of two sculptures and spent several sessions with groups of children bombarding them with drawing activities in which they expressed their ideas about a local farm and the town in general. As his own ideas were developing about the sculptures he shared these with the children. This allowed for a reciprocal sharing of the elements of the form and details of the works that evolved. Both sculptures demanded many hours of work on the sites. In so doing he reinforced another important element, that of working in public situations. His activity on the sculptures, not surprisingly, acted as a magnet to the people who lived around the area and to passers-by and he was thus able to open up lines of communication on the work. On one day he was approached by a man who became very interested in the work and who, thereafter, came out every day. This man was a recently retired gamekeeper and had moved into the town after a lifetime of rural activities. He had, it seems, not left his house once until the work on the sculpture had aroused his curiosity enough to make him step outside.

Two non-professional photographers, Peter and Aase Goldsmith who live in Glenrothes, began several years ago to become more involved in the new town. They have followed projects of mine from inception, through the work process to final execution; recorded the work of the group of craftspeople who live and work in the town; have collaborated in exhibitions with the 'town artists' and the craftspeople; recorded historic elements of the town. These activities, and much more besides, serve to show how involvement with these two photographers has been able to open up new dimensions not only for the craftspeople and town artists but also for the townspeople and for themselves. Their dedication to their work and ability to be on hand at the right time to catch a certain unrepeatable moment has created a unique record of some aspects of the life of the town.

NON-PROFESSIONALS IN PLANNING AND BUILDING

From the wider aspect of who actually conceives and designs our built environments, there are encouraging signs of moving away from rigid professional protectionism. For example, the Taller of Bofill in Barcelona. This is a building team producing some very exciting works not only from a visual point of view but also from a social one. The team is unusual because it is a multi-cultural group comprising of people from disciplines other than architecture i.e. a literary critic, a poet, an artist; another from the theatre and another, unqualified, from engineering.

The initial creativity is the important first step in every project and the ideas team in Barcelona usually takes the form of what could be described as a creative bombardment of the site and problems of the project. The team is led by Ricardo Bofill, son of an architect, who 'refused to qualify as an architect on the grounds that the beaux-arts education he was offered in Barcelona, the post-international style education offered elsewhere, even the technology-based course he started in Geneva, would merely equip him with precisely those methods which other architects were using in foisting onto the community the kinds of architecture it did not want'.[2] However, there is the movement which propagates the ideas of self-build where the architect becomes an advocate enabling individuals to build and even design their own forms of shelter. The work and writings of John Turner recommend themselves to study in this area of activity.

Since the Skeffington Report on participation in planning, evidence seems to point to the fact that much lip service is paid to its recommendations. This usually takes the form of plans and models of proposals being exhibited and the public being asked to comment. Only those members of the public experienced and articulate enough to understand and comment on such proposals make any kind of contribution. Often, however, these contributions are consigned to a file or the wastepaper basket and the original proposals proceed unchanged. Nevertheless there are hopeful signs. Planning workshops, usually set up in urban renewal areas and staffed by zealous young planners, seem to be making some headway.

Two examples of activities with which I am familiar recommend themselves to implementation elsewhere. The Craigmillar Festival Society, which operates in a mid-wars housing estate in Edinburgh, exerts some control over planning, building and social development in the area. It has been in operation for fifteen years and in that time has shown what can be achieved by self-help by establishing itself as a political force to be reckoned with, as well as stimulating wide ranging cultural and social activities. In aiming to achieve Liaison Government, a community newspaper is distributed to over 7000 households and, among the many items, notice is drawn to the monthly meeting at which is discussed current policies, works and problems. Nine working parties gather information from the community and feed the monthly Planning Workshop while annually there is held the Craigmillar Convention and the Craigmillar Musical. The latter uses a popular medium to provide a platform to focus attention on a range of themes pertinent to the progress of the community.

The Festival Society operates fiftyseven neighbourhood projects ranging from a street volunteers network to residential holidays. An information office, with a 'one door' approach to problems, employs over 140 people and manages community transport, an education unit, a swimming pool, newspaper, arts and sports, annual festivals, and a wide variety of community buildings. For this proven track record, the EEC recently awarded the society a £¼ million to further promote its activities. The energy and incentive for this development has come from within the community, spearheaded by Helen Crummy, and it is for me one of the most important examples of an area of multiple deprivation, pulling itself together by its own apron strings. The Assist project in the Govan district of Glasgow, organised by the Department of Architecture at the University of Strathclyde, has pointed the way towards the renewal of inner city tenement dwellings threatened with demolition. Taking a group of traditional stone built tenements, consisting of the notorious Glasgow 'single-ends' (one room and shared toilet facilities), the householders with the project team acting as advocate have transformed the 'single-ends' into comfortable flats each having their own toilet and bathroom. To do this the person density of the blocks had to be reduced by natural wastage and the provision, where desired, of alternative housing elsewhere. The necessary space was thus released on each floor to make it possible to reshape the areas into flats which meet modern standards.

CONCLUSION

Two related elements seem to emerge in all of this. The first is the recognition that creativity and imagination are essential for the development of our society and second is the importance of rediscovering the uniqueness of the individual and the creativity that exists in each of us. Other town artists have been appointed in places such as Stevenage, East Kilbride, Livingston and Rochdale. As members of the planning departments they can help to inject creativity into the planning/building process and create opportunities for communities to contribute to their own environments.

Community Artists, who are now quite numerous in this country, act more directly as cultural animators within the community itself. Their work is a direct reaction to the failure of art education in our school system. They offer the opportunity for people to discover their own ability through self-expression, bringing with it an enrichment to life denied to them by their living and working environment: 'Creativity is for the gifted few; the rest of us are compelled to live in environments constructed by the gifted few, listen to the gifted few's music, use the gifted few's inventions and art, and read the poems, fantasies and plays by the gifted few. This is what our education and culture condition us to believe; and this is a culturally induced and perpetuated lie'.[3]

To my mind, the natural development of all of this is, for example, in the public and rented sector of housing and therefore within the majority of the community, a sequence from user participation, tenant control leading ultimately to the option of self-build. In building one's own house, leisure and work unites to produce that high degree of self-fulfilment so necessary in creating the developed individual.

REFERENCES

1. Weber, J. (1977) *Towards a Peoples Art*. E. P. Dutton, New York
2. Broadbent, G. (1973) *Architectural Review*, November
3. Nicholson, S. (1974) *RIBA Journal*, February, p. 25

9 BLACK ROAD, MACCLESFIELD

An example of self help rehabilitation

by Rod Hackney

The policies of mass clearance and comprehensive redevelopment, which reached a peak in the 1960s, have halted and, on reflection, many large schemes proved disastrous beyond all measure.

Apart from the astronomical cost, about £70 000 a unit over the sixty year loan period, the new tower and medium storey block has failed to improve upon the rows of terrace houses that were bulldozed to make way for them. The general result is a multitude of unpopular and expensive modern units, doubtfully constructed and planned and, worst of all, now posing a whole new range of social management problems. Indeed, some of the worst are proving so expensive to maintain to an acceptable standard that they could go the way of similar housing in St Louis in the USA, where the decision was eventually made to demolish a rambling medium rise housing estate as the only real economic solution to the problem. Recent building on the open spaces in this country, originally left for the continuation of the high and medium rise housing policy, has taken the form of the more acceptable two and three storey terraces which, hopefully, will alleviate some social problems created by high rise building. Nevertheless, they are still expensive substitutions for the dwellings they were meant to replace.

Now that most of us acknowledge that the country's financial position is a delicate one, it is understandable that housing funds, like all other aspects of the economy, have had to be cut back. Expensive clearance and redevelopment has failed and small scale infill and rehabilitation has become the alternative solution, both as a financial and social necessity. The Housing Act 1974, still the prime act today, emphasises the need for public participation in future programmes, but how many housing agencies, particularly the local authorities, can honestly say that their endeavours to engage public participation go beyond a few well publicised meetings? Indeed, how many officials are there who actually regard the general public as more of a spanner in the machinery of the local authority administration?

One might also ask, are the public at large willing or even able to participate in the manner outlined in this housing legislation?

Unfortunately, if some working relationship is not effected between the professionals and the public then, on the next swing of the housing pendulum, the Government would have every reason to state that, together with the programme of rehabilitation, the participation programme had failed miserably. With the Industrial momentum increasing, lubricated by North Sea oil, the only sensible course would then be a return to a more controlled product, that of replacing the old housing with new building on a large scale. The 1960s all over again, but this time with years of blighted backlog to catch up on. This situation must not be allowed to occur. All authorities concerned with housing and the public must make a go of the participation and rehabilitation clauses in the Housing Act 1974.

Despite the limited financial budget available, there is a good chance that many inroads into solving the housing problem can still be made during this next decade by emphasising the practical benefit of public participation. This should not in any way infer the reduction of standards, after all they have never really been that high anyway, compared with other European countries. Start reducing standards anymore and one might as well completely remove the distinction between fit and unfit property and then statistically there would be no housing problem. All the three million or so slums would then be considered fit and those that were empty be made available for the homeless. The housing problem solved overnight without a single improvement being carried out! However, the real situation *would* remain and millions of people would be living in houses which fall below a politically acceptable level of tolerance. The Housing Act 1974, which may well have been an interim political measure to tide us over our financial bankruptcy, could therefore, with public participation, prove to be a whole new way of tackling the housing situation. It will involve the owner occupier, tenant and landlord to an extent never really envisaged by most of the people involved in the housing sector. It will require confidence on the part of the residents concerned and foresight on the part of the officials.

With shorter hours being worked and less overtime required, the climate seems opportune for residents to get involved with self-help on an ever increasing scale. Indeed without it, local authorities will only be able to scratch the surface of the housing problem. Unless you have public participation, the finances available can only be spent in one of two ways: either spread thinly over many houses, giving those attended to nothing more than a glorified 'paint and make good' job, or given to a few privileged areas to produce reasonable schemes of improvement but leaving the majority of housing unattended to; producing blight at an unprecedented rate.

Take a look at the building operations involved in improvement and repair. A large percentage of them do not require skilled training. Those jobs could easily be done by the house occupier in a building programme, providing he is willing and able. It is a matter of cooperation and coordination between the public, the skilled worker and the professional manager. It does not mean that builders will lose out on the work available. The skilled trades would still be needed, although they may be acting in the capacity of sub-contractors rather than general contractors. Neither does it mean that professionals will be ousted, although their role will become one of public relations and personnel management rather than the straightforward application of specialised skills they were trained for. Standards need not decline with self-help. On the contrary, as the example which follows illustrates, they may very well improve! Costs will be greatly reduced and a more worthwhile exercise will have been carried out with those most intimately involved in re-habilitation, that is the residents, having played a major role in the housing improvements and repairs. Think of the extra social benefits which might accrue, of the pride of the participants in the scheme and of a reduction in vandalism. Real public participation will go a long way towards guaranteeing the success of the programme.

To help to understand this train of thinking, the example of the Black Road General Improvement Area in Macclesfield, Cheshire, is now outlined. The Macclesfield Experiment is the first completed scheme of self-help rehabilitation in this country and in many ways it foreshadowed the legislation outlined in the Housing Act 1974. The account is written in chronological order to help explain the progress of the scheme from the start to finish.

Macclesfield is an old established town which experienced considerable growth in the first half of the nineteenth century with the construction of two and three storey terrace cottages for the workers of the town's textile industries. Although many of these original houses have been demolished, the majority remain and most are in need of some form of repair and improvement. Others were in such a bad state of repair that the local authority could see no other alternative but to consider them only suitable for full scale clearance. Those in the Black Road area of the town, on the lower slopes of the Peak District and bordering the Macclesfield Canal, were considered to be some of the worst. They were all built about 1815.

In 1968 the Council prepared a case for the clearance of over three hundred houses in the Black Road area in order to clear the bulk of unfit property and promote a comprehensive scheme of redevelopment incorporating new semi-detached houses and accommodation for old persons. Because of insufficient funds no action was taken on this scheme and both slum clearance and new house building were suspended generally throughout the town by the Council.

Subsequently in 1972, Macclesfield Council decided to resume its programme and the Black Road area was one of four areas to be cleared first. This fact was publicised at a Town Hall exhibition in June 1972. The residents of the Black Road area had made representations to their aldermen and councillors in 1968 and enquired about their fate during the four years that followed. This exhibition, however, spurred them on to formalise their organisation. They established an Action Group in order to present their own alternative points of view to the Council and the towns-people.

THE ACTION GROUP

The Action Group first circulated a petition to find out where most of their support lay and to test local feeling about the Council's clearance plans. They quickly learnt that most people in the affected area would like to stay and in one specific part of the area all the residents expressed their alternative wish to improve their homes rather than have them demolished.

The Action Group decided to concentrate its case in the area where it was guaranteed unanimous support. They argued that it was important to set a precedent and then other similar schemes could follow suit if similar support was forthcoming. They met both elected representatives and local government officers and explained their alternative improvement ideas. Most of their summer evenings were spent visiting the homes of the fortyeight aldermen and councillors in Macclesfield. All along, the Action Group avoided any personal criticism of the local government officers and the elected representatives and refused to get involved in local party political bickering. They enlisted the support of their local Member of Parliament and extended an invitation to him to visit the area, thus securing front page coverage in the two local newspapers.

Car stickers and campaign posters were prepared by the Group and distributed throughout the Town. Public meetings were held to gain the support of the public and local influential groups and visitors were encouraged to attend weekly Group committee meetings. A publicity team was also set up to continually feed the local press with news items and thus kept the townspeople informed of progress. The Group also received considerable support through the column of the 'Readers Letters' page of the local newspapers. In short, the Group made out a very convincing case to illustrate their preference for improvement of their homes rather than having them cleared. They adopted a slogan: KEEP IT UP, BLACK ROAD.

THE RESIDENTS' TECHNICAL REPORT

The Action Group asked their resident architect, Rod Hackney, and their resident builder to prepare a technical report on the condition of the thirtyfour houses in the pilot area. They also appointed their own surveyors to inspect in detail all the houses concerned and to assess repairs and itemise a list of improvements required to bring the houses up to the necessary standard to give them a new lease of life. The Action Group included in its report outline proposals for declaring their area a General Improvement Area and their proposals included a comprehensive list of environmental improvements for tidying up the area around the houses. As 'qualified persons', they are allowed under Section 28 of the 1969 Housing Act to present a technical report to the Council for their consideration. This they did in September 1972. Their fiftyfour page report, outlining the case for improvement and not clearance for their area was printed and a hundred copies circulated to all elected representatives and local government officers. Other copies were sent to the local and national press and all parties who the Group considered would help them in their campaign.

THE COUNCIL'S RESPONSE

The report was well received by all concerned. The Planning and Development Committee and the Housing Committee met in October 1972 at a special joint meeting to consider the report. They decided to recommend the setting up of a Housing Strategy Group consisting of local authority officials from the former Slum Clearance and General Improvement Area working parties. Their first priority was to consider the case of the Black Road area residents and make recommendations for the full Council to consider. The economic criteria affecting older housing had changed radically with the 1969 Housing Act. The expansion of the improvement grant system had shifted a much greater share of public investment into improvement and repair of both older houses and their surroundings. In the same Act, cooperation between residents and the local authority was encouraged in order to decide upon the desirability of area improvement and to gauge the amount of local residents' support for the implementation of general improvement schemes. These were the points the residents highlighted in their report. They acknowledged the poor condition of their homes, but balanced this, they said, by their unanimous call for improvement and promised guarantees that all the residents would improve their homes if given the chance by the local authority.

The Housing Strategy Group spent six months in its preparation of recommendations. They first asked the public health department to re-inspect the Black Road properties. They searched out the Department of the Environment's opinions and they later checked the credibility of the Action Group's guarantees of support. The public health officers found that while the bulk of the properties in the Black Road area were still considered in such a bad state as to be only suitable for clearance, they concluded that there was a concentration of improvable properties within the boundaries of the area outlined for improvement by the Action Group. The Department of the Environment's reaction to the Group's proposals was that the houses were borderline cases for improvement, and that environmental improvement potential was limited compared with other general improvement areas in the north-west of England. They went on to say that 'resident solidarity and an ambitious scheme of environmental improvements has been noted . . . to such an extent that whilst reservations about detail proposals, scope and cost still exist, social argument cannot be excluded in the balance of physical deficits and potential'.

They left the final decision to the Council, who then spent time meeting the Action Group and gauging for themselves the scale of support for improvement. In their report they quoted three major points that had to be considered when determining the future of the Black Road Area:

1) The residents of the Action Group still accept that their houses are viable homes and consider them capable of improvement at reasonable cost to give a life of at least thirty years.

2) Residents' confidence is matched by their willingness to invest in the dwellings.

3) Legislative and economic conditions have altered sufficiently since 1968 for the local authority to reconsider their earlier decision to clear.

The Housing Strategy Group also acknowledged the residents' proposals for carrying out the scheme on a self-help basis. The Action Group had indicated that they wished to manage the actual house improvements and environmental works. Residents' labour was available to carry out certain tasks and the Action Group had an architect who could manage the programming of the entire operation. With their own management they calculated that the average cost of house improvement works would be £2000 per house and £8500 was estimated for the cost of the environmental works.

THE DECLARATION OF A GENERAL IMPROVEMENT AREA

In February 1973 the Housing Strategy Group submitted their

recommendations and, subsequently, in April 1974 Macclesfield Council declared the Black Road Area the first general improvement area in the town. Amongst the Council's resolutions were:

1) That the Town Clerk be authorised to complete the necessary legal documents.

The Action Group had earlier agreed to sign dedication documents agreeing to take up improvement grants. They had also participated in a proposal to give up their private land for environmental works. This was then prepared by the Town Clerk and the Action Group's solicitors, signed by all the owners, the Mayor and Town Clerk and then registered under the Cheshire County Council Act. This protected the residents from any difficulties that may have arisen if any newcomers were to later reside within the boundaries of the improvement area. The Action Group also changed its name to the Black Road Area Residents' Association and formed themselves into a trust organisation and voted in four trustees to administer the improvement scheme and subsequent maintenance of the environmental improvements.

2) That the Community and Health Services Committee recommend to make the area a Smoke Control Order in respect of the Houses in the general improvement area.

3) That the Local Authority authorise an expenditure of £250 per house for environmental works.

The residents later calculated that if they had contracted out their ambitious scheme it would have cost about £23 000. Residents' labour and only contracting specialist work out to individual contractors, i.e. stone walling, brickwork, asphalt laying, reduced this amount to £8500.

4) That the Housing and Estates Committee be asked to make accommodation available for rent to the occupants of the Black Road area properties as temporary accommodation whilst the improvements were being carried out.

The residents had indicated that they could make certain alternative accommodation available but it fell short bearing in mind the limited time in which the improvements could take place, i.e. the residents expected to complete all their house improvement work by June 1974 when the grant levels would be reduced from £1500 to £1000. In addition, the officers concerned with temporary accommodation were able to phrase the wording on their rent books for temporary accommodation in such a way as they could argue that the accommodation provided was similar to a hotel room and therefore solved the problem of the possibility of a temporary resident wishing to 'sit' once they were in a Council house.

5) That the Council be prepared to give maximum improvement

grants where appropriate . . . and that the chairman and vice-chairman of the Housing and Estates Committee be given delegated powers to approve grant applications.

This helped facilitate quick expedition of the residents' grant applications and thus insured smooth continuity of the improvement works. The Council agreed to make maturity loans available for the first time in Macclesfield to the hardship cases in the Black Road area. For others they promised loans to cover the improvement costs over and above the grant amount. In short, the Council endorsed all the proposals of the Black Road residents plus additional proposals to safeguard the implementation of the scheme. It was now up to the residents to prove themselves and carry out their improvement scheme.

Whilst the Council had been making up their minds about the area, the residents had been busy finalising plans for the expected declaration of a general improvement area. The most important achievement was to persuade most of the sitting tenants to purchase their homes from the owners. In 1969 the Council had surveyed the area and found that 76% of the residents were tenants. In 1972 this figure had been reduced to 40% but, by the time the area had been declared an improvement area, only 10% of the residents were sitting tenants. The rest were all owner occupiers. This large scale movement towards owner occupation was partially as a result of the Action Group's confidence in investing in their area prior to it being declared for general improvement. Whilst the area was threatened with clearance, house prices were very low but the Action Group had managed to get all the sitting tenants to buy prior to the increase in house prices that was bound to come when the Council's clearance proposals were replaced with plans for improvement. In one particular terrace, the sitting tenants were able to raise £1600 for the five houses in which they lived. Although this was not a large amount the Action Group's financial advisers, working with the agents of the landlady, were able to work out that £1600 invested in an annuity policy would bring the landlady twice as much in interest compared with the rent she would receive, plus the advantage of not having to maintain the houses and, of course, not having to improve five houses when the improvement scheme began. The £1600 was not divided equally by five, but rather made up of amounts the sitting tenants could afford, i.e. the two pension-age sitting tenants contributed £200 each. The younger couples therefore paid more for their houses. These Robin Hood financial arrangements worked a treat and, in addition, the Council was pleased that the actual residents would get the grant rather than the absentee landlord.

THE SHOW HOUSE

Both the Council and the residents needed convincing quickly that the works would start immediately after the improvement declaration was made. The architect agreed to improve his house first with the help of the other residents and a local contracting firm. The improvements of this house also helped 'educate' the other residents in such pursuits as chimney breast demolition, house replanning, carpentry, etc., so that they had a little experience when it came to doing their own houses and also helping the elderly residents who would require assistance when their houses were being improved.

After three months, the Show House was complete. The Council was impressed with the first conversion and so were the residents. All interested parties were invited to an 'open house'. As well as local government officials and elected representatives, builders were also invited with the view to offering them negotiated contracts for some of the other properties for works the residents themselves would not be carrying out. They were also able to see the desired standard of workmanship and visit the other houses which were to be improved.

THE RESIDENTS' PROGRAMME

Whilst drawings and specifications were being prepared for all the houses, roofworks were begun and the Council agreed to pay interim grant payments for part of this. This allowed complete terrace re-roofing prior to the actual internal house improvement works starting. The architect drew up itemised specification clauses for each house and contractors were asked for itemised prices. This meant that individual residents could see where the costs lay and could also see from the nature of the price breakdown where their labour could be best utilised to save the most money. Some contractors were a little sceptical of the approach, especially as there was an abundance of work in the town at the time. Most refused to participate but, nevertheless, the residents managed to secure all the assistance they required and in addition got the builders to also agree to penalty clauses and completion dates for each house.

The resident builders agreed to help carry out one complete terrace. Another small local contractor agreed to take a second terrace and a larger firm from the town took the third terrace. The former two turned out to be great successes in that they were able to adapt to the strange site management conditions and residents participation in the improvement works. The third, larger firm, proved more difficult and unable to accommodate the wishes of the residents in the same way as the two smaller firms. This resulted in all kinds of difficulties including delays in the completion.of the works with subsequent mortage offer lapses, lengthy stays in temporary houses by the residents and, indirectly, a reduction in the standard of site workmanship. In the case of this larger firm however, slight recompense appeared in the quality of the workshop joinery, such as stairs. Nevertheless experience has shown that in this self-help scheme larger contractors cannot participate in the same manner as smaller firms because of the long chains of command and inflexibility.

Mention has been made of mortgages. No scheme of this nature can be attempted without the full financial backing of a local authority. Building societies refused to contemplate financial assistance towards the improvement of 160 year old terrace housing. The local authority, on the other hand, could not declare a general improvement area and then not back it to the hilt with financial aid. Everyone who needed assistance in the Black Road area got it. The elderly took up the maturity loans. The less well-off younger people, option mortgages, and the remainder either took advantage of normal mortgages or, as in a few cases, they paid cash. When figures were submitted by the contractors they were, of course, higher than those figures submitted in the original residents' report. Apart from inflation, the residents had up-graded their requirements with many deciding upon central heating at the last minute. Average mortgages, to cover the costs of the works, over the £1500 grant level were about £1300–£2000 and the average maturity loan, about £600. These figures suggest that the elderly paid less for their house improvements. This is true as, in general, less work was done to these homes and not because they were in better condition but because the elderly did not want as comprehensive an improvement job as the younger residents. In addition, the local authority agreed to interpret the improvement of the elderly residents' houses rather liberally thus again reducing cost. This manifested itself in the upgrading rather than complete replacement of staircases, the maintenance rather than raising of low door head heights, etc.

Once a mortage offer had been given by the local authority it was up to the owner to keep to the agreed figure. If he wanted extras then the amount would be calculated with the contractor and then the owner would have to put in more man hours to meet the additional costs. Residents found that much of the contractors' site time is spent in non-skilled pursuits, work that really anybody can carry out if given the direction and explanations of what is required. It was the responsibility of the architect to programme all this and ensure that the owners and contractors were equally aware of what each was required to do. Most of the residents worked on the building site during the evenings and at weekends. In the case of a few, they took time off work to complete their house improvements. In the case of the elderly, the residents pooled their labour and demolished chimney breasts, out houses, etc., and then later participated with house decorations.

ASSESSMENT OF THE SCHEME'S SUCCESS

Now that all the house improvements are completed the results can be assessed. No one house is the same. The completed improvements reflect the individuality of each occupant. It would have been much easier to standardise the scheme, just like many similar schemes throughout the country, but in Black Road perhaps the greatest single success is the individual house types produced. The windows and doors are different. There are many types of staircases, some open-riser, others solid-riser. Some kitchens have large areas of floor units, others breakfast bars. Some houses are open-plan, some have all the improvements accommodated in the original house structure, whilst others chose to extend either in the form of a one or two storey extension. Some residents decided upon a shower cubicle rather than a bath and most chose gas wall mounted balanced flue boilers, whilst others preferred solid fuel central heating though others, again, decided upon more conventional forms of house heating. Even with this apparently anarchistical design approach to their house improvements, the overall appearance of the improved houses still reflects the period in which the houses were built and, in addition, their commonsense approach has helped the residents avoid the easy trap of ruining the house proportions by changing the original window sizes. Instead the existing window and door proportions have been kept and no-one has inserted bow-windows or gone for porches over their doorways.

The local authority on their part have acted responsibly in their interpretation of the building regulations. Rigid and inflexible standards have not been asked for. No 'Parker Morris' recommendations here, and no attempt to make the houses into something they were never designed for. Shared external manholes and soil vent pipes, relaxations on room heights, etc., have all helped to make the scheme possible. The local authority have shown an admirable approach to the difficult task of site management of this self-help scheme and the resultant improvements have satisfied everybody. In short, this was not a simple task of up-grading the houses to the twelve point standard as laid down in the 1969 Housing Act, but rather a detailed endeavour to accommodate the wishes of all the individual residents at the same time as giving their old homes a new lease of life and an individuality in which they could justifiably be proud and call their own. The results are there for all to see.

The same management skills were shown in the carrying out of the environmental works and now that these are completed they are complimentary to the individual house improvements. Off-street car parking has been provided, seating and play spaces, tree and shrub planting, new rights of way and private garden areas. The sloping site has offered many excellent opportunities to make exciting changes of level in the layout of the footpaths, ramps and steps. In addition, surface drainage of the internal area of the site has been provided, all the new water service drains are located within the internal parts of the site for easy maintenance, and the residents' own off-street lighting has been installed.

The scheme has generally been completed on time, in spite of all the site management difficulties and also the effects of the 'three day week'. The completed scheme is a credit to all concerned: the residents, the local authority and the contractors. It has managed, in Macclesfield at least, to show what a unified group of residents can do when they decide to carry out a single-minded goal and put aside their personal differences in order to see through the implementation of a scheme of general improvement. It has shown what happens when the same group of residents and the local authority work together, with mutual respect and trust, to see a scheme through. Both the Black Road residents and the Macclesfield Council can feel justly proud of the success of the Black Road Area General Improvement Scheme No. 1.

LESSONS FOR OTHER AREAS

It is worthwhile trying to evaluate the success of the Black Road scheme to see if other areas can be similarly affected and to see if the lessons displayed in Macclesfield can be utilised elsewhere in the country.

Firstly, the presence of a 'qualified person', as referred to in Circular 65/69 from the Ministry of Housing and Local Government, within the affected area was of immeasurable value when it came to negotiations with the Council and later the contractors. There is therefore an argument here for calling for 'professional' residents in future areas of General Improvement or Housing Action. That is, people willing to give all their time to helping implement the housing improvement programme. Further, the rectangular site chosen for the pilot scheme proved ideal in its internal arrangement of spaces for a successful environmental improvement scheme. It proved that the limited view of including traffic management to existing roads in any general improvement area is not imperative. Indeed, it showed that without any works to the surrounding roadways a successful environmental scheme could concentrate on simply tidying up the 'backs', the areas between the terraces and making the house improvement and environmental improvements compatible with each other.

By concentrating on a small compact area and making sure that all the houses were improved, the Group were able to ensure that their houses, being within self-contained boundaries, would not prejudice future plans for immediately surrounding areas. The scheme would no doubt have failed if a large pilot scheme had been chosen and only random house improvements within each terrace carried out. The Group decided at the outset to establish a successful precedent. Once this had been achieved they then expected the future to take a similar course as long as the financial incentives were still available for house and area improvement.

The manner in which the Group tackled the Council, and their emphasis on cooperation with all concerned, undoubtedly persuaded local government officials and elected representatives to listen more willingly to their ideas. Their insistence on avoiding criticism of individuals within the local authority had a great bearing on the outcome of first their fight to save their homes and, subsequently, their successful management of the general improvement area. Rather than sit back on their laurels, once they had saved their homes, they simply transferred the energy displayed in their campaign to the practical implementation of the house and area improvement scheme. They wasted no time and thus avoided the possibility of residents becoming impatient and perhaps losing interest.

Lastly, they embarked on a campaign to save their homes knowing that they were right in what they wanted. They were willing to sacrifice personal gain to see the joint effort succeed. In many respects they took most of the people they dealt with by surprise. The local authority was very sceptical when the campaign first began and it is perhaps true to say that not until the actual improvement scheme was well on the way did they realise the determination of the residents. The Group's single minded aim to get on with the job of improving their homes and the energy they displayed in achieving this aim, guided by their basic common sense attitude, were the hallmarks of their achievements.

CONCLUSION

Success breeds success and other groups of residents in Macclesfield, who had been keeping track of events in the first general improvement area, began to consider if their houses could be similarly treated. A group of residents further north along Black Road approached the residents of the completed improvement area and questioned them on the workings of the scheme. After an initial residents meeting they decided to approach the architects' drawing office (established now at 214 Black Road, where the author worked) and asked if a technical report could be prepared recommending the area for retention and the declaration of another general improvement area. This report was completed in September 1975 and was submitted to the Macclesfield Borough Council for consideration along with the residents' social survey. The residents' group adopted the name, 'Black Road Area Residents' Association No. 2' and the reports called for the declaration of 'Black Road General Improvement Area No. 2', an area of similar size and property to the original improvement area (if not a little smaller in size and perhaps in worse condition).

The Council wasted no time in investigating the area to see if they could go along with residents' wishes. The official report was completed in November 1975 and it endorsed the residents' proposals, recommending improvement of the area rather than clearance. Other points included for similar legal tie-ups to be obtained from all residents, owner occupiers, landlords and tenants. The Planning Department also became involved as it was suggested in the technical report that the second improvement area be declared a conservation area at the same time. In addition to the normal implications of a conservation area, there was also the availability of extra funds for environmental improvements, and this would come in handy for works to surrounding roads as most of the environmental improvements contained within the scheme were to be spent within the common courtyard between the houses.

The implementation of The Black Road General Improvement Area No. 2 thus began, with completion expected in 1978. The Council also considered other parts of Black Road within its overall policy for the area and allowed residents of another block of houses of similar size to the other two, to apply for grants for individual house improvements. Here, no funds were considered necessary for environmental works. Other blocks of houses are still scheduled for clearance, especially where the tenants are looking forward to being rehoused by the Council into new houses or flats. Black Road No. 1 has been made part of a conservation area along with the complete length of the Macclesfield Canal which runs parallel to Black Road.

In other schemes, in the process of being carried out by the author and his assistants, the lessons of the Macclesfield schemes are being tested on a much larger scale and the future will determine if the small intimate approach can be adopted in the larger urban areas of British cities. There is always the risk of the government of the day changing legislation so that rehabilitation will perhaps not always be recommended policy. It is therefore very important that where schemes are begun, they are in areas where success can be expected, if not guaranteed. As this is perhaps expecting too much in these days of economic uncertainty, it is therefore imperative to plan larger areas of Housing Action and General Improvement in a small way by breaking down the areas in question into parts which are then concentrated upon in turn. Small blocks of units or lengths of streets should then be improved as a group and then the effort shifted to the next block or group, as at Macclesfield. This way will mean that if legislation changes the improvements that have been carried out are 'safe' for at least thirty years (the minimum life of an improved property) whilst those properties not improved could be the subject of modified legislation. This will not be the case in say a hypothetical example where a general improvement area has been declared containing many hundreds of units and only spasmodic house improvements have been carried out, i.e. two or three units in each street. There is a risk here that if the scheme fails or government legislation changes then even the few improved units are not safe from possible demolition.

Mass improvement policies can be as inhuman as mass redevelopment policies. The small scale approach, as at Macclesfield, is perhaps one example of the recommended method of improving larger areas. The breakdown of large schemes into manageable units, say a street of forty houses or a block of thirtyfive units, with the management skills adopted in the improvement areas in Black Road applied to each small unit, will go a long way to consolidating successful improvement areas, retain the human management scale and allow residents the opportunity of becoming fully involved with the improvement programme.

10 DESIGN AND COMMUNITY INVOLVEMENT
A local authority perspective

by Michael Tempest

This is a personal and individual interpretation of the work of a Local Authority — Nottinghamshire County Council. To understand the way ahead, it is necessary to understand the point we are now at. It does seem incredible to think that in 1927 the Cambridgeshire County Council adopted the policy to design schools for the whole community.

Henry Morris, the brilliant and far-seeing Secretary of Education, proposed that the Secondary Schools of rural Cambridgeshire should become village colleges forming the community centres for a group of villages and providing for active educational and recreational life of the area. Architects started to take an interest when the fourth of the Cambridgeshire projects was opened in 1939, designed by Walter Gropius and Maxwell Fry. It is amazing that it has taken until now for the idea to really bite. The 1944 Education Act stated 'it shall be the duty of the Local Authority for every area, so far as their powers extend, to contribute towards the spiritual, moral, mental and physical development of the community'. Gordon Bessey, the Director of Education for Cumberland, developed the principles laid down by Morris. Wyndham School, Egremont, designed by the County Architects, clearly sets out to achieve a centre for both child and adult recreational/educational activities and needs. It is from these early projects that one realises that not only is the community school concept impressive in itself but it provides a basis for trying to develop community links and involvement.

Nottinghamshire County Council, in 1965, set up a Joint Development Team of Architects and Education Officers to prepare a brief for planning a number of large comprehensive schools. Their studies revealed considerable need for public usage of facilities. The first of these projects to open was that of Bingham in 1969. All the projects had a strong emphasis on sport, influenced by the circular 'provision of facilities for sport' issued by Ministry of Housing and Local Government (MHQLG) and Department of Education in 1964 and by the strong influence of the County's own Education Department. The first four joint-use Comprehensive Schools were established at Bingham, Balderton, Carlton and Worksop. These

Centres provided facilities for public use mainly outside of school time and included sports hall, squash courts, gymnasium, swimming pools, learner pools, refreshment areas, licensed bars, theatres, concert halls. Outside provision included football, cricket, rugby, hockey pitches, dry play areas, running tracks and tennis courts. In addition, the Carlton project provided a ski slope, target golf and bowls.

Several variations of this first mark of joint use have since been developed at Chilwell, Selston, Kimberley, Retford, Southwell, Rushcliffe, Rainworth, and Keyworth and Sutton Centres. These Centres were a result of an opportunist approach depending on the foresight of Members and Officers in expanding the facilities at schools to make them available to the public. From taking the decision to proceed with the policy, they were implemented very quickly and with a great deal of trust. It depended on considerable goodwill by the County Council and the District Councils. These schemes fulfilled a clear if limited basic need established through the foresight of a small number of Members and Officers who had a reasonably clear view of the community needs, although there was differing degrees of public participation in evolving the schemes, particularly the latter variations.

PUBLIC PARTICIPATION AND ITS EVALUATION

As a first example of public participation, I shall describe the scheme at Southwell, a small country commuter town ten miles north-east of Nottingham.

The Southwell scheme. This scheme was linked with the expansion of the new secondary school to provide a village hall, restaurant and bar facilities, meeting rooms/club rooms for the many clubs, societies and organisations of the town. This was a conscious move away from the sport biased centre and, although it did provide squash courts and was linked to the existing town swimming pool on the same site, it was mainly established to provide facilities for clubs, groups and social education and drama type activities. This provision was arrived at after detailed discussions by Senior Officers with a small cross-section of the well organised clubs and societies of the town.

This study showed that already there was a severe need for a community hall, for which a Trust Fund had already been established. Discussions also took place with the MHOLG, which again reinforced the view that there was a need for a variety of meeting rooms, areas for things like a creche in association with mother groups, women's institutes, drama, choral and music groups.

Some of these, like the Women's Institute and mother groups, would require facilities during the school day.

This project has had management teething problems and it is still too early to constructively assess its success. Nevertheless, the buildings and facilities are well used. It is clear from this early example that participation by the public was mainly through the structured clubs and societies and the knowledge gained by Officers on earlier projects developed within the County. It did not necessarily reflect a totally balanced community opinion. This I feel to be less important than the fact that it does provide a modest centre from which links or spokes can be extended to the community to involve them firstly in the affairs of that community and then possibly, through future building programmes, meeting the expanding needs of that community by using it to establish the design requirements.

The Sutton Centre.   The Sutton Centre scheme was the most significant next development towards the fully integrated community school. It was the first opportunity to develop a major project that was centred in a community. It was also the first time that a fairly exhaustive feasibility study was carried out involving considerable community involvement.

While considering a site for a new comprehensive school for the town, it was discovered that one half of the centre of Sutton-in-Ashfield was being developed for a shopping precinct and the remaining half of the town centre was in the ownership of Sutton-in-Ashfield Council. The idea to build a school on the periphery of the town was dropped and an agreement was reached with Sutton-in-Ashfield Council to build a community school in the town centre. At last, the authorities were able to achieve a school in the heart of an existing community rather than isolated on the periphery. Historically, this had been almost impossible to do because of the high land values which had forced schools to develop on the edges rather than in the heart of towns.

From the outset it had been realised that this scheme was going to be a very significant step forward in the Authority's thinking and, because of this, Chief Officers and Senior Staff were involved in the exhaustive public participation exercise. On the 15 September 1970, Senior Officers of the County Council met the Development Committee of the Urban District Council to discuss the possibility of a major town centre development of a recreational, cultural and educational nature at Sutton-in-Ashfield. It was agreed that the County Council should undertake a feasibility study for consideration by the two Authorities. The County Council was asked to carry out this study and produce a report. The study would try to establish the nature of the existing community in Sutton-in-Ashfield and to understand the patterns of employment, social life, religious and cultural, sporting activities, and the shopping habits. It was anticipated that a picture of existing facilities would emerge together with a guide to the deficiencies and future needs. In addition to this, it would be necessary to decide whether the site was suitable for this development. From October 1970, for a period of three months, Chief Officers and Senior Staff met many groups and organisations to discuss the life of Sutton-in-Ashfield and what the hopes and aspirations of the people were. During this concentrated period of public participation, discussions took place with the following groups:

The Local Urban District Council; Medical Practitioners; Councillors; Teachers and Staff of Schools of Ashfield; Youth Officers and Leaders and Members of the Youth Clubs; Young Persons from Sutton-in-Ashfield on probation; Organisations such as the Rotary Club, Towns Womens Guild and Voluntary and Welfare Associations; Members of the Local Churches; Voluntary Staff of the Family Planning Association; Local Dramatic and Choral Societies, Ladies of the Toc 'H' Branch of Sutton-in-Ashfield; the Managers of the Department of Employment; the Workers Education Association; Nottingham University Department of Adult Education and the Professor of Community Health at the University; all Departments of the County Council and Medical Officer of Health for Nottinghamshire and the Probation Officer; the Careers and Youth Employment Officer; Representative of the Department of Education and Science in London; the Department of the Environment in London; Gordon Bessey, Director of Education for Cumberland, and the Headmaster and Staff of Wyndham School, Egremont, Cumberland; the Organisers of Further Education for Cumberland and the Director of Development, Killingworth, Newtown, Northumberland; the Head-master of Killingworth Comprehensive School, and the Further Education Youth Tutor for Killingworth; the Head of Countersthorpe Upper School and Community College, Leicestershire; Monsieur Sanouillier, Mayor and Monsieur G. Baudon, Councillors of Yerres, France and Madame Moselle Roux of the Staff of La Maison Pour Tous, Yerres, France.

In addition to these organised discussions, there were many long debates with various unclubables of the town, particularly the children who frequented the coffee bars and chip shops, the leather jacketed motor bike riders and their girl friends. Meeting these groups on their own ground was certainly an interesting experience for all parties. I suppose the generation gap was so great that they were able to talk more freely with 'these strangers who came from down south, Nottingham city'.

The organised groups, naturally enough, tended to promote their own interests and needs. Lack of time prevented consultation with the various sporting organisations. The general impression was that sporting activities of Sutton were not in any fundamental way different from other communities in Nottinghamshire and, in view of the experience gained on earlier projects, it was felt that this was the least crucial area for investigation and discussion, added to which the Area Sports Council provide excellent advice concerning sporting needs for specific areas.

The town of Sutton-in-Ashfield lies approximately fifteen miles north-west of Nottingham City and is a town traditionally based on the mining industry. Although it does fall within the declining western areas of the Nottinghamshire and Derby coal fields, the area is trying to re-establish itself and attract new industries to replace the old mining one. These new industries include light engineering, plastics and hosiery, but the continuing importance of mining, and the fact that a number of new industries are also adopting shift work, means that life in Sutton-in-Ashfield is dominated by shift work. So, to this type of general backcloth of employment in the town, a pattern of the sort of town it was became apparent from the Feasibility Study, and I will discuss, in a little more detail, the patterns of social life that did emerge.

'There is nothing to do in Sutton' was one of the very frequent comments made by those who were interviewed, particularly the young. One young man on probation added with more insight than he realised: 'if there were, we would not be here now'. There was a considerable number of organised groups, particularly among women, but despite this they only represented a small proportion of the total population. An example of this was the young people belonging to youth groups mainly linked with churches. Representing no more than 10% of the fourteen to twentyone age group, most of the clubs were open for one night per week. The young expressed concern that all there was to do was watch television, to attend one of the small number of discotheques, to 'hang about on Portland Square', or to spend time in the local pubs. With the last bus returning from other towns, or Nottingham, at 10.30 pm it meant that participation in activities in other towns was limited. The youngsters particularly expressed the view that they would like to attend evening courses providing that they were not the structured type of course where you had to attend for twelve or twentyfour weeks. What they really wanted was somewhere they could drop in for a class on a 'pay-as-you-go' basis, but have access to people with skills in specific subjects.

Many of the older organised persons groups had extreme difficulty in finding suitable accommodation. Fund raising for the upkeep of premises, which may well not be worth the investment, took up much of the effort which could have been going into promoting the aims of the various organisations. Many of the needs of these organised groups could be met by providing rooms for meetings of ten to twelve, or as large as 120 persons. Most of the organised groups were largely confined to women. The men of Sutton-in-Ashfield tended to be 'non-joiners'. The attraction for the working class men were the Miner's Welfare provision, the public houses, the various sporting clubs and the popular pursuit of fishing. What was abundantly clear was the almost complete absence of facilities for family activities. It was felt that this was where a major contribution could be made to the life of the town. There was nowhere in the town where one could adequately hold dances, dinners and exhibitions. People expressed the view that there was a need for a place where they could get a snack or a meal in pleasant surroundings, and this was certainly borne out by those who carried out the survey. Because of the types of industry in the area, the level of handicapped persons and aged persons tended to be high. There was a good deal of voluntary help being provided, but they did lack suitable accommodation. There existed a strong tradition of drama and choral work and there were well organised Dramatic and Choral Societies.

As previously mentioned, little time was spent considering sport through public participation. It was apparent, however, that with two good swimming baths in the centre of Sutton it would be unnecessary to provide any additional swimming facilities. And, because of the high level of shift work, the expressed view was that there would be a demand for daytime adult education classes. This view mainly came from the evening centre teachers and members of the evening centre classes, as well as from the Nottingham University's Department of Adult Education and the Workers' Educational Association. Classes could be provided for unemployed men, housewives and employees of large manufacturing concerns of which some are becoming increasingly willing to promote day release for employees for educational purposes. The University and the Workers' Educational Association were of the opinion that this demand could build up to a number of three hundred daytime places in adult education classes.

In conclusion, Sutton had been presented to the team as a town lacking in facilities for recreation, for cultural pursuits and for social activities; the town needing a centre and, particularly, a civic centre. It confirmed our belief that it was necessary to provide the school facilities in the town centre to compliment the new commercial development. This small example of part of the study was conducted by means of indepth discussions with persons and groups on their home territory to try and build up a detailed pattern of the life of Sutton-in-Ashfield. It enabled free discussion to take place and it enabled ideas to be developed in a very relaxed manner. Inevitably, the techniques used did not reach every member of the community but, nevertheless, I feel that this method is very much more effective than the circulated questionnaire with a highly structured question content. Although one can reach virtually the whole population with the printed questionnaire, inevitably there is a very poor response and only the questions set are answered. If it is anything like the forms I fill in, none of the questions are the ones that I want to be asked in the first place!

Participation by the organised groups directly affected the design of specific areas like the theatre. The solutions for the less clearly defined spaces, however, which may well be used by the largest cross-section of the community, were influenced by the early discussions only and a continuous involvement by the public did not take place in these areas. I cannot fully support the view that it is possible to arrive at design solutions through total public involvement. The design of a building, other than small units like houses, becomes so complex that it is impractical to involve the public beyond the point of establishing their needs. It would be possible to work with a selected Community Committee in the form of a client group, but they would have to be able to take and make decisions within the constraints of the building and economic processes. To some extent these groups already exist in the form of elected representatives to Local Authorities and they should be aware of their community needs.

The main accommodation now provided at the Sutton Centre includes provision for ultimately 1200, plus school places with additional space for sixth form school facilities, a youth service and adult education provision. A Day Centre for the aged and physically handicapped caters for fifty to sixty persons. The Centre has social, refreshment, craft and hobby areas. There is a very significant advantage of this link as it offers a permanent opportunity for school children to participate with these groups of the community. Also included in the scheme are the Probation and Youth Employment Services and the Area Social Services. There is a theatre financed jointly to provide seats for 250 people. The sports facilities include a gymnasium, sports hall, squash courts, a four lane bowls rink and an ice rink. The scheme did not include a swimming pool, as previously mentioned, and, therefore, in architectural terms, it was extremely difficult to devise a building without this major focal point as a centre of attraction. The swimming pool is traditionally the natural attraction for boy to meet girl. It was finally felt that a comparable substitute was the ice rink which provided exactly the same focal point and visual stimuli. Whilst everybody who was asked thought it would be a splendid idea to have an ice rink, it certainly had not been put forward very strongly by the public as a basic requirement, but it has proved to be successful.

The importance of the Sutton Centre scheme was such that it was felt essential to carefully monitor its progress when it became functional in order to achieve maximum feedback. On most buildings and for most architects this is totally lacking and the architect has to rely on infrequent visits to the building to see how things are working out. It was agreed that a full-time Research Worker would be employed to study the way Sutton Centre develops in the community. This appointment is for a five year full-time study with administrative back-up. The scheme is being financed jointly between the Department of Education and Science and the County Council and is being supervised by Nottingham University. The Researcher, who is a sociologist, started his appointment in the Autumn of 1976.

The school has now been operating since September 1973 and the sport facilities started to operate for public use in February 1977. This phasing in of the public facilities is helpful in monitoring its affect both from the now established school and of the community. At this point in time, it is too early to make any realistic assessment of how the building is fulfilling the requirements of the community and the affects it is having on that community. The Research Worker will look at how the school and community integrate with each other and how actively it is a 'community school', what the school is achieving, whether the educational pattern is different because of the involvement of the community, how the Centre is influencing Sutton, and what the public think? A weekly inventory of events and people is being kept and is being monitored. Already the Researcher is beginning to see interesting interaction of the community and school. For example, mining shift workers come into the premises during the day to have their coffee with the fifth form and the physically handicapped adults.

The success of the scheme depends very much on the dedication of the teaching staff and the leadership skills of the headmaster, who have all been doing a tremendous job since the school first opened. The headmaster has to steer the educational process in the right direction and to avoid collisions with the community interests. The building itself can make many contributions towards the integration of the community and one example of this is the simple design of rights of way through the school which stimulates interest of adults to enter the hitherto forbidden territory of school once they have left it as a teenager. It is felt that the building ought to be a centre from which its influence, as a network, spreads out gradually to the community. But already, because of its attractive facilities, it is drawing people in from greater distances, possibly beyond its desirable influence, and this may be a disadvantage in the longterm.

The building already has adults, teachers, helpers, voluntary workers and pupils operating at the same time. In addition, there is the Users Association, as well as parents and governors. Approximately fifteen hundred adults have a direct link to the school through the population of nine hundred children. Four hundred adults use the Day Centre and they too have their family connections. It is these sorts of findings which will be invaluable to both designers and administrators for future community development. Studies are being made to ensure that activities generated in the Centre are not in opposition to similar functions in the town. The Research Worker already confirms with my own feelings that this project is a first step in achieving a constructive movement forward through community involvement and the building design can considerably help to create the right atmosphere to bring a community together. However, although the building has extensive facilities, it can only be the first step in community development. Also, I do not believe that buildings should be totally flexible and able to cope with any situation. The design of space is crucial to human needs of security, comfort, function, and so on.

The objective is for the Research Worker to thoroughly emerse himself with the people of the Centre and sub-centres which are already emerging in the community of Sutton, and beyond the Centres influence spreads outside of the Sutton boundaries, and to feed back the information to designers and administrators. The designer rarely has the opportunity to be involved in this type of research work and obtains feedback mainly from infrequent visits, normally in his own time, to the buildings he has designed.

The Rushcliffe Leisure Centre.   This scheme opened in 1976 and the main feature of the Centre was the provision of a leisure pool. The facility was provided as a direct result of detailed public participation. From the outset a detailed feasibility and public participation exercise was carried out on similar lines to that of Sutton and initially it was clear that a swimming pool headed the list of priorities for facilities. Because of the enthusiasm of a very small nucleus of keen swimming clubs, however, it was also considered necessary to provide a pool for national standard competition swimming. Yet after many hours of discussion with many people, it became clear that something very different to the early concept was wanted by the majority of people who intended to use the Centre.

The need to cater for the whole family, the need to eliminate the strict division between bathers and spectators, and the need to be able to provide social swimming, paddling and direct access from a beach, particularly for the very young and the physically handicapped, were apparent. As a result, the end product was very different to the first ideas expressed. However, within the scheme it has still proved possible to make provision for competitive swimming, although on a more modest scale than the Olympic swimmer would hope to see. I think this is a good example of a major influence by a public participation exercise on a main provision. Again, this Centre is linked to an existing school and incorporates additional education accommodation within it.

The primary school and the community.   The philosophy of the community school has been based on the link between the school and the community and for a long time it had been felt that the secondary level of education was the most suitable link to develop. For major facilities I think this is still a sensible conclusion. Nevertheless, there is a more subtle relationship with the community in the primary school than there is in the major central provision. In a small town it is reasonable to think of one large community, but in a larger town or a village there are small communities quite often forming part of a larger community. Smaller communities in the past related to the church, but now the primary school becomes the focal point in the community.

In terms of community involvement and participation, I think the principle of a first stage Centre, from which a net spreads out, is even more valid when based on the primary school. It has more meaning in its relationship to a small community and more people identify the primary school serving their neighbourhood. This first stage Centre, or series of Centres in the case of a small town, can be the basis for developing community concepts which in turn can lead to further development and building and can act as a collecting point to develop these ideas. For me, the modern well run primary school is one of the most exciting buildings that I go into and I am always highly stimulated by them. The building itself has a small cosy and acceptable atmosphere even to the most introvert person. It is not so impersonal as the large comprehensive school and is more suitable for the less formal requirements for meeting within small communities. Its major advantage for local use is that it is normally well within most people's walking distance of home and most people will have children or friends' children who have been to the primary school and have direct or indirect contact with it. The school will have its finger on the community pulse.

Many primary schools now allow mothers and other adults into the

school to help with day-to-day running of affairs. The primary
school should be closely linked with the adjacent housing developments and, by linking it with other facilities such as local shops and a
pub, this can all help to make it an important focal point within the
community. In addition, the school playing fields are now becoming
available for outside recreation and the fences are beginning to
disappear. The 'Keep-Off' signs are beginning to go, the doors are
beginning to open. Several primary schools in Nottinghamshire have
been developed to incorporate joint provision for use by the community.

Hucknall Edgewood Drive Primary School.   An opportunity
arose at a primary school site in Hucknall, a town on the north-west
edge of Nottingham City. When site investigations were being
carried out it became clear that the whole area was to be developed
for housing. Unlike a new town, we did not have total control of
development and, therefore, we found ourselves with the almost
impossible task of bringing together the District Councils building,
the local developers and the County provision. Working closely with
the Department of Planning and the Director of Education, we were
able to establish the basic concept of the community school. Then
followed long and difficult discussions with several private developers
and their architects, both of which changed several times. It was
possible to develop a community school and playing fields more
closely related to the shops, pub and housing. The final realisation of
this laborious struggle still has to be achieved as both the shop and
housing developers have gone bankrupt. The school itself received a
financial contribution from Hucknall District Council, now part of
Ashfield District, together with a Sports Council grant. The scheme
consisted of the expansion of the physical education facilities so that
the larger hard area could be combined with the apparatus area to
enable games such as badminton to take place. A learner teaching
pool was provided and a small toddlers pool which can easily be
supervised by mothers. A lounge and parents watching area is adjacent to the pool with a large glass panel for viewing. Opening off
this area is the coffee bar and reception which leads through into the
club room and creche facility with access onto an enclosed courtyard.
It can be used for nursery play. Some of the entrance area was
originally designated for library use, but agreement has now been
reached whereby the library facility is linked to the central resource
area of the primary school, which provides a very much better facility
than first envisaged. There is a craft and hobbies workshop provided
with adult size benches and equipment, in addition to normal
provision one finds in a primary school with a majority of smaller

scale furniture. The pottery kiln can also be used by adults. It is intended that this space be used for hobbies, small scale repair work, jewellery making, pottery, woodwork, and so on. It enables adults to use the facility during the day and, when not in use by adults, can be used fully by the school children. For example, if a person is on shift work or retired they can come and work on their own or even possibly demonstrate their skills to the children.

The site is open with direct access for the public. It is intended that the grass pitch be used for fairly informal games of conventional team type and that the more informal, 'smaller children', play areas be used by children during and after school hours. There is a hard play pitch which is floodlit for evening use. Also incorporated on the site is a balancing pond, part of which is the drainage system to the housing scheme. As an educational resource for the school, the pond will have plants and normal pond life.

Little public participation took place on the Hucknall scheme because of the limited time and resources available. I feel, however, that this is less important if you accept this as a first stage towards community involvement and creating a focal point to move onto the next stages.

CONCLUSION

The four very different schemes I have described are examples of the different degrees of public involvement in the decision making process. Several important factors are now clear to me and my colleagues in Nottinghamshire, now that there are, in addition to the smaller schemes, over twenty major centres in operation. We found that no two communities are the same and that buildings, people and resources should reflect these differences as far as possible. When involving the community, their subjective and emotional views should not be under-rated. It is also vital to have a face-to-face, and as informal as possible, discussion with groups and individuals on their home ground. I would never have thought the Darby and Joan Club would get excited about horse riding, but the old lady's eyes lit up and she was keen to have a go.

The Authority must also be clear, before entering into any public participation exercise, on the limits of its resources. It is no good producing a super plan which cannot be implemented. The public, rightly so, become cynical of this type of report. The ability to implement ideas is one of the most difficult tasks for both the designers and administrator. Techniques for the management of centres which involve community participation are still in their infancy. It is in this area that considerable thought needs to be applied. Restrictive practices can soon develop to erode the community principle.

Management must be self-motivated towards the ideas of community development and leadership. This is vital to its success.

THE FUTURE

Having looked at some examples of community involvement in Nottinghamshire, I shall now take a brief look at what I think the near future offers. There is going to be a greater need for Local Authorities to consider their limited resources and to decide how to maximise their use. It is important that all resources are looked at very carefully, particularly before they are discarded when they have gone out of their current usage. Although I feel that there will be an ever increasing need for places for people to meet and learn, the already emerging social changes are beginning to indicate changing needs. The present scramble to secure alternative energy sources may conceivably succeed, in which case there will be an acceleration of the use of finite and natural resources. Social change is inevitably going to swing away from the consumer society concept if society is to survive and this will mean less work rather than more. It is reasonable, therefore, to assume that education, cultural and leisure activities may well escalate. At present we have the phenomena of a falling child population and, therefore, a decline in school places. One of the reasons for this, of course, is the fact that education is restricted to the privileged few between the ages of five to eighteen years old.

There are people now being paid not to work and people being retired, in many cases, with their mental abilities as good as ever they were. These people could come together in schools, or whatever we choose to call them, and a new form of school process would begin to emerge. The buildings to meet these needs must form the centres of communities whether large or small and now is the time that we should be planning and constructing these facilities for the future. I think that by carefully studying an existing town, and sounding out its needs at grass roots, it is possible, even in these hard times, to create facilities from the massive stock of buildings in public ownership. The critics of the 'school' concept maintain that people resent coming into schools, but many of them have never themselves been in a good modern, well equipped school with dedicated teaching staff and well motivated and stimulated children. These schools are exciting. They are pleasant and comfortable places to be in, having a good scale and informality about them. The older school and school buildings, which most people are familiar with, throw up fears of exposure to ignorance of a subject brought about by the teaching techniques employed. In a self-motivated situation, backed up by a variety of teaching skills, all these worries fade away.

Finding out becomes a pleasure. After a time at one of these centres people discover they have skills that other people have not got and are able to pass these on to others with the result and satisfaction it gives them. If this is the way we are going, then what has to be done?

In trying to understand communities one must first identify what a community is and where its boundaries are, why they exist and how they can alter, and so on. It will be necessary to identify what a community is trying to do and what it needs to do it. It may be a simple and clearly defined need, like a swimming pool, but there will be the more difficult type of accommodation to define in the form of a variety of meeting facilities and areas for access to resources, which may well include books, slides and films, specialist equipment for things like joinery, metalwork, jewellery making, etc. This is where an interdisciplinary team, the community team, will need to be involved. I think to gain most success the team should establish itself in the heart of the community for say a period of six months. Ideally, I think this should be formed as a second stage after a first stage centre has been established and has been operating for some time. This is the concept that I described earlier and enables the team to more clearly identify the existing structure of the developing network. The team should be based either at the centre that is identifiable or in the centre of the community so that the community has direct access to them. It should have the characteristics of a shop or possibly more like a public library, which offers a service and sufficient facilities to enable the public to sit alongside the professional as the work is developing. After the six month period, as ideas emerge and are put forward, it will be important for those directly involved in implementing them to either remain in the community or be in very close contact with them so that the developing ideas will emerge as a result of community collaboration.

Local Authority offers scope for exploring, developing and producing projects involving total communities. It is by no means as simple as it sounds, of course, and does necessitate being linked with an Authority that has the framework in which people of similar attitudes of mind can work to achieve success. For the future progress of community development it is also important that the barriers that still exist between departments in Local Authorities must be further broken down. The Local Government intelligence network in the United Kingdom must rank with the best of any commercial organisation and offers infinite scope for obtaining knowledge from all parts of the country and again this must be used more frequently. All the ingredients are there for success, it is just up to the people involved.

RESEARCH

Most of the chapters in the previous section have been concerned with research to some extent. However in this section, research is the main focus although, as the chapters illustrate, the type of research is not viewed as separate from the planning and management of projects—the action—as is the case with the more traditional approach.

Chapter 11 points to the necessity for a greater emphasis on the integration of research with action and with community involvement. In noting criticisms of action-research, the author argues that much of this is due to a misunderstanding of the approach and of what can be realistically expected from its use.

The next chapter by Chris Horn discusses the achievements of a project—the Sunderland Quality of Life experiments—in involving the public in both the planning of leisure projects and the evaluation of the action. One important lesson to be drawn is that it can be distinctly advantageous to link action and research.

Chapter 13, by George Smith and Phil Topping of the Social Evaluation Unit in Oxford, discusses some of the pressures which have given rise to action-research. In drawing lessons from the Educational Priority Area Projects and the Community Development Projects, they stress the importance of distinguishing the different types of action-research projects and of planning the organisational structure accordingly.

Considered together, these chapters support the value of action-research in the field of community involvement and leisure.

11 THE INTEGRATION OF RESEARCH, ACTION AND INVOLVEMENT

by John T. Haworth

In the sphere of leisure and related community welfare, traditional methods of research and provision can be valuable but there is also a need for an increased emphasis on innovatory approaches. An important reason[1] for this is that services and facilities are not always in agreement with the requirements of the community, particularly in working class areas. A recent report by the Department of the Environment,[2] for instance, showed that when sports centres have been provided in inner city areas in the hope of improving the quality of life for residents generally, they are often used mainly by the middle classes.[1] Use by working class people can be inhibited by geographic, economic and social factors. In other cases, working class residents may not perceive such centres as being for them.[3] Yet relevant public provision is needed, since commercial provision, while important, can be too limited in choice and at times too expensive.

Although it may be argued that rectifying the imbalance in the distribution of leisure resources and opportunities across groups is the job of the politician and policy maker, this presumes they are aware of ways to achieve this, even where they are willing to try. This is not always the case. It is known, for instance, that disadvantaged groups are also groups which are politically weak.[4] They lack information and in many cases the skills to play the political game as conducted by those in power. Yet how to change this to give opportunities for all sections of the community to have an effective voice in provision, while preserving the minimum acceptable level of efficiency and organisation, is not always known or appreciated. One innovatory approach to research and provision worthy of increased emphasis is the integration of research with policy making (action) and public involvement. This chapter looks at some important general aspects of this approach.

ACTION-RESEARCH

The integration of research with action is not a new approach. Action-research has been used for a number of years in both work and in some areas of community development.[5] In the leisure sphere, however, it has only been used in limited cases, with the exception of the recent Leisure and Quality of Life Project.[6] Compared with the emphasis placed on traditional approaches, this use of action-research in leisure is still very new.

There are, of course, many ways of conducting action-research and more than one definition has been offered.[6,7] No single method can serve as a detailed model for all action-research. The range of projects tackled and the differing skill levels of the people involved precludes this. For example, while some groups may find it possible to specify their objectives without too much difficulty, as in the Sunderland Project, others may find it very difficult to articulate the nature of their problems. Initially, all that may emerge is an indefinite cry for help. Details of the use of action-research have to be determined with regard to the nature of each particular project. However, there are some general features. For example, unlike traditional research, action-research is concerned to a greater or lesser extent with trying to bring about change, as well as attempting to evaluate this. The Educational Priority Area Projects, for instance, were concerned with, amongst other things, trying to find ways to help schools in deprived areas as a means to compensate for the existing economic and social problems. Likewise, the Community Development Projects were concerned with the problems of multiple deprivation and the need to find ways of ameliorating social problems. And to quote a final example, the Leisure and Quality of Life Studies[6] were designed to promote self-help in leisure and associated areas of community development.

A related distinguishing feature of action-research is that, unlike much traditional research, it is not, in general, now concerned with verifying the causes of events. Instead, it provides mainly factual feedback about results, comparing these with planned ones and identifying failure where possible. Action-research also provides ongoing feedback which can be used as a regular aid to the modification of policies, particularly in local situations. Similarly, it can help in clarifying the aims and objectives of organisations, modifying these, if necessary, in the light of results. It can be used to generate and test new forms of action. Finally, national policymakers, perhaps at times somewhat overambitiously, have viewed action-research as a way of field testing experimental policies before large scale implementation. This has, of course, not been the only reason why national policymakers have used action-research, as Smith and Topping elaborate in Chapter 13.

Although action-research has been used in a range of major projects, it has not been without difficulties, and it has not gone short of criticism.[7,8] Many of the difficulties and criticisms, however, can be allayed by a better understanding of action-research and of what can be realistically expected from its use. A consideration of this follows.

DIFFICULTIES AND CRITICISMS

The difficulties and criticisms of action-research tend to cluster around three interrelated points: evaluation; general applicability of findings; and implementation of projects.

Evaluation.   One criticism of action-research is associated with objectivity. In action-research the researcher is part of a team and is involved in the planning and implementation of action as well as its evaluation. The researcher may also be part of a management committee concerned with the objectives and philosophy of the project. In the author's experience, the researcher may well be expected to join in discussions on these matters, as well as provide advice on the methods of evaluation of the work. The researcher may also be expected to become involved in the problem situation the work is trying to tackle. He may be expected to offer advice on the action where he thinks this may help a project succeed or prevent it from failing. In addition, he may have to help develop initiatives, develop skills of advocacy for a certain course of action, anticipate the possibility of untoward rejection of the findings of a project and try to find ways of collaborating with people to prevent this. [7]

This close relationship between the planning and implementation of action, on the one hand, and the evaluation on the other, has led to the criticism that the action-researcher cannot remain objective and hence cannot, for example, ensure unbiased evaluation. Some field workers involved with both action and research have attested to this difficulty. However, this criticism need not be applicable to the same extent when the researcher is trained in the importance of being objective and recognises the importance of research. In fact, one of the main benefits a research worker can bring to a project is his objectivity and willingness to try and ensure that objectives and goals are as clearly stated as possible, even if these have to be broad and continually reviewed, and even if it takes time for them to be articulated. And equally important is his insistance on the use of appropriate methods of evaluation. Indeed, as Chapter 12 by Chris Horn intimates, the close involvement of a research worker with the action side of a project may greatly help in the choice of appropriate and sensitive methods of evaluation. This can significantly outweigh any advantage gained by having an 'independent' evaluator, who may not be so perceptive of the complexities of the situation. Of course, the research worker will need to struggle continually to be objective and to be realistic concerning the claims made for the work done by the team. But this is not confined solely to action-research. A related criticism concerning objectivity is that in action-research the evaluation cannot be independent of the actions of the researcher if he is involved in the planning and implementation of the project. However, many action-research projects would not try to make this claim and would acknowledge the implications of this for the general applicability of their findings, as discussed later in the chapter.

Besides having a full-time research worker, an action-research team may also have the part-time assistance of an 'outside' person, perhaps from an educational institute. While this may be a factor in helping with objectivity, its main value is more in the addition of supplementary research expertise since the person is also likely to be involved in the management and work of the team. This additional research support may in fact be very welcome to the team since one of the real dangers facing the researcher is overwork due to excessive involvement in the many aspects of the work of the team. In some action-research projects the field workers may also be involved to some extent with the research. In this case it becomes even more imperative that the whole team is convinced of the values of the research element and is intimately involved with the discussions on the planning, evaluation and reviews of the work.

Another criticism of action-research is connected with the nature of the aims and objectives of projects. Many action-research projects tend to have broad aims and objectives such as the improvement of social conditions. In pursuit of these aims, programmes of action may change rapidly, old ideas may be dropped and new ones adopted. As Smith and Topping point out in Chapter 13, these features can be anathema to conventional researchers. In order to determine the causes of events they emphasise narrow, precisely stated objectives, stable programmes of action and precise results. Community workers, however, have pointed out that demands facing them are often likely to cause specific goals and objectives to be reviewed. A good community worker may need to change direction abruptly in order to take advantage of an altered situation. Scope for innovation is needed in community work practice. It is thus very difficult to have a situation where a researcher sets specific goals to be evaluated afterwards.[9] This can, in some cases, also apply in the leisure area.

It is because of this recognition of the complexity of the situation, rather than a failure to understand the requirements of conventional research, that many projects have broad aims and why many workers emphasise the importance of integrating research with action in order to retain flexibility while still monitoring and appraising the situation. This does not mean, of course, that there is never any scope in action-research for some precision in the definition of aims and objectives, or for the collection of quantitative as well as qualitative data. Chapter 12 by Chris Horn illustrates that this can be possible. Similarly, retaining broad aims does not mean that there is no scope for logical thought and analysis. Chapter 13 by Smith and Topping, for example, advocates the importance of distinguishing the nature of projects and planning the organisational structure accordingly. However, what the integration of research with action does mean is that in general there is little scope for the rigid detailed specification of projects to try and determine casual inferences. Such tools of the social scientists, as probability sampling, attitude scales, battery tests, control groups, and complex routing questionnaires, may have to be sacrificed along with the demand for large amounts of data. 'Definitive' evaluation is becoming recognised as a chimera which requires resources beyond normal prudent budgeting and unrealistic assumptions about human behaviour.[5]

The ideological framework surrounding a project is another important factor concerning the evaluation of action-research projects. The discussion of aims and philosophies of a project, particularly if these are broad, can raise fundamental points about the relationship of the project to social and political values. Often, courses of action are based upon various philosophical assumptions and values. These must be discussed by members of the team, otherwise conflicts can occur and the research may end up just evaluating the assumptions on which the action is based.

Discussion of such topics has to, of course, be sensitive. Agreement on values and courses of action need not necessitate all members of a team sharing the same shade of political philosophy. At the same time it has to be accepted that the discussion may result in a project criticising existing social policies and orders. Not all projects operate in politically sensitive areas. But a danger does exist that the issue of values can be neglected, even though relevant, in order to present evaluation as 'objective' and 'independent' to secure funding. Such a course of action only subjugates projects to a form of control based on the values of sponsors.

A factor related to this issue of ideologies and values is the question of whom the evaluation is for. Evaluation can be for many clients including central government, local government, independent agencies and voluntary groups, etc. Each may have its own requirements based on different priorities and values. As discussed later, these must all be recognised if evaluation is not going to favour one particular group. These points concerning evaluation are intimately connected with the second major difficulty concerning action-research, namely the general applicability of findings.

General applicability of findings.   One of the major criticisms levelled against action-research is that it does not produce definitive findings of general applicability and that its use in general policymaking is limited. This, however, is to misunderstand the reasons why action-research is often advocated. Policy formation, in fact, results from the synthesis of many diverse influences and research findings are not always one of these. At times, findings can appear far too late to be taken into account. Allying research and action can be one way of ensuring that research is one of these influences. Although this may apply particularly to local situations with which much action-research is concerned, it is also relevant directly to the National situation. The research worker in an action-research project is often in direct contact with policymakers. Providing he is aware of the many reasons why a project may have been introduced, he may be able to exert influence.

Action-research also recognises the dynamic complexity of social situations and behaviour and, as such, aims to produce findings of some value in similar situations. A much more modest and realistic objective than determining definitive findings and cut and dried solutions to problems. However, this does not mean that the insights produced by action-research are not relevant directly to National policy. The Leisure and Quality of Life Studies, for example, show that they can be. In demonstrating the enormous potential for self-help in the leisure sphere in four different communities, it is a reasonable, even though not a definitive, supposition that this applies to other communities in the UK and that the methods used in the studies may have a chance of success in these communities. Of course, success is not guaranteed and the onus is still on each community to be innovative. In taking account of the findings, national policy could be formulated to encourage widespread use of the approaches used in the studies and provide skilled personnel, possibly on a regional basis, to help implement schemes. [10]

Action-research studies can also be of significance nationally in that they may stimulate people to try various courses of action which have been successful elsewhere. They may suggest new ways of doing things as well as point to difficulties experienced with some projects. Again, none of this is given as a recipe for success. Anyone using this information has to consciously think about his situation and consider which of the various options should be tried. Of course, these kinds of 'relevance by demonstration', with the implication that some help with implementation may be needed, may not fit entirely the desires of central government administrators. The cost of giving help may be questioned. However, in some cases, national bodies are beginning to face up to this and are not demanding that policies are tested which are independent of the help of the action research team. [11]

Implementation of projects.   Action-research projects, by their nature, are not always as easy to implement as policy without research, or research without policy. Cooperation is required between a range of people from different backgrounds. But if some of the pitfalls are recognised, and there is a willingness to cooperate, action-research projects can be successful.   Action-research programmes have to be introduced by negotiation and persuasion. This makes them particularly vulnerable to political climate. Political change at either national or local level can significantly affect a programme. While policymakers will be readily aware of this, research workers must also take it into account. Similarly, the possibility of programmes being affected by local or central government policy developments has to be recognised.

The establishment of action-research programmes can take time, particularly in the early stages. An interdisciplinary team may have to be established and links forged with clients such as voluntary groups, local authority departments and national bodies. The danger exists that insufficient time may be spent on the discussion of the aims and objectives of projects and the methods of evaluation. As programmes develop, the pressure for action can also result in the research worker having inadequate time for the necessary analysis of data and write up of reports. In short, the danger exists that action-research can become an attempt at instant problem solving without consideration of broader issues or, as some have put it, all action and no research. Sponsors have to be prepared to allow more time for research than is strictly required for action. The researcher must be given time to relate the work to other studies, sponsors must also be prepared to accept the provisional nature of findings and the need for further work. This does not, of course, mean that research must unduly constrain the action. As mentioned previously, researchers must avoid using inappropriate research designs. They must also recognise that action personnel and policymakers may be concerned that research may be using considerable resources in time and money, while not ensuring worthwhile findings. Joint discussion is obviously essential to maintain some balance between action and research appropriate to the particular project.

Discussion may also be needed in order to allay the possible fear of action personnel and others involved in the project that evaluation will be a criticism of their abilities. Steps must be taken to point out that some failure in projects is only to be expected and that without monitoring there is no possiblity of improvement. In return, research personnel cannot expect to stand aloof from problems of action and refuse to enter discussions or offer suggestions. As a general guide to the implementation of action-research, both action and research personnel should be established at the same time so that goals, objectives and evaluation can be planned together from the beginning. Action and research personnel should also form part of an integrated team in order to promote free discussion. There should be agreement on the roles, responsibilities and functions of each part of the team, even though aspects may be shared. Finally, cooperation between the action research team, the sponsors and other participants is crucial. A management team representing these elements is important in trying to ensure this, and for handling conflict if it does arise.

COMMUNITY INVOLVEMENT

A final topic for consideration is the question of the involvement of the community in action-research projects. Public participation in projects has been a general feature of action-research. One reason is the desire to encourage local initiatives, but another is the concern as to what happens to a community group when the action-research personnel are withdrawn. An aim of many projects has been to train the group to enable it to continue the project. However, this has not often included training the group in research. Yet this can be important.

Greve[12] maintains that the case for involving residents in identifying issues, formulating measures, conducting activities, handling resources, monitoring and evaluating processes and results is just as tenable in relation to the research aspect of a project as it is to the action side. Passing on research skills and attitudes can be an important contribution to community development.[13] Research training can help the community clarify aims and objectives, determine how far these are being reached, and where they are not, and hence help in their redefinition, if necessary. And, it can do this on the terms of the community.

Often community research has been done on rather than with people. Evaluation of projects has not always taken account of the values and priorities of the residents, which at times may not be the same as those of the action researchers, the local authority, the sponsors, or indeed other local groups. Involvement of the community in research may not prevent values and priorities conflicting, but it may at least bring them into the arena for open discussion, with evaluation highlighting the benefits and costs for different groups.[14] Involvement of the community in research may also help members of the community construct a case for support of their project, as Chapter 12 illustrates. Of course, there is the difficulty that involvement in research may only be taken up by the more articulate members of the community. But the important factor is what is done with the skills on behalf of the community rather than representativeness. Action-research groups will need to adopt a policy of trying to reach other members of the community.

Involvement in research may cause difficulties where it forces groups to acknowledge failure. This may endanger the growth of confidence. There is also the difficulty of confidentiality of discussions. Interaction could, at times, be stifled if confidentiality is not assured. However, it is also necessary to take into account the principle used in the Sunderland studies: 'that if community involvement is to be genuine, and responsibility realistically delegated, then there should not be an element, such as evaluation, which is carried on outside the normal areas of operation' (see Chapter 12).

CONCLUSION

While action-research is not the only valid approach to research and provision in the sphere of leisure and community development, it is one worthy of high priority. Equally, while it may not always be appropriate to involve community groups in action-research, it would seem that many more projects could do so with mutual benefits to all concerned. Certainly undertaking research with rather than on people will have far reaching effects on the conduct of research and, hopefully, on the nature of provision.

REFERENCES AND NOTES

1. Other reasons are given in:
   Haworth, J. T. (1976) Leisure research: a new direction. In *Leisure and the Community* by Haworth, J. T. and Veal, A. (eds). Leisure Studies Association, Centre for Urban and Regional Studies, University of Birmingham
2. Department of the Environment (1977) *Recreation and Deprivation in the Inner Urban Areas*. H.M.S.O., London
3. Pearson, L. F. (1976) Working class non-work time and social policy. In *Leisure and the Community* by Haworth, J. T. and Veal, A. (eds). Leisure Studies Association, Centre for Urban and Regional Studies, University of Birmingham
4. Home Office Deprivation Unit (1975) *Local Government: Approaches to Urban Deprivation*. Occasional Paper No. 1. Institute of Local Government Studies, University of Birmingham
5. For a brief review of British action research in the community see:
   Batty, A. (1977) The action research background to the leisure experiments. In *Leisure and the Quality of Life: Volume 2*. H.M.S.O., London

6. Department of the Environment (1977) *Leisure and the Quality of Life: Volume 1 and 2.* H.M.S.O., London

7. Rapoport, N. R. (1970) Three dilemmas in action research. *Human Relations, 23,* 499–513

8. See for example:
Town, S. W. (1973) Action research and social policy: some recent British experience. *Sociological Review, 21,* 573–598

9. Young Volunteer Force Foundation (1976) *Evaluation Theory and Community Work.* YVFF, London

10. The Government have distributed Circular No. 92/77 (Department of the Environment) to Local Authorities informing them of the findings of the Leisure and Quality of Life Studies. A film is also available. However, to date, there do not seem to be any plans to help authorities implement the findings.

11. A project on community education, for which the author is research director, is attempting, on a regional basis, to find better ways of utilising resources by making available the skills of a small interdisciplinary team. The funding bodies recognise that if the work is successful, one implication may be the need to establish similar teams in each region.

12. Greve, J. (1975) Research and the community. In *Community Work 2* by Jones, D. and Mayo, M. (eds). Routledge and Kegan Paul, London

13. For an example of research involving the public as co-investigator see:
Robertson, I. (1976) *Community Self-Surveys in Urban Renewal.* Manchester Monograph No. 4. Department of Adult Education, University of Manchester

14. Smith, G. (1975) Action research: experimental social administration. In *Action Research in Community Development* by Lees, R. and Smith, G. Routledge and Kegan Paul, London

12 RESEARCH AND COMMUNITY INVOLVEMENT

by Chris Horn

As with many government backed projects which develop over a number of years of internal discussion, the Quality of Life Experiments[1] were a response to a number of pressures. Economic restraint was taking hold in the early 1970s and leisure, the Cinderella of local and central government, was facing severe problems. At the reorganisation of local authorities, more formal responsibility for leisure provision was to be adopted but it was still to be divided between several departments, usually education, social services, and leisure or recreation. Also it seemed likely that leisure time would increase at a faster rate than resources could be directed towards leisure activities. Some increasing measure of self-help was inevitable. This was also assisted by the idea that leisure could be used to rebuild community identity and feeling in redeveloped and newly established areas. Greater use would have to be made of existing capital resources as funds would be severely restricted and, therefore, more dual use policies would have to be translated into effective practice.

To emphasise that cooperation would have to take place at national as well as local levels, the Quality of Life Experiments were jointly funded by the Department of the Environment, the Department of Education and Science, and relevant local authorities in the districts of Sunderland, Stoke-on-Trent, Clwyd in North Wales and Dumbarton in Scotland (in the last two areas the Welsh and Scottish offices were involved). Each area undertook its task in its locally developed style, but each started with the same terms of reference, namely:

> To take part, in conjunction with the Department of the Environment, the Department of Education and Science, and the Scottish and Welsh Offices and in association with the appropriate bodies for arts and sports in a two year experiment designed to contribute to improving the quality of life locally, by ensuring the optimum use of existing leisure facilities, cultural, recreational and sporting, and the addition of new facilities and their development so far as practicable within the period; to undertake by means of a coordinated approach, bringing in the full range of local organisations and interests concerned, both public and private (including industrial and commercial), and having due regard to the spare time activities, interests and potential support of local residents; and to

evaluate and report the results for inclusion in a report for general publication.

The remainder of this chapter refers solely to the experience in Sunderland where the experiment was retitled Experiment in Leisure Project, or ELP for short.[1]

THE ESTABLISHMENT AND STRUCTURE OF ELP

Firstly, the central government departments selected a chairman (the Leader) of the steering committee (known as the Project Team). He was the very experienced chairman of the Sunderland Council of Social Service, an umbrella organisation for all voluntary social agencies in the district. His merited reputation was very important when ELP attempted various innovations in its operation. Secondly, an officer of the local authority was seconded to the experiment to act as an administrator. After sounding local opinion, a full Project Team of twelve members was invited to join the experiment to act as the central decision making body. All had considerable experience in the management and promotion of leisure in the public, private and voluntary sectors. After discussion of the terms of reference it was agreed that a coordinator and evaluator should be appointed. The latter post was very significant as it set the learning element at the forefront of the experiment. It was also felt that a coordinator was more appropriate than a director since the Project Team, which formally included the three officers, were to respond to initiatives rather than dominate the whole experiment.

By early 1974, all the above had been assembled and ELP was firmly underway in Sunderland. At this stage, several important decisions were taken. No opinion survey would be taken in Sunderland (which has over 300 000 inhabitants) as the key to ELP was to be 'learning by action'. The Project Team was uncertain of the value of opinion surveys in the field of community leisure activities as its growth depends on the discovery and support of enthusiastic individuals, who are small in number, and unlikely to be identified in any opinion survey in the whole Borough. A suggestion to mount a full publicity campaign and employing an advertising agency was also rejected. It was correctly assessed that, with three good local daily newspapers, two regional television networks, and two local radio stations broadcasting to the Sunderland area, ELP could generate its own publicity. Each of the media was stimulated to cover the start of the experiment and word-of-mouth reinforced this beginning. The message was a simple one. ELP had a large project fund of £200 000 and was looking for ideas for spending this sum of money. Needless to say the response was immediate and eventually the ELP Project Team considered over one hundred and fifty ideas of which thirtynine eventually were given financial support. After some early discussion with the financing sponsors, it was agreed that maximum flexibility within the normal rules of public accounting should be given to the Project Team. Part of the function of ELP was to demonstrate the full limits of flexibility for the use of public funds.

In order to emphasise the 'learning by action' principle, the Project Team agreed that a procedure was required for dealing with applications and ideas. However, this procedure was developed during the period when the Project Team considered the first applications. The adopted procedure was thus built on actual experience and expected capabilities of the Project Team and project proposers, most of whom were members of the public operating in a voluntary capacity. The agreed procedure (see Appendix) had three stages, as follows:

Stage 1: A project proposal form was completed outlining the basic aims, organisation and initial estimates of a project. Providing the Project Team felt the idea showed some potential, the project was passed on to the second stage.

Stage 2: A worksheet was completed in consultation between the proposer and ELP staff. This document covered any changes in the aims and the proposed organisation of a project, a more detailed costing of the activity and the procedures to be adopted in the evaluation. Once this was accepted by the Project Team the project was funded, operated and evaluated. At the conclusion of the funding period the next stage came into operation.

Stage 3: A project analysis was written by the evaluator which referred to the original expectations for the project, levels of achievement and recommendations for future operations. This report was discussed by the Project Team and project organisers participated fully in these sessions.

The above system is a good example of the interaction of the evaluation process and the general administration needs of the experiment. The evaluation demanded that the aims and operation of the project were clearly understood before a project commenced and this clearly assisted the organisers of a project, especially those who were attempting something for the first time. This process also established the evaluator and evaluation as integral parts of ELP operations. A detailed knowledge of the project ensured that any data collection was sensitive and appropriate both to the project activity and the capabilities of the organisers.

The projects supported by ELP covered a wide range and included arts, sports, recreational, cultural and community activities. It is interesting that while ELP itself was able to operate corporately, and with great flexibility, its reporting back to the sponsors of the experiment, the central government departments and the two local authorities, Sunderland Borough Council, and Tyne and Wear County Council, were inevitably constrained by the existing structures. Thus, the evaluator reported to a Central Research Advisory Group in London on the research findings of ELP while the Team Leader reported to a Steering Group more concerned with the management of the project. Locally, at the end of the project, responsible bodies had to be located for taking charge of the physical assets accumulated by ELP and also some projects required a continuation of financial support. At times the heterogeneous character of some of the projects was threatened when new financial support was obtained, i.e. a community use of a school's project had elements of recreation, community activity and education, but its later funding came only from the education committee.

Although perhaps not fully appreciated during the life of ELP, a, fundamental principle was being applied in the allocation of funds, administrative support for projects and their evaluation. The activity itself was at the heart of all the processes. Once the nature of the activity was established, the administration and financing, as well as the evaluation, were moulded around this core to ensure as little disruption as possible. One example of this was the use of small money floats or advances. Retrospective claims are a common practice in public finance, but this would have been restrictive on those voluntary groups and individuals with insufficient private resources to support expenses even over short periods of time. As an independent body, standing between the public auditor and the project organisers, the Project Team could operate effectively as a middleman. In particular, the new activities supported by ELP benefited greatly from the flexibility and ability to react quickly to unforeseen small expenditures. This assisted the creation and maintenance of enthusiasm in the difficult early development of several projects.

THE LESSONS OF THE ELP EXPERIENCE

The projects financed by ELP included fifteen neighbourhood play schemes, a peripatetic theatre company, three outdoor activity centres and central equipment pools, several types of transport pools, community use of schools, bands in parks, board games centre, information office and mobile information vehicle, adult education project, community arts, subscription concert series, workingmen's clubs' fetes, Olympic gymnastics club, film making, playbus and a stage lighting and audio equipment pool. The following table shows the numbers involved in all the various activities supported by ELP.

Full-time employees*	28
Members of committees/individuals responsible for the management of project	256
Numbers of individuals actively helping the organisation of projects	989
Estimated number of individuals participating in all ELP projects	78 495

*NB: Even in those projects where full-time staff were employed, a voluntary management committee retained ultimate control of the project.

Within the great variety and scale of activities, several themes emerged and each will be discussed within the context of a particular project. It must be emphasised that these themes are interdependent and many projects could be used to exemplify each theme.

Role of the enthusiastic individual.   From the very start, ELP was impressed by the amount of enthusiasm displayed for outdoor pursuits (mountaineering, trekking, canoeing and camping) in Sunderland. A total of nineteen formal requests were received from a wide range of groups including schools, scout groups and private individuals. Before ELP began its operations, Sunderland had one education authority outdoor centre and another run by a voluntary organisation of school teachers with a combined annual capacity of 3000 bed weeks. School outdoor activities were limited due to the lack of adequate equipment and a similar situation existed in groups such as the scouts and guides. After one year of ELP funding of over £50 000, the level of activity was raised very significantly. Two new outdoor centres were established and support given to the existing voluntary centre and the four centres had a combined annual capacity of 11 000 bed weeks. A centrally stored equipment pool, available to private individuals and schools, supported 18 000 man days of activity by over 4000 persons. The appointed full-time coordinator was coping with over a hundred enquiries per month connected with outdoor activities.

The rapid development in outdoor activities was only possible through the great efforts of the individual voluntary leaders at each of the centres and the full-time coordinator. It was agreed by all, at the conclusion of ELP funding, that the sympathetic and positive support given to all those involved in a voluntary capacity by the ELP staff and the full-time outdoor activities coordinator was very important. Although all those involved had experience in outdoor pursuits, few had any related administrative experience. Both centrally and at each of the three centres, a management committee of mainly volunteers was established to be responsible for the assets (valued at over £50 000) created by injection of ELP funds. Each committee offered a balance of support ranging from technical matters (legal and financial), to expertise in specific outdoor pursuits. The additional presence on the committees of local councillors ensured access to local authority funds for ongoing financial support. In the debate which preceded the commitment of the local authority for future financial support, great reliance was placed on the information gathered from the evaluation of the project. The evaluation helped to determine the levels of activity and their impact on the local community especially the young.

At the centres much of the labour for the renovation and construction of facilities was provided by volunteers or older school children on craft experience courses. One outdoor centre was developed by a leader at a YMCA and the centre acted as a focus for the overall expansion of activities, especially for young people in an area which had previously lacked such facilities. Indeed, after two years a small manufacturing firm was eventually established making fibre glass canoes, employing local people who had been initially involved in a voluntary capacity. ELP was fortunate that its terms of reference allowed it to risk such a large sum of money on several individuals whose ideas were largely untried. The gamble was not so great, however, as ELP could offer very flexible but also firm support from its full-time officers. It is difficult to conceive that any sample survey could have unearthed the potential which was realised in this project. Furthermore, an excessive demand for planned estimates of predicted activity would probably have led to a target being set that was lower than the achieved position. The existence of the ELP money bag acted as an effective catalyst in stirring the imagination of those involved in the development of outdoor activities, as it offered some genuine hope that their ideas could be realised. In subsequent years it was feasible for each of these activities to settle down to a more predictable pattern of development, although the availability of similar funds to ELP would probably encourage further eruptions of creative ideas.

Leisure and community development. Although the Education Committee had a policy of dual use for school premises when ELP began in Sunderland, it had decided that it could only be implemented on purpose built sites. ELP provided a small fund of £2500, shared between three schools, for experiments to take place of the feasibility of the immediate implementation of the dual use policy. As in the overall ELP project, the initial brief for the development at each school was in a general form and encouraged each to develop according to local resources, both human and physical. Part-time evening principals were appointed at each school to act as catalysts around whom the early developments could take place. All those appointed were teachers at the respective schools, No precise plan hindered the early growth and eventual character of each after hours scheme.

One of the schools selected was a comprehensive in the middle of a large council estate housing over 10 000 people. Before the ELP project less than ten adults from this area were registered at evening classes. One officer in the education department interpreted this as clearly demonstrating that there was little interest in the area for evening activities on school premises. An alternative interpretation was that this low level of participation was a reflection of the inappropriateness of existing evening class provision relative to the needs of the area. The rapid development of the ELP scheme soon showed the latter interpretation to have been correct.

Three features of this development were responsible for its success at attracting weekly over three hundred people, including about a hundred children, to its wide range of activities. Traditional evening classes require the payment of a full term's fees at the start of the term. In this instance, an entrance fee was paid on each evening attended and thus when people were unable to attend they saved the entrance fee. This permitted broken sequence was catered for by the leaders of each class. Secondly, the content of the classes was decided by those attending. As the finance of the organisation, under the responsibility of a Users Committee, was locally determined it was possible for heavily subscribed classes to support small minority interests. This local control enabled both the content and level of teaching to be sensitive to local needs and potential. The final feature was the range of activities which were deliberately selected to encourage all members of the family, mothers, fathers, children and grandparents, to attend these sessions. Activities were sometimes designed to cope with a great variety of age ranges or, more simply, activities were designed for specific age groups. Many parents were thus able to enjoy evening classes without leaving children at home. Mid-evening breaks for refreshments and announcements further emphasised the social function of this development. One group of mothers also realised that families with very young children could attend if a creche was provided. A rota was established to provide a creche.

The evaluation of this project had two guiding principles. Firstly, it should inform the Users Committee about the characteristics of their operation, numbers attending, class sizes, home addresses, attraction of family activities and the financial structure. Secondly, as they would be making a bid for future ongoing public support, the evaluation should assist the advocacy of their case to the education committee. Attitudes of teachers and caretakers, the attraction of a new audience for after hours use of schools, and the compatibility of extended evening use and daytime school use of facilities were all important. This approach proved successful on two fronts. The Users Committee and those attending responded to the demands of evaluation by giving up time to devote to it and encouraging others to participate. Also, the results of evaluation fed back ideas into their operation, especially in their commitment to attracting family groups and ensuring they served minority groups such as the elderly.

The three schools included in this project differed greatly in available resources. One was a former old secondary school, the second school had a significant proportion of its facilities destroyed by fire months before the start of the project, and only the third school was a fully equipped comprehensive. The project also demonstrated the latent tension with the local authority structure between education and leisure in this field of after hours use of school facilities. ELP had no such established divisions, but when further public support was requested it proved impossible to get the local authority to behave corporately. The Education Committee wholly supported the scheme once the Leisure Committee backed out, partly through a fear of being overwhelmed by education. Yet, at the local level, these differences are unreal and irritating when they affect the future of activities which are legitimate and important.

When several projects were linked by their area the concentration of their combined impact on the community was very significant. In a poor inner city area the establishment of a neighbourhood play scheme not only provided much needed activities for children in school holidays and at weekends, it also gave confidence to a group of mothers organising the play scheme, added credibility to the efforts of the community worker who supported the mothers in the early stages, and offered an incentive and example to others in the area to start other activities. A community arts project funded by ELP led to the painting of a gable and depicting a former chandlers shop which had been a focus of attention in the area. To some extent the initiation of a tenants' association and greater local responsibility and influence ·for local residents can also be attributed to the momentum set up by the ELP projects. A similar sequence of events took place on the council estate with the after hours school use project — a play scheme and adventure playground were funded by

ELP. One additional and crucial point must be made. None of these activities were imposed or planned in this fashion. Each sequence arose out of the gradual evolution taking place in the areas and as such the community was able to keep pace with the development.

Evaluation role in community leisure activities. At times it is assumed that an evaluator should be independent and the evaluation removed from the day-to-day operations of an activity. In the ELP project the opposite of that situation was agreed upon at the start and a fully integrated approach was adopted. There were three motives for this decision. Firstly, it was felt that all the activities would benefit from the feedback from evaluation and its impact would be more constructive if those involved in the project activity were involved in some way in the evaluation. Secondly, the evaluation itself would benefit as the involvement of the evaluator would assist the development of a sensitive and sympathetic approach to the problem of the evaluation capacity and potential of a project. Thirdly, if the community involvement was to be genuine and responsibility realistically delegated then there should not be an element, such as evaluation, which was carried on outside the normal areas of operation.

These motives led the evaluation to take on a particular character. Administrative records were extensively used as data sources for all projects. Possibly the best example of this was the management of a leisure transport pool of mini-buses available for self-drive hire by groups in Sunderland. A form was devised, for completion by the responsible leader, which was primarily governed by the terms of the insurance cover but which also satisfied all the evaluation needs for this project. Project organisers were able to influence the style of evaluation. In the play schemes project, the mothers found the idea of precoded questionnaires both impersonal and unattractive. Open ended questionnaires were thus employed and an excellent response was received and, for certain purposes, the answers could be coded at a later stage.

An important factor also influencing the effectiveness of the evaluation process was the willingness of the ELP Project Team to accept failure either in part or for the whole of a project. If failure to achieve cannot be identified then logic decrees that a project has been successful and no change is required. Further, the existence of the evaluation process as an integrated part of the ELP operation led to evaluation, itself acting as a spur towards greater achievement. Knowing that evaluation reports would be written generated an atmosphere where all were fully striving to achieve their goals. Mention has already been made of the increased power of advocacy given to a group with access to evaluation material. Nearly all projects supported by ELP accepted this as the normal process as they had been directly involved in its design and implementation. At the termination of ELP funding, each project organiser or organisers were invited to a Project Team meeting to discuss the project analysis. This maintained the confidence of those involved as they were able to comment on this evaluative verdict on their efforts. It was agreed by all involved that this final element in the exercise set the seal on an approved and very effective process.

CONCLUSION

The ELP in Sunderland attempted to break new ground in the methods of funding and administrative support given to community leisure activities. It can be dangerous to draw wider conclusions from one experiment. However, much of the experience does offer clear pointers and examples from which other situations may be able to benefit. It is important to first emphasise the unusual features of the Sunderland situation before outlining the major lessons that emerged. The ELP was funded jointly from central and local government sources and thus was not responsible to any single authority. As an experiment it was not under the usual political pressures faced by local authorities and, in particular, this permitted the funding sponsors to suggest that all projects did not have to succeed. The ELP was thus allowed to gamble more than traditional funding bodies. The only element in the organisation imposed by the funding sponsors was the inclusion of the evaluation of projects and the experiment as a whole. Bearing these features in mind, the following major conclusions emerged from the work in Sunderland:

1) Within communities there is a reservoir of creative and administrative talent which, given sympathetic support, can be responsible for significant contributions to life within these communities.

2) When the funding and organisation of community leisure activities is viewed in part as a learning exercise, the dynamism and need for change and flexibility generated by these activities is more easily catered for.

3) Within this atmosphere, evaluation has a natural and integrating role. Initially it can assist the clarification of realistic goals and it can assist the learning process as the activity develops. Change and adaptation then become natural processes rather than features which cause unnecessary difficulties.

4) When evaluation has this approach it becomes an activity in which all can and want to participate. Both qualitative and quantitative data can be collected. Administrative records provide a

valuable source of evaluation material when examined carefully. The active involvement of all organisers of projects in the evaluation design and the discussion of its findings ensured the effective use of this part of the ELP approach. It is certain that the advocacy for future financial support by project organisers was improved significantly by the availability of the evaluation reports. The possible identification of failure, itself, gave the reports greater credibility especially those where 'success' was identified.

5) Probably the most important feature of the ELP organisation was the great importance attached to the individual characteristics of each project activity. Financial, administrative and evaluation requirements were all tailored to suit each activity. In evaluation, some organisers were keen and capable of completing question- naires, but in others there was insufficient time for such an elaborate system. It should be remembered the majority of those involved in ELP were unpaid volunteers and the maintenance of their en- thusiasm and involvement was crucial to the success of the Sun- derland experiment.

At the conclusion of the experiment in Sunderland it was felt by those involved that the approach had proved successful. The unusual features of the ELP organisation, as well as the traditional features, had been integrated within its operation. On reflection, success was based on the maintenance of a balance between the various pressures imposed by the ELP structure while retaining an environment which actively promotes enthusiasm, creativity and hard work. Leisure should be fun and enjoyable and any support it receives will be more effective if this is appreciated.

REFERENCE

1.   Department of the Environment (1977) *Leisure and the Quality of Life: Volume 1 and 2*. H.M.S.O., London

Appendix 1

DETAILED EXAMPLE OF THE ELP PROCEDURE

The example quoted is the project which assisted the expansion of the operations of the Sunderland Playbus. The Playbus had been operating in Sunderland for a short period and was organised on a volunteer basis. Originally the bus had been bought and converted by the members of the Sunderland Round Table.

STAGE 1: PROJECT PROPOSAL FORM (completed by the applicant)

a) *Project name*: Expansion of Sunderland Playbus
b) *Date of proposal*: 3rd July 1974

c) *Proposer*: Patricia E. Collinson, 8 Claremont Avenue, Roker, Sunderland.

d) *Co-proposer(s)*: Jean K. Archbold, Dr A. Lillington (paediatrician), Mr Alan Wright (Tyne and Wear PTE, General Manager)

e) *Aims* (be as specific as possible): Not only to provide those play facilities essential for the emotional and intellectual development of three to five year olds in deprived areas of the town, but also particularly to develop use of language by encouraging older pupils, parents and other adults to come into the bus and talk with the children on a one-to-one basis. We aim to reach a hundred and fifty children per week by extending the range of the bus to areas like Pallion, the Garths, etc., and so through increasing the understanding and skills of parents more satisfactory school/family relationships will be established later on. No fee is charged.

f) *Money requested*: £3000

g) *Items of expenditure:* (1) Salary for organiser £2150; (2) Driver's fee £200; (3) Maintenance of vehicle £400; (4) Running costs £100; and (5) Renewal of equipment £150.

h) *General organisation of the Project*: The bus parks at a different site each day. It is hoped to extend this to both mornings and afternoons. The driver collects it after two hours and returns it to the bus garage. Approximately fifteen children per session use the play facilities. The lower deck is for sand, water play, painting, drawing, etc., the upper for story reading, table top games, Wendy house, etc. A toilet and wash basin are on the bus. The bus is used during school term times but could be extended in use to holiday periods too. A full-time organiser is essential from September to coordinate helpers, renewal of equipment, finance, etc.

i) *Other sources of income*: May 1974: £150 — Social Services; Spent May–July: £80–£70 left in bank account; Other sources: Nil (we have approached other organisations but have received no definite promises to date).

STAGE 2: WORKSHEET

Once the Project Team accepted the Project Proposal the ELP officers and the project organisers held further discussions and a worksheet was jointly prepared for approval by the Project Team. The Playbus Worksheet, headed 'Expansion of the Sunderland Playbus' (prepared for Team Meeting, 18 September 1974) was as follows:

Responsible body: Playbus Organiser and Experiment in Leisure Officers.

Background to Project: Until now the Playbus in Sunderland has been run mainly on a voluntary basis but the demands upon it and the lack of funds have resulted in the approach to Experiment in Leisure. To date, from information received from the local authority on priority areas, the bus has been parked for one session each day, on a regular basis, at certain points in the town and local children have been encouraged to use the play facilities on the bus which comprise sand, water play, painting, drawing, etc., on the lower floor and story reading, table games, Wendy houses, etc., on the upper deck. A toilet and wash basin are also provided on the bus.

Aims: The principle aims of the project are:

a) To provide play activities in areas of the town where there is a shown need and where they are not provided by another agency.

b) To establish the need for the facility, hopefully to obtain adoption by the local authority at the conclusion of Experiment in Leisure, particularly having regard to the cost of the erection of purpose built buildings.

Project description: An advertisement would be issued locally for a full-time organiser within the salary scale for Nursery Teachers. The person appointed would mainly work from home but office facilities would be provided in Stockton Road.

The scheme would generally continue to operate as before, i.e. on a rota basis parking at a specified point in priority areas in the town. Consultation regarding selected areas would take place with local known agencies to determine areas of need. Arrangements would be made to accommodate, where possible, other demands for the use of the bus. The project, under the auspices of Experiment in Leisure, is costed on the basis of one year's operation, possibly from November 1974 to November 1975. The organiser would arrange for each daily visit and, as a minimum, the voluntary attendance of three adults which would comprise one trained person in nursery or similar work, one mother and one mature school girl or student of a local college (i.e. graduates waiting to take a Dip.Ed.).

The play facilities previously outlined would be varied and new toys introduced. Additionally, the children would be encouraged to take milk, the cost of which, since the Playbus is registered with the Social Services Department, is fully reimbursable. Approximately a hundred children each week would be expected to make use of the Playbus (see table on opposite page).

The organiser would be paid by Experiment in Leisure and all expenses paid through the Experiment in Leisure office, excepting that a petty cash imprest of £15 would be arranged to cover the cost of the purchase of small items of equipment.

Evaluation:

a) An evaluation form would be completed for each day's activities and this would be prepared in conjunction with the evaluator.

Financial arrangements: Costing:

Salary of organiser	£2250 (approx)
Car and telephone allowance	300
Driver's fee	250
Vehicle maintenance	400
Running costs	150
Equipment	150
Total	£3500

The form would be completed by the qualified person working on the Playbus for that day.

b) The evaluation would also concentrate more specifically, in some instances, on particular children and parents, on an anonymous basis, looking into family background and assessing extent of reliance on presence of parent, language problems, length of time taken before strong parental ties were broken, extent of play with children of different age groups, extent of movement within the bus, extent of own initiative to play, attitudes towards play facilities.

c) Attempts would be made to encourage the parents of older children, together with the elder brothers and sisters of the children, to arrange organised parties on the ELP Nature Bus.

d) The organiser of the Playbus would cooperate with the ELP Nature Bus in introducing plants, stones and other items of interest to develop appreciation.

e) An assessment would be made of the extent of use of different types of play facilities.

f) A comparison of impact would be made between the running of the Playbus up to the present time (from research material already available from thesis studies) against the running under a full-time organiser.

STAGE 3: PROJECT ANALYSIS

When the funding period ended the Evaluator prepared a project analysis. This attempted to relate achievement to earlier ambitions expressed in the project proposal form and worksheet. The following project analysis headed Expansion of Sunderland Playbus: Project Analysis, was discussed at a Project Team meeting at which the project proposers and the playbus organiser participated fully in the discussion on the lessons learnt and the next steps for future support of the Playbus:

Proposers/source (proposal form and worksheet): For the twelve month period before the application to ELP for funds, the Playbus in Sunderland had been organised through volunteer efforts. The approach to ELP was made to allow the Playbus to operate to a fuller capacity and so satisfy the demands that had become apparent in its early work.

Project description (worksheet):   The scheme was generally to continue to operate as before, i.e. on a rota basis parking at specified points in priority areas in the town. Consultation regarding the selected areas would take place with locally known agencies to determine these areas of need. Arrangements would be made to accommodate, where possible, other demands for the use of the Bus. The play facilities would be varied and new facilities introduced. There would be five morning and afternoon sessions for the Playbus per week during school terms. The Bus was designed to cater for ten children at each session.

Achievement (reports by J. Archbold, Playbus Organiser): In the twelve month period financed by ELP, the Playbus has operated for fortyfive weeks both in and out of school term time. The seven week non-operational period was caused by the delay for repairs to the vehicle. The Playbus, quite naturally, has a low priority in relation to the work of the Passenger Transport Executive. Usually, during term time, six sites have been visited each week. Four of the sites have been visited twice a week, with the remaining two being visited only once a week. Considerable use has been made of the Playbus facility during school holidays. Neighbourhood playschemes, local groups and the community arts organiser are among those who have made use of the Playbus in these periods. During a full operational year the facilities of the Playbus were enjoyed by about two hundred children and it supported approximately four thousand child sessions during this time. The main effect of the supply of funds from ELP has been to enable the Playbus to increase its working capacity by over 225%.

Aims and examination of aims (worksheet and evaluation):

a) To provide the play activities in areas of the town where there is a shown need and where they are not provided by another agency — *achieved*. The need satisfied by the Playbus can be of two types. Firstly, there have been areas where there has been a demand for playgroup facilities, but the lack of suitable buildings has curtailed their development. Secondly, the Playbus has gone into areas to illustrate the use of this type of activity for mothers and children of a preschool age. It is hoped in both circumstances that the Playbus activity will lead to permanent facilities and organisations being established. This has occurred in the year of ELP sponsorship.

b) To establish the need for the facility, hopefully to attain adoption by the local authority at the conclusion of Experiment in Leisure sponsorship, particularly having regard to the cost of the erection of purpose built buildings — *achieved*. The final details of

Finance:

	Estimated	Actual
Salary of Organiser and Supervisers	£2250	£2350
Office & administrative costs	300	165
Driver's fee	950	925
Vehicle maintenance and running costs	550	475
Equipment	150	210
Total	£4200	£4125

the continuing support are still under negotiation. The principle has however been accepted.

Examination of financial arrangements: After the original worksheet estimates had been approved, two changes were agreed at later stages by the Project Team. The division of the Organiser's salary between the Organiser and the individual play session supervisors led to only a small increase in the actual spending. This was caused by the extensive use of the Bus during school holidays. The original figure for drivers' fees had been set at an unrealistic level. The payment to the driver of £2 per session has proved to be satisfactory.

Project organisation (worksheet): The full-time Playbus Organiser was responsible for the day-to-day management of the operation of the Playbus. This was to involve the selection of sites, the selection of children to attend the Playbus, the arrangement for trained supervisors for each session, the maintenance of the Playbus itself, and any other useful contacts to be made with other organisations in the interests of the Playmobile Association.

Evaluation of project organisation (evaluation): Because of one year's experience using volunteer effort to organise the Playbus activities, it has been possible to compare the effectiveness of volunteer effort and paid work in this particular field. The increase in the working capacity, over 200%, with the payment of an organiser and supervisors speaks for itself. It has allowed the fullest use of a resource paid for initially by voluntary contributions and a small sum of money from the local authority. The Playbus cannot be compared with other more usual playgroups. It operates in areas with two types of difficulty (as mentioned above). The payment of both Organiser and Supervisors ensures a continuity of service which is most important in these types of environment. From the working of the Playbus during this year of ELP sponsorship the experience would indicate that the role of the Organiser is almost a full-time one. The work involved in organisation, supervision and the driving of the Playbus demands a considerable amount of time to be devoted to them. It is difficult to conceive of the Playbus operating on a continuous similar level without a similar amount of money being available for the payment of staff.

Experience/recommendations (evaluation):

a) In terms of the individual children attending the Playbus, progress in their social and educational development has been observed. The Playbus is well suited to managing with small groups of children who, in larger playgroups, may find themselves overwhelmed by the size of the group.

b) For some mothers, the work on the Playbus, or simply being able to bring their children to the site, has led to new friendships in the local community. The majority of the mothers find that the attendance of their child at the Playbus enables them to do work which is not easy when the child is at home.

c) Rates of attendance at the Playbus vary markedly between the different areas which have been visited. In the more deprived areas, a great deal of effort is needed to generate confidence and enthusiasm for the playgroup concept. In better off areas, where the problem is lack of facilities, the playbus can be a very effective focus for a demand for facilities.

d) The use of the Playbus during holidays has permitted many organisations to benefit during these periods. This is yet another example of making a facility even more available for a wider use by the community.

e) Now that the Playbus has operated to its probable full capacity, it is possible to relate the initial capital expenditure to provide the facility to the ongoing running expenses necessary to make effective use of such a facility. While many voluntary and charitable organisations can find the resources to provide the physical facility, it must be remembered that for a full and effective use other sources of finance must be found if full use is to be made of the original volunteer efforts.

[The author (C. J. Horn) was evaluator on the project and completed his report on 31 October 1975.]

CONCLUSION

At the termination of ELP funding negotiations between ELP, the Borough of Sunderland, and the Sunderland Preschool Playgroups Association led to the continued support of the operations of the Playbus within the overall support for playgroup activity in the Borough.

13 ACTION-RESEARCH PERSPECTIVES AND STRATEGIES

by George Smith and Phil Topping

The idea of linking social research and government more closely in the development of new social policy is long established. An irresistible aim, as Halsey[1] argues, for social scientists and administrators alike. But, in the past two decades, debate on how to achieve these closer and more effective links has grown more intense with the rapid expansion of social research, the increased pervasiveness of government policy into almost all aspects of social life, and the related shift in policy from merely regulating development to a more active intervention and the direct promotion of change.

Many devices have been tried to draw research more tightly into the policy making process — direct commissioning of research studies and closer contractual ties between the research contractors and their customers in government; the promotion of research and evaluation into the effectiveness of existing policy; and the growth of specialist social policy research units, in and around government, firmly committed to influencing policy rather than more distant academic objectives. One device that promised much was the idea of action-research or experimental social administration (field-testing and assessing new programmes on a pilot basis before large scale implementation). During the 1960s and early 1970s, action-research became an increasingly fashionable tag to attach to a wide range of very different activities that somehow combined elements of action or research. Following the Educational Priority Area project, financed by the Department of Education and Science, and the Social Science Research Council, launched in 1968, and the twelve Home Office Community Development Projects in 1969, almost every government department concerned with social policy set up its own action-research scheme — the Department of Environment's Inner Areas Studies and Quality of Life projects, the Home Office's Neighbourhood schemes and Comprehensive Community Programmes, and the Cycle of Deprivation studies from the Department of Health and Social Services, to name a few. Each project has had a different mix of action and research and a different organisational structure, as lessons were drawn from earlier experiments, but all have at one time or another been loosely grouped under the title of action-research.

It is now over ten years since the Plowden Report[2] confidently launched this development. 'Research' it proclaimed, 'should be started to discover which of the developments in educational priority areas have the most constructive effects so as to assist in planning the longer term programmes to follow'. Since then, optimism has given place to pessimism and disillusion about the contribution research can make to the formation of more effective policy. Turning knowledge into action has proved far harder than merely getting researchers and practitioners to sit down together. Even the apparent consensus over the right general direction for policy development has evaporated. It is no longer a question of testing the most effective of an agreed set of options. Assumption that policy development was on an ever upward and onward path has been severely undermined by the recent cut-back in government expenditure.

As a result of this experience, we are far more knowledgeable about the problems of linking research to action[3,4,5,6], but far less sure of any more positive prescriptions of where to go from here. Inevitably this lack of certainty is reflected in the changing position of research. In several of the more recent action-research projects, research has been effectively demoted to a subsidiary role, no longer a major partner assessing the success or failure of the whole enterprise. Government departments are no longer queueing up to launch further projects. Action-research, in many areas, appears to have promised much and delivered little.

In such situations the best way forward is often to carefully review the preceding stages. It is our view that many different activities were too easily grouped under the single heading of action-research. The many different groups involved have worked with very different expectations of what could be achieved. Part of the disillusion stems from applying expectations, drawn from one approach, to projects which never remotely resembled this method. For example, applying the criteria of a strict experiment with precisely measured outcomes to a project which was never more than a broad exploration of some major social problem.

In this chapter, we want to underline some of the different types of action-research by drawing on experience from the Educational Priority Area and Community Development Projects. To do this we begin by tracing the origins of action-research and then briefly outline the context of action-research projects and the many different groups involved, each with their own expectations of what an action-research project may entail. Finally, we identify a number of different types of projects and their likely outcomes.

THE BACKGROUND OF ACTION-RESEARCH

The growth of action-research represents an alliance between many different interest groups. These groups join the enterprise at varying stages of its development, adding their momentum or bringing a change of direction. Some are involved at the outset (e.g. social scientists and administrators) for, in the 1960s, action-research appeared to be one solution to the dilemmas they faced. Others (politicians or pressure groups) can see the advantage of the new device, once it has been developed, and they, too, may join in. However, for others (local authorities, where projects are based, or local people in project areas) involvement is often involuntary, but once the project is underway they may be able to influence its programme and development.

Before turning to a more detailed description of these different interest groups, it will be helpful if we outline more precisely what we mean by action-research projects. These can be characterised as relatively small scale projects operating in more or less real-life situations. They are likely to have separate action and research personnel and sometimes separate teams responsible to different organisations, as in the Community Development Project. The purpose, through a mix of action and research, is to draw out from pilot activities the practical lessons or findings for some more general application. The precise mix of action and research is rarely specified. In some projects, action may be little more than a token change and the main emphasis be on research studies. In others the reverse is the case. However, we would rule out, from consideration on the one hand, the social psychological experiment which collects together otherwise unrelated people to test a research hypothesis and, on the other, the evaluation of a large scale policy change where there is no prospect of research directly influencing the way policy is implemented. Action-research projects have been described as 'limited liability commitments' to experimenting with new techniques, new roles or organisational change where the ideas are as yet only vaguely specified, or perhaps more frequently where there is likely to be opposition to more widespread change.

What does action-research offer the different groups we have identified? For administrators the idea of 'experimental social administration' is clearly attractive for it appears to offer a more rational alternative to the large scale implementation of politically determined but untested policy. It goes beyond that other device for generating a commitment to change and a consensus of ideas (the commission or committee of enquiry) by actually experimenting with solutions, not merely listing possible courses of action. Effective 'experimental social administration' would undoubtedly have strengthened the administrator's hand in providing authoritative advice on the development of policy.

Action-research projects, however, have two more specific advantages for administrators committed to some degree of change. First their set-up permits a broad programme, cutting across normal departmental boundaries. Indeed projects such as the Community Development Project explicitly included interdepartmental coordination at the local authority level among their objectives. Curiously, the parent bodies of many of these projects (central government departments) are themselves departmentally bound. To sponsor wide ranging action-research projects is one way forward — a way perhaps of staking out new territory. Hall [7], for example, suggests that one motive behind the Home Office's Community Development Project was an attempt to strengthen that department's claim to take over responsibility for the social services following the Seebohm Report [8].

The second advantage, particularly where projects are sponsored by central government, is the opportunity to by pass intervening levels of administration. In the early stages of the Community Development Project, local project directors met with the central Home Office team far more regularly than with their employing local authority. And each of the Inner Areas Studies was directly linked to a minister in the Department of the Environment who was chairman of the local steering committee. Again this must appear to offer attractive advantages to those whose policies are normally mediated through a large number of intervening groups which may block, reinterpret or misunderstand the original objectives.

For the social scientist concerned in policy research, the development of action-research was the next obvious step. For evaluation and assessment of existing policies highlights problems and weaknesses. The first stage was to propose solutions, the next to try them out experimentally. Inside almost every social researcher is an 'action-man' trying to get out. Few can resist making policy suggestions, though the number prepared to put them to the test is inevitably smaller. Action-research thus provided the researcher with a chance to make practical and useful findings, and a sure supply of resources from sponsors.

However, there is another important technical strand. Conventional surveys and studies are almost bound to produce a static picture and, from this, causal relationships are hard to establish. One way forward, to try and determine the ordering of events, is complex statistical procedures. Another is to set up experiments which, by changing relationships, are likely to reveal causal links. Clearly, action-research projects could provide this experimental context and, importantly, the resources and legitimacy for introducing change. Politicians can hardly be accused of inventing the idea of action-research, though once developed it can easily become the device of the moment. Several projects, despite their tiny resources and scale, have generated high levels of political interest and attention. After all, each local Educational Priority Area Project only had some £8000 per year to spend. Not a large sum even in the late 1960s.

The announcement of new projects has been carefully timed to extract the maximum publicity. The Inner Areas Studies Project was launched in a prominent fashion by Peter Walker in 1972 and the Comprehensive Community Projects were unveiled shortly before the second election of 1974. Some may interpret this as part of a smokescreen, an apparent show of brisk and purposeful activity to head off pressure for more substantial change — a new way of buying time. Others may, more realistically, see it as a way of testing the climate of opinion, generating some consensus in policy areas where there is not widespread popular pressure for radical change, particularly policies of redistribution to poorer, more disadvantaged groups or areas.

Action-research projects naturally attract those who have strong commitment to change. The Educational Priority Area Project had close links with those who had pushed the idea of educational priority areas in the Plowden Report [2]. The Community Development Project gradually shifted from its design as a large scale social experiment to something closely resembling a pressure group, openly pressing for an increasingly radical approach. National pressure groups, too, have increasingly made use of research to strengthen their impact on the national debate and it is not surprising that they have moved into the action-research field. For example, the Shelter Neighbourhood Action Project (SNAP) in Liverpool did so as a way of extending this influence and demonstrating that they have an effective programme to put forward.

These then are some of the pressures that gave rise to action-research and ensured its rapid expansion. Their influence can be seen in the many similar characteristics and problems shared by action-research projects. We will briefly refer to four of these features.

Firstly, action-research projects have generally had vague and diffuse goals. They are almost always linked with those nebulous but attractive areas of social policy where imagination has outrun the ability to translate ideas in practice, i.e. Community Education, the Community School, or Community Development, as answers to the problems of the inner city. Nothing less than a 'reaffirmation of western democratic ideas, as John Greve [9] commented on the objectives of the Community Development Projects. These broad goals allow local teams enormous latitude to select programmes appropriate to the local problems of their own interests or skills. Community Development Project Teams were able to redefine the overall programme by pointing to contradictions and inconsistencies in the original objectives, and arguing that the causes of local problems lay not in the immediate area or its population, but in wider inequalities in the social structure.

Second, action-research projects are based in particular areas and are inevitably drawn into local commitments and relationships. Most, too, contain among their formal objectives the development of local involvement and participation and the notion of community. In many projects, the style of operation has been consciously to avoid the 'top down' imposition of ideas and action, characteristic of most policy development, and instead to foster local initiatives, local determination and control.

Third, almost all action-research projects have been concerned with the problems of poverty or inequality, though few were explicitly set up to tackle this head on. The original objectives of the Community Development Projects were to improve the coordination of local services, increase the sense of community and encourage self-help groups and participation in local services. Such a programme of community development, it was argued, would be a radically new approach to the problems of deprivation, though any major impact on poverty remained the responsibility of 'the onward march of familiar general policies'. Perhaps here again, in this tangential approach to the major problems facing development areas, is further evidence of the reluctance to openly support a programme of redistribution. Even the pilot project has to be restricted to some more marginal aspect.

Fourth, almost all action-research projects have experienced major difficulties in the relationship between action and research. The first few years of the development project were marked by frequent disputes and breakdowns as research teams withdrew or transferred from one institution to another. The diffuse goals, the rapidly changing programmes, as old ideas were dropped and new ones adopted, and the emphasis on local participation and control (all attractive characteristics to many of the action side) were anathema to conventional research where precisely stated objectives and outcomes, stable programmes and centralised decision taking are essential components. Much has been written on these conflicting positions, but perhaps less on the alternative patterns and relationships between action and research that emerged as experience has built up in different action-research projects.

ACTION-RESEARCH IN PRACTICE

In comparison with many of the later projects, the Educational Priority Area Project had a relatively simple structure. Though each project contained both action and research staff, both sets were employed through the same university department. There was thus far less opportunity for the institutional frictions that marked the early stages of the Community Development Project. The Educational Priority Area also developed directly from the Plowden Report[2] and was influenced by the large scale experiments in compensatory education in the USA. As a result, the project began with considerable agreement about the problems it set out to tackle and some of the solutions that were available. For example, the importance of preschool education as a way of raising standards of performance, and the need for parental involvement to strengthen links between home and school. Though there was a little uneasiness about this second objective among some local schools, there was a general consensus about the desirability of both these programmes. Local projects were thus relatively free from local or national pressure to adopt one line or other, though there was strong opposition to the idea of introducing structured language programmes at the preschool level. This proposal therefore had to be abandoned in the London project area.

The first stage in each local project was the collection of baseline data in a standardised form, covering information about pupil performance in schools, teacher morale and attitudes, and parental interest in education and contact with schools. In one sense the information collected contained few surprises and had no fundamental effects on the direction of the local action programme, as much was already known about the educational performance in the Priority Areas. It was more a question of mapping in the particular selected areas and, later, comparison between the four projects districts underlined the very different characteristics of those areas loosely grouped together as deprived. But, at the start, the data collection served to confirm previous analysis rather than redirect attention to new problems. This diagnostic phase took only a few months, at the beginning of the three year project, while action programmes were being developed.

Two forms of evaluation were distinguished at the early stages of the project. The first would approximate as closely as possible to the experimental method. This would require an action programme with clear-cut and measurable objectives, action that continued long enough to have some chance of making an impact, and a population which regularly took part. Education, with its compulsory attendance, relatively fixed groups and agreed objectives, frequently provides an appropriate context for research of this kind and there is a long history of educational research on which to draw. Several of the Educational Priority Area Projects set up experiments to assess the effectiveness of preschool education, or special curriculum for other age groups.

However there was clearly a second type of action with a far less specific programme and objectives. One example might be an attempt to establish the feasibility of introducing parents or other non-teachers into schools. Another, the programme of 'community education' strongly supported by the Liverpool project [10] and another the multi-purpose education centre at Red House set up by the West Riding project [11]. In these examples, formal assessment of their effectiveness is clearly premature for it is not possible to predict exactly which groups will be involved, or the likely effects. Conventional research techniques cannot sensibly be applied, though there are other forms of research (e.g. social anthropology) which may provide alternative methods.

Faced with such programmes, research in the Priority Areas either tended to throw in its lot with the action, 'go native', and take on the role of an additional advocate, or attempted to compile a very general description of the development of the programme—research as 'contemporary history', as Marris and Rein [3] termed this method. The Educational Priority Area Project included a mixture of these formal and informal methods. Local projects were relatively free from pressure to adopt one method or another and there was little attempt by projects to challenge their original brief or the central assumption that educational change in the Priority Areas was a worthwhile objective.

Though the Community Development Project was conceived at the same time as the Educational Priority Area Project, and for much the same reasons, its history and experience has been totally different. For the former project, it has been far more closely entangled in the central government machine, remaining a direct responsibility of the Home Office, though action teams were employed by the relevant local authority and research teams by a university or polytechnic. Most social research projects experience substantial swings of fortune, as public interest in their subject matter ebbs and flows. This Project's position, close to government, has magnified these changes. It has experienced from the Home Office a firm central direction, *laissez-faire*, and, in turn, indifference and hostility. Even at one stage the announcement of an apparently similar project, the Comprehensive Community Programmes, was made by the same Home Office department. A sure sign, according to American project folklore, that the game was up and the older project doomed.

Part of the explanation for Community Development Project's frequent change of direction and programme may lie in the need to remain competitive and to underline that it was not necessarily bound to the outdated ideas of its founders as newer and more fashionable projects were unveiled. Though seen as experiment at national level, the scale of this Project, at the local level, meant that it was treated as a real resource by local authorities and its location and management were decided accordingly. Originally the Home Office had envisaged that local projects would be responsible to a local steering group, comprising representatives from local government, central government departments, local voluntary agencies and local groups. Local authorities, however, were far keener to make them directly responsible to a standard council sub-committee, to which a limited number of outsiders might be coopted. Close links with the local authority also acted as a constraint on the action programme. Almost every project was involved in one or more major collisions with their authority and two, in Batley and Cleator Moor, were prematurely closed down. Even those such as the Liverpool project, which followed a relatively conventional form of community development, had carefully to balance their work in the community with resident groups against the negative impact of such community action on the local authority.

These difficulties merely heightened the problems of research, already facing problems enough with the separate action and research teams at the local and national level. There was a very diffuse set of goals with local action teams frequently committed to local determination and control over their programmes. Research grants for the Community Development Project Research Teams were very substantial by the standards of the time and at first, like local authorities, universities and polytechnics, they pressed strongly for conventional research activities. The result was at best friction between action and research and, in many cases, complete breakdown in the first projects as the Research Teams pressed for the necessary conditions for formal evaluation studies. In some cases this friction continued throughout the Project, but, in most projects, active collaboration between action and research teams was established, or at least a *modus vivendi* achieved. The results suggest a range of action-research strategies, offering alternative approaches to that of formal assessment or informal reporting.

In practice, there have been very few formal evaluation studies in Community Development Projects and, where there have been, they have been restricted to a particular aspect of the project, i.e. the take-up of welfare rights following a local campaign in Batley[11, 12], the effectiveness of local information centres, or the response by local people to a new service. Most of the action in the development projects are wide ranging, unpredictable and scattered, and therefore impossible to evaluate in any formal way. It is a major task merely to keep pace with what is happening and try to establish links between one event and another. One method of final reporting is to present an account of the project's development (a form of 'contemporary history'), but one that sets the action firmly into its social and political context and may rely on formal research studies to illuminate particular details of the description. For example, the pattern of local participation in project activities. [13]

In the original specification of research in Development Projects, its task, in the first phase before action programmes were set up, was to diagnose local problems. Most projects have used standard survey methods to analyse local conditions, the problems of school leavers in the Liverpool area, housing in Birmingham, and employment in other areas. As projects moved away from the 'social pathology' approach to deprivation, where individuals and their relationships are the prime target to tackle the wider structural problems in housing and employment that threatened their areas, this form of analysis began to play an increasingly important part. For with these major problems, it was no longer possible to mount pilot programmes with the limited 'social action' money available. Better perhaps, to concentrate on building up a lobby for change, by analysing the problems and using the material collected as a lever. This could be both a professional activity (carefully conducted surveys or other forms of research) or carried out by local groups. In Liverpool, for example, several tenants' associations carried out surveys of their blocks to find out residents' preferences in any improvement programme. Perhaps this form of action-research marks the full circle. For research having started out as an independent, detached assessor of the action, has now come to be seen as one of the services that a community project might offer local people.

TYPES OF ACTION-RESEARCH

The experience of the Educational Priority Area and Community Development Projects underline the many different forms of action-research that have been developed as the original model proved too limited. In particular, many of these development projects have occurred, despite the complex organisational arrangements, as action and research teams were able to combine in a concerted attempt to analyse the problems facing the local area. The original research brief for the Community Development Project implied that teams would progress through these different phases of development thereby suggesting a series of different styles. Yet it is doubtful whether teams, which had come together to conduct a joint analysis, could easily separate again into those who were to initiate action and those who were to assess it. In practice, project teams have stuck closely to one or another type of action-research.

First, we can consider the diagnostic project. This attempts to find explanations for problems which have public attention. In the large scale action-research projects, these are likely to be as general as the problem of inner city decline, or multiple deprivation, and where there is unlikely to be a simple answer or solution. The skills required in a diagnostic project are primarily those of the researcher, i.e. collection of data, analysis and interpretation, though action-research strengthens the local focus of this work. The national programme of the Community Development Project anticipated that local projects would begin with a diagnostic phase, but perhaps more a diagnosis of the right strategy for the local context than a free hand at diagnosing the general problems. The Community Development Project was intended to experiment with new techniques of reform at the local level, leaving the structural problems of society to 'the onward march of familiar general policies'. In the event, many of these development projects spend much of their time refashioning the diagnosis by showing that 'broad general policies' were not only failing to tackle the problems, but were often further contributing to its decline.

The second type of project is the exploratory model, envisaged as the second stage of the Community Development Project, and is very different in style. The objectives are still broad, the means of reaching them unclear, but the emphasis is on action. A wide range of initiatives will be explored with the intention of following up the most successful. The premium is on mustering all available resources to develop some momentum. The skills required are those of securing cooperation from the local groups, mobilising local resources, generating enthusiasm and weaving a web of commitments and responsibilities. Direct project control over the content and direction of the action will be low.

Research can play a support role in this type of project. For example, mounting small scale surveys to show that need for change existed or the use of surveys to stimulate community and resident groups, often by revealing a degree of consensus about local problems which increased the sense of local identity. Assessment, here, will be based on teasing out a description of the sequence of events, how far momentum was maintained, and ideas picked up and replicated elsewhere.

If the exploratory approach produces effective results, then the project may move into a demonstration phase, channelling resources into a few selected schemes with a view to demonstrating their suitability for wider application. This implies an increasing degree of control over the action and here it becomes more meaningful for research to concentrate its attention on measuring process and outcomes, rather than merely keeping pace with its development. Information can either be fed back on some regular basis to the action team or, more formally, through reports. A more rigorous version of the demonstration project is the experimental model where a formal test of effectiveness is set up. For example, the testing of a preschool programme with clear, measureable objectives.

At the other end of the scale comes what might be termed the political model where the solution is apparently not in doubt, though support for any wider programme of action is missing. The project can thus take on the role of a pressure group for a particular policy or idea. Several development projects, in part, adopted this approach as they moved to a more radical analysis of social problems. Here they focused on the structure of society, particularly the problems of capitalism, as the major determinant of inner city decline and urban deprivation. Several of the interproject reports, published by the Community Development Project, start from this premise, though the detailed accounts of local conditions they also contain suggest a far more complex analysis.

CONCLUSION:

Action-research has not fulfilled its original claim to be 'experimental social administration', producing neat field tested policies for wider implementation. The closest it has so far come to this ideal is probably the impact of the Educational Priority Area Project on the expansion of nursery education. But, as we have suggested, this approach is itself based on a highly rational model of policy development, which is hardly supported by any studies of how policy is actually made. Several of the developments in action-research we have described, are partly attempts to come to terms with this reality. A recognition that pressure, timing and the right contacts are far more important than a comprehensive research paper a few years late.

Action-research may not have justified its original claims but, as we have shown, it has underlined the many different ways that research can contribute to more effective action. It was unrealistic to expect that the same project could rapidly shift from one type to another in a short time. In future action-research projects it will be important to clearly identify the most appropriate type of project and plan the 'organisational structure' accordingly.

REFERENCES

1. Halsey, A. H. (1974) Government against poverty in school and community. In *Poverty, Inequality and Class Structure* by Wedderburn, D. (ed). Cambridge University Press
2. Plowden Report (1967) *Command Paper: Vol. 1 & 2.* H.M.S.O., London
3. Marris, P. and Rein, M. (1972) *Dilemmas of Social Reform.* Routledge & Kegan Paul, London
4. Shipman, M. (1972) *The Limitations of Social Research.* Longmans, Essex
5. Rein, M. (1976) *Social Science and Public Policy.* Penguin, Middlesex
6. Smith, G. (1975) Action-research: experimental social administration? In *Action-Research in Community Development* by Lees, R. and Smith, G. Routledge & Kegan Paul, London
7. Hall, P. (1976) *Reforming the Welfare: The Politics of Change in the Personal Social Services.* Heinemann, London
8. Seebohm Report (1968) *Command Paper 24 7 168.* H.M.S.O., London
9. Greve, J. (1975) *Comparison, Perspectives and Values: Some Observations on the Study of Social Policy.* Inaug. Lect., University of Southampton
10. Midwinter, E. (1972) *Priority Education.* Penguin, Middlesex
11. Smith, G. (1975) *The West Riding Educational Priority Area Project.*
12. Taylor-Gooby, P. (1977) Welfare benefits advocacy in Batley. Papers in *Community Studies No. 11.* Department of Social Administration and Social Work, York University
13. Topping, P. R. and Smith, G. (1977) *Government Against Poverty: Final Report of the Liverpool Community Development Project.* Department of Social and Administrative Studies, Oxford